# HAWAI'I CHRONICLES

✦

# HAWAI'I CHRONICLES

Island History from the Pages of *Honolulu* Magazine

EDITED BY
BOB DYE

A Kolowalu Book
University of Hawai'i Press
Honolulu

© 1996 University of Hawai'i Press
All rights reserved
Printed in the United States of America

96  97  98  99  00  01    5  4  3  2  1

**Library of Congress Cataloging-in-Publication Data**

Hawai'i chronicles : island history from the pages of Honolulu magazine / edited by Bob Dye.
    p. cm.
"A Kolowalu book."
ISBN 0-8248-1829-6 (alk. paper)
    1. Honolulu (Hawaii)—History.  I. Dye, Bob, 1928–
II. Honolulu.
DU629.H7H39  1996
996.9'31—dc20                                              96–7380

University of Hawai'i Press books are printed
on acid-free paper and meet the guidelines
for permanence and durability of the
Council on Library Resources

# Contents

Acknowledgments ix

Introduction 1

## I  Beginnings

Volcanic Origins 11
  *Gavan Daws* / November 1988

Land of Gods 17
  *Martha H. Noyes* / February 1993

## II  Explorers and Exploiters

The Manila Galleons 25
  *Herb Kawainui Kane* / November 1982

The Lost Hawaiian Island 33
  *Victor Lipman* in collaboration with
  *George Balazs* / November 1983

Capt. George Vancouver: The Forgotten Explorer 43
  *Herb Kawainui Kane* / May 1985

The First Haole on Maui: La Perouse, the 53
Humanitarian Explorer
  *Mirka Knaster* / May 1986

The Rape of the Fragrant Trees 63
  *John P. Wagner* / November 1986

The Life, Death, and Rebirth of an Island 71
  *Victor Lipman* / November 1984

Contents

## III  Travelers and Their Tales

The Inevitable Visiting Writer                                    83
  *Tom Horton* / November 1980

Mark Twain in the Sandwich Islands                                97
  *Tom Horton* / November 1979

Jack London and Hawaii                                           113
  *A. Grove Day* / November 1984

The Mauna Kea Killing                                            121
  *Joseph Theroux* / November 1989

Life and Death at the End of the Chain                           129
  *Brian Nicol* / January 1986

The Hawaiian Education of Henry Adams                            141
  *Alfred L. Castle* / November 1981

An Artist-Adventurer in Turn-of-the-Century Hawaii               149
  *Pat Pitzer* / May 1987

## IV  Places, People, and Prejudice

The Path of Progress over the Pali                               159
  *Rick Stepien* / November 1980

The Notches of Nuuanu Pali                                       169
  *Gerard Aulama Jervis* / November 1982

Ainahau: A Paradise for a Princess                               173
  *Marilyn Stassen-McLaughlin* / November 1986

The End of Hope                                                  185
  *Barbara Del Piano* / January 1995

We Will Eat Stones                                               191
  *Martha H. Noyes* / January 1993

The Lynching of Katsu Goto                                       197
  *Gaylord C. Kubota* / November 1985

The Defiant Leper of Kalalau Valley                              215
  *Wray Jose* / November 1982

Contents

Wedding of the Year: 1893   223
*Bob Dye* / November 1993

## V  Pearl Harbor and War in the Pacific

Death in the Depths: The F-4 Tragedy   233
*Peter F. Stevens* / November 1990

Pearl Harbor Reopened: The "Seaman Z" Story   241
*Edward Oxford* / November 1984

The Battle of Niihau   251
*Brian Nicol* / November 1979

The Forgotten Internees   257
*Susan Morrison and Peter Kneer* / November 1990

The Day After: December 8, 1941   267
*Thelma Chang* / December 1991

The Night They Bombed Tantalus   275
*John J. Stephan* / November 1980

Contributors   283

# Acknowledgments

The editor and publisher gratefully acknowledge the permission of The Nature Conservancy to reprint "Volcanic Origins" by Gavan Daws, originally written for *Hawaii, The Islands of Life* © 1988, The Nature Conservancy of Hawaii, by Gavan Daws, and captions by Samuel Gon III; and to David Pellegrin, president and CEO of Honolulu Publishing Company, to reprint articles written by Victor Lipman, Brian Nicol, and Pat Pitzer.

The editor has made every effort to obtain permission from the authors holding the copyrights to the articles appearing in this anthology. In a few instances, these efforts have not been successful. The editor and publisher offer their apologies to any of the contributors they were unable to track down, recognizing that every endeavor was made to trace them. Copyright remains within the original copyright holder of each article.

# Introduction

✦ "Hawai'i has an incredible, fascinating past," says Brian Nicol, a former editor of *Honolulu*. "From the blood of Hawaiian warriors flowing in the Iao stream to the blood of U.S. servicemen shed on December 7, the stories are magnificent and spellbinding. The cast of amazing characters is endless: Robert Wilcox, Father Damien, the queens and kings, Thalia Massey, Mother Waldron. No place on earth has anything like the true stories that make up Hawai'i history."

The first issue of *Honolulu* Magazine appeared in July 1966. On the cover was a color photograph of Jacqueline Kennedy, Governor Jack Burns, and socialite Cecily Johnston watching the Kamehameha Day parade from the balcony of Iolani Palace.

The cover was a last minute replacement for one that was used a month later and made an even clearer statement of the magazine's intent. That cover showed Waikiki restaurateur Michele Martin, picnic basket in hand, tripping the light fantastic with two nymph-like creatures who were awash in saffron-colored gowns. If readers would turn the page, the editors promised Chez Michele would reveal "How to Stuff a Zucchini."

The editors were Cynthia and David Eyre, and their editorial budget was $250 an issue. David Eyre recalls that he paid two to three dollars for verse and twenty-five dollars for an article. The magazine was mailed to more than twelve thousand homes in affluent island neighborhoods. *Honolulu* was free to those on a select mailing list. Placing the slick magazine on a coffee table was supposed to be like flashing a "Gold Card" to signal that the reader had made it financially. Another thirteen thousand copies went to subscribers on the mainland and to newsstands.

*Honolulu* was the successor to *Paradise of the Pacific*, begun in 1888 under royal charter from King Kalakaua to promote tourism. The king also used the periodical to introduce Hawai'i to his foreign consuls, most of whom had never set foot in the country they represented. To

## Introduction

educate them, *Paradise* carried articles on Hawaiian history. The articles proved so popular that the November issue of the magazine came to be devoted to the history of the islands and marketed as a Christmas gift for friends on the mainland.

After seventy-eight years *Paradise of the Pacific* "vanished for simple lack of support," says David Eyre. "Its able editor was fighting a monster in demographics. Half its circulation resided on the mainland, half in Hawai'i. An advertiser didn't know whether to say 'Fly Pan Am to San Francisco' or 'Fly Pan Am to Honolulu.' And an editor didn't know whether to write about 'The Mongoose vs. the Rat' (which intrigued mainlanders but bored locals) or 'Frank Fasi Does It Again' which locals loved and mainlanders didn't understand. In quick sum, it was a no win jumble." The editorial content of the new magazine, the Eyres decided, would be "total local."

The first *Honolulu* Holiday Annual edited by the Eyres carried an article on the effect of World War II on Hawai'i business by Malcolm MacNaughton, David Eyre's boss at Castle and Cooke. And there were articles by two of Hawai'i's favorite newspaper columnists, "Ode to the Roadside Stand" by Bob Krauss of the morning *Advertiser* and "Poi Tastes like Library Paste" by Jim Becker of the afternoon *Star-Bulletin*.

Cynthia and David Eyre worked out of their home, from desks at separate ends of the house. They did not consider editorship of the magazine as full-time work. Cynthia continued to write travel articles for major American newspapers, and David remained as public relations director at the kama'aina firm on Bishop Street.

Softly romantic photographs of beautiful Hawaiian women came to grace the covers of *Honolulu*, and they reflected the image of Hawai'i that readers liked. Jim Becker says that "the Eyres produced a magazine for those people who came to Hawai'i to become part of the community, not simply to be in the sun. Those readers wanted to know how Hawai'i got to be the way it is." David Eyre says, "We published what I call 'sentimental history.' They were short pieces, so we could provide our readers with more variety."

The readers, it seemed to the editors, could never get enough stories about Hawai'i. They were what James Michener calls "nesomaniacs"— "crazed island-lovers who surrender their life to 'the spell of the Pacific.'" Nicol says, "The sun, sand, and surf may be the reasons so many people come to the Islands, but the culture and heritage are the rea-

## Introduction

sons so many people stay. I, for one, could never get enough Hawai'i history."

Magazines, more than newspapers, reflect the interests and personalities of their editors. When the Eyres retired from *Honolulu* Magazine in 1976, they were succeeded by Jeri Bostwick, who edited the magazine for just a year, too little time to put her personal imprint on *Honolulu*. But under new management, with Dave Pellegrin as editor, the change was dramatic.

A Harvard graduate, Pellegrin first came to Hawai'i in 1969 on an East-West Center grant. He subsequently worked as a writer and editor for the *Advertiser* and for the Associated Press in Philadelphia and Hong Kong. In 1976, he was working in Barbados as a UNESCO adviser to the Caribbean News Agency when he heard *Honolulu* Magazine was for sale. With the financial assistance of the Pellegrin family business, a publishing company in Wisconsin, Honolulu Publishing Company was formed. Dave returned to Hawai'i, along with his father, George, and together they revamped the magazine and converted its circulation from "controlled" to paid.

"Dynamic as hell" is the way veteran newspaperman Jim Becker describes Dave Pellegrin: "His magazine definitely had an impact on this city." Pellegrin says, "I wanted to publish a magazine for people who read for pleasure. That meant I had to find good writers. Most of the better writers in Honolulu were working for the two daily newspapers, but the papers had new rules that forbade them to write for me, or anyone else who competed with them for advertising revenues." The prohibition still holds. "There should be a diversity of voices," says Dave Shapiro, managing editor of the *Star-Bulletin*. "Besides, if one of my reporters has a good story, I want to publish it." Some of their reporters disagree. Although the distinction is disappearing as newspaper feature stories more and more imitate those in magazines, magazine writing differs from newspaper writing, they point out. Besides, they claim their byline in *Honolulu* promotes their newspaper.

Pellegrin adopted the newspapers' policy as his own. Dan Boylan, a professor who was then a contributing editor to *Honolulu*, remembers an early morning "terroristic telephone call" from Dave, to castigate him for reviewing a book for the *Advertiser*. "Nobody will pay two dollars to read you in *Honolulu* when they can do it for thirty-five cents in the *Advertiser*," Pellegrin bellowed. Boylan muttered that a freelance writer was *free* to write for anyone. "Not if your name is on the

## Introduction

masthead," Pellegrin growled. "I have first refusal rights on everything you write."

Pellegrin sought out talented part-time freelance writers as full-time editors—Pat Pitzer who edited *Show and Tel*; Victor Lipman, an advertising salesperson for the downtown *Daily Planet*; and Brian Nicol, a teacher at La Pietra girls' school. "They were first-rate feature writers," says Boylan, "and Nicol and Lipman were among the very best writers in all Hawai'i."

As the size of the magazine grew, Pellegrin added other freelance writers as contributing editors. Among them were former *Advertiser* three-dot columnist Tom Horton to write the back-of-the-magazine essay "Afterthoughts," broadcast journalist Richard Borreca to comment on politics, and me, a former aide to newspaper-baiting Mayor Frank Fasi, as media critic.

"With Pellegrin in charge, *Honolulu* went from a chronicler of society to a city magazine with a social conscience," says Jerry Burris, now the *Advertiser*'s chief editorial voice. "Those were the golden years of *Honolulu* Magazine," says Boylan. "With Pellegrin as editor and Nicol and Lipman as his associates, the magazine was a dream for a writer. Excellent writers themselves, they encouraged other writers and were always supportive. They never told you what to write but showed you how to write it better. Nor did they squeeze your copy to fit a hole. If your story ran twenty pages, they made room for it. I felt privileged to write for those men."

With the addition of other publications, the corporate demands on Pellegrin's time became greater and he relinquished the editorship to Brian Nicol in February of 1982.

"I love to read history; I love to research it; I love to write it," says Nicol, who has a master's degree in history from the University of Minnesota. "Because the magazine had such a long and remarkable history in the Islands, I felt it should be the ongoing showcase for Hawai'i history. What better place to tell the story of Hawai'i than in a century-old publication that was witness to a great deal of that story."

The 1980s was a boom decade for Hawai'i and the magazine, recalls Nicol. "Healthy ad revenue flow meant more ad pages, which meant more total pages, which meant more room for stories." In those days the Holiday Annuals never went below two hundred pages, and Nicol made the annual a "Hawai'i history keepsake."

In 1990, Pellegrin won one of the first Lifetime Achievement Awards

Introduction

from the City and Regional Magazine Association in recognition of his "extraordinary commitment to magazine excellence." He was then only forty-seven. Over the years, *Honolulu* has consistently had one of the highest market penetrations of any city and regional magazine in the country.

There have been many other awards. *Honolulu* won the prestigious William Allen White Award for editorial excellence in 1990, 1992, and 1995, and each year receives the Pa'i Awards from the Hawai'i Publishers Association for the quality of its writing, and Pele Awards for design from the Hawai'i Advertising Federation.

I chided Dave over lunch at the Outrigger Canoe Club that he and Nicol could call his Holiday Annual a "Hawai'i history keepsake," but I thought of it as the ghetto of Hawaiian history, because on its pages appear almost all of the articles about our islands' past. I argued that history should be in every issue. "I know that Hawaiian history is popular; our reader surveys have told us that," he says. "But a timely story always takes precedence over a timeless one. An editor doesn't feel any pressure to rush into print with a story about an incident from the eighteenth century."

During the past thirty years *Honolulu* has published as many articles about Hawaiian history as the *Hawaiian Journal of History* has. In one year, 1989, the *Honolulu* Annual alone carried sixteen articles on Hawaiian history to the ten articles in that year's *Journal*. "*Honolulu* is to be commended for bringing Hawaiian history to a broader audience," says University of Hawai'i Professor Paul Hooper, himself a historian who has contributed to the magazine. Other academicians from Hawai'i to contribute articles on the Islands' past include Jacob Adler, Dan Boylan, Al Castle, Gavan Daws, A. Grove Day, and John J. Stephan.

Helen Chapin, author of *Shaping History: The Role of Newspapers in Hawai'i*, says *Honolulu* has made "a big contribution to documenting Hawai'i's history. The scholarship is original. The articles are very readable, and presented in a lively and interesting way." History professor Dan Boylan also praises the articles for being "readable" and unlike the "constrained and dry as dust articles turned out by my academic colleagues."

John Heckathorn, the current editor of *Honolulu*, is in the mold of Pellegrin and Nicol. He left the staid academic life of the University of Hawai'i at Manoa campus for the rough and tumble of downtown jour-

## Introduction

nalism in June 1985. He first came to Brian Nicol's attention when he won a runner-up prize in the magazine's fiction contest in 1983 and was published the following year. When Nicol found out that Heckathorn was as good a cook as he was a writer, he asked him to author a dining column. "Dining" was an immediate success, and Nicol offered Heckathorn full-time employment. "I was an unpublished novelist (*Animal Soup*) and going nowhere. I jumped at the chance to work for someone who at least read my writing, and even liked it."

Brian Nicol returned to the mainland in 1990 and was replaced by Ed. Cassidy, the magazine's promotion director. "I wanted the magazine more involved in community events, and Cassidy had the promotional instincts to make it happen," explains Pellegrin. One of the first things Cassidy did was to tell Boylan, who by then had established a reputation as Hawai'i's most respected political commentator, that his column would only appear occasionally. Boylan promptly moved to a weekly publication, and *Honolulu* lost its political bite and editorial balance.

Cassidy, an energetic and exuberant man, came to the magazine from the movie industry and saw the two communication forms as similar. But the direction in which Cassidy pointed the magazine was not popular with many readers, and they groused about it. When Cassidy departed the editor's chair in 1993, he praised *Honolulu*'s editors, artists, and salespeople in a column titled "Making Magazines" (August 1993). He did not mention the magazine's writers—staff or freelance—but did praise the fiction of John Heckathorn, who replaced him as editor. During his tenure, Cassidy appeared to be more interested in storytelling and promotion of the arts than in journalism.

"Heckathorn is moving the magazine back toward a more serious journalistic force in the community," says Burris. "He has a lively intelligence and the heart of a sybarite, an editor who views the world with good humor on a full stomach." Boylan also sees the magazine returning to its former glory: "I'm pleased Heckathorn's editor because he's first a writer."

Will the kind of history published in *Honolulu* change? Heckathorn seeks articles that plunge readers into the dangerous waters of contemporary history, rather than to seduce them into the security of a romantic past. "As Hawaiians fight to take back their history from the control of men like *Advertiser* chairman Thurston Twigg-Smith, our pages will become a politicized battlefield," he predicts.

Introduction

Haole writers of Hawaiian history, even the celebrated A. Grove Day and Gavan Daws (both of whom who appear in this anthology) and the venerable Ralph Kuykendall, have been attacked for their "Euro-American" bias by Hawaiian nativists and their admirers. Following A. Grove Day's death in 1994, the *Advertiser* printed a "critical appreciation" of his work by poet Rob Wilson. He noted that Day "took an exclusionary approach to mapping Pacific cultures—call it "the Pacific as seen and narrated by 'great white visitors'—that is now being challenged and undone by indigenous, hybrid and ethnic perspectives."

Will the new Pacific writers submit to *Honolulu*? Heckathorn certainly hopes so. Sue Yim, recently retired from editing the *Advertiser*'s feature section, likes writing for *Honolulu*. "Magazine writers have greater freedom to develop a style, to express themselves in their own voice," she says. Though too few Pacific writers submit to *Honolulu*, Heckathorn believes that out of the Hawaiian Sovereignty Movement will come native Hawaiian voices who will interpret Hawai'i's past in new and disturbing ways on the pages of *Honolulu*.

*Honolulu* is the only general interest magazine published in Hawai'i that carries Hawaiian history on a regular basis and for that reason counts many of the best writers of Hawaiian history among its contributors. I have selected twenty-nine of their articles. They range from the islands' volcanic beginnings to the bombing of Pearl Harbor. Accounts of contemporary Hawaiian history have been left for another volume.

Readers may note an apparent inconsistency in the use of the okina (') throughout the text. The editor chose to follow faithfully the articles as they originally appeared in *Honolulu* magazine. The magazine has evolved from limited use of Hawaiian diacritics to its current policy of incorporating Hawaiian orthography into all of its articles that use Hawaiian words. The selections appearing in this anthology reflect the editorial policy of *Honolulu* at the time the selection was written.

# I
◆
*Beginnings*

# Volcanic Origins

## GAVAN DAWS

*In a new book from* The Nature Conservancy of Hawai'i, *the noted author of* Shoal of Time *and* Holy Man: Father Damien of Molokai *takes us back to the beginning, to the firepits of Island creation.*

✦ The only way to get to know a volcano, Thomas Jaggar believed, is to live with it.

He built his home on stilts, wedged into a crack in an immensity of dark volcanic rock on the southeast flank of the island of Hawaii—latitude 19° 5' 47" N, longitude 155° 15' 37" W at an altitude of 4,000 feet, precisely so that he could go to bed at night and wake in the morning snug within the rim of the most continuously active volcano in the world.

After breakfast he would stride through the mountain mists to the cliff face of the crater of Kilauea and clamber 200 feet down a rope ladder, to stand with nothing between him and the firepit Halema'uma'u. Here he was, Thomas Augustus Jaggar Jr., a human being of the early twentieth century, with his blood heat set by evolution at 98.6 degrees Fahrenheit, wearing the necktie of a serious volcano scientist, measuring the level of a perpetual lava lake that simmered and bubbled and fumed in his eyes. Molten lava, pushing right up at him out of the Earth's magma, 1,800 degrees and more at the surface. Primordial heat, searing the bare skin of his unbearded, unguarded face. Jaggar loved to teeter on the very edge of personal physical

---

First published November 1988.

scorching. He lived and breathed volcanoes. He sniffed his breakfast egg with its faint sulfurous smell and wondered if the egg of all life might be volcanic in origin, if evolution went back beyond the living embryo to the chemistry of volcanoes, sulfur, hydrogen, oxygen, carbon dioxide, ingredients of the egg, ingredients of the volcano.

He smelled out volcanoes wherever they were on earth. At Bogoslof in the Aleutians he saw hot lava tumbling into the ocean, the beaches aroar with sea lions, the steaming air above screaming with birds, life and deadly volcanism flourishing together. At St. Pierre in Martinique, molasses and Caribbean rum flowed like lava in the streets after Mount Pelée laid waste the town in 1902, and Jaggar saw human beings dead by the hundreds, close up; a baby dead in an iron cradle, a big fellow dead on his back in a deep baker's oven—the flesh shriveled and drawn away from his joints by the heat—not of baking but of volcanism. In Japan he had himself rowed out in a little skiff to look down over a hot lava tongue licking the sea floor below. He trailed a thermometer in the boiling water. All about him floated dead fish, belly up, boiled. If the tiny boat should capsize, Jaggar—the preeminent American volcano scientist of his day, with three degrees from Harvard and a worldwide reputation, geology professor to the young Franklin Delano Roosevelt—would boil. He loved every moment of it.

In the furious world of volcanic eruptions Kilauea was as gentle and generous as a volcano could be, active almost perpetually, giving out especially liquid lavas that often fountained spectacularly, making for wonderful viewing, but not normally going off with a deadly bang. People most times ran toward Kilauea to watch, rather than away for their lives. And when the volcano was quiet, tourists could saunter down into Halemaʻumaʻu with an egg in a pan and fry it on moving lava and write home about this strange, entertaining breakfast, being sure before mailing their postal card to scorch its edges a toasty Halemaʻumaʻu brown.

Everything that made Kilauea an ideal tourist attraction made it ideal for continuous scientific study—Jaggar's life passion. Early in the twentieth century, when he was climbing to the world peaks of his profession, only one permanent volcano observatory existed on the face of the Earth, at Vesuvius. Jaggar argued that the United States should have its own observatory, and for the sake of the best science it should be located at Kilauea. There, as nowhere else in the world, a volcano could be studied in all its phases—before, during, and after eruptions. And

## Volcanic Origins

the resident observer—of course—should be no one but Thomas Jaggar. Jaggar was the primordial force behind the Hawaiian Volcano Observatory. He started work in 1912, in a little seismometer vault dug out of ash and pumice, rimside, five minutes from his house. He observed nonstop. He was forever designing new monitoring instruments (though none of them ever matched the fine tuning of his collie dog, Teddy, a domesticated sensing device who always knew before anyone else when Kilauea was preparing to perform). In good times Jaggar could readily raise research money, public and private. In bad times he raised pigs to meet the payroll. Good times and bad, he published scientific papers continuously, like an intellectual lava flow from Kilauea, an outwelling that pushed the world science of volcanology ever forward into the twentieth century.

Jaggar had a wife named Isabel. On his endless expeditions across newly cooled volcanic rock she looked after the food. She took dictation for his close-up eyewitness reports of eruptions. Thomas died before Isabel. She had his body cremated, respectably committed to controlled flame, and later, when she felt the moment was right for her own private ceremony, she secretly scattered his ashes in a greater fire— the perpetual fire of Jaggar's life, Halema'uma'u at Kilauea.

Always think in millions of years, said Jaggar, and everything is in motion to one who senses slow motion. Think of the Hawaiian archipelago in million-year motion.

The islands, all of them volcanic, were formed in turn by upwellings from an eruptive hot spot below the ocean floor. Then in turn they were rafted away with the slow, slow movement of the huge Pacific Plate over the Earth's mantle, 70 million years of geological time travel, north and west across the Tropic of Cancer, worn by wind and rain, sinking gradually under their own weight as they went, oldest first, back beneath the surface of the sea.

Today there are eight major islands and more than 120 smaller islands, pinnacles, reefs, and shoals. The oldest and farthest to the north and west have disappeared below the sea and are now underwater seamounts. Kure and Midway are atolls with coral reefs and highest points of no more than a few score feet. More than 1,500 miles south and east of Kure, offshore of the island of Hawaii, a new island is forming. Still a half mile and several thousand years of time yet below the ocean surface, it already has a name: Lo'ihi.

Most recently emerged of the main islands is Hawaii, often called the Big Island. Shaped by five volcanoes, it shows the huge creative force of volcanism. Mauna Loa, still active, rises more than 29,000 feet from the ocean floor, 13,677 feet from sea level to summit. It is 10,000 cubic miles in bulk, meaning it is the biggest single volcanic structure on Earth—a hundred times bigger than Shasta or Fujiyama, indeed the biggest such feature in the solar system anywhere between the sun and the planet Mars.

The Hawaiian chain exists in the most profound oceanic isolation on the face of the globe, more than 2,000 miles from the closest continental land mass.

Life had to come from far away, blowing in on the winds, floating in on ocean currents, rafting in on logs swept from the continents, touching down with migratory birds on their transoceanic flights.

In this sterile island world of volcanic rock and salt spray, plants established themselves only at the rate of perhaps one species in each hundred thousand years. No amphibian or land reptile successfully crossed the ocean to Hawaii. No oak, no pine, no sequoia. No big game animal came from America or Asia, nor any beast of burden. In 70 million years only two mammals settled in: one for land, a hoary bat, solitary, nocturnal, reddish-gray, and weighing less than an ounce; and one for sea, a monk seal of primitive habits.

The volcanic shapes of the islands were sculpted by wind and weather, and a varied physical foundation was laid down upon which an enormous range of life forms developed. A mountain peak on Kaua'i, Wai'ale'ale, is the wettest spot on Earth (at least the wettest where anyone has maintained a rain gauge). Other, higher summits—Haleakala on Maui, Mauna Kea and Mauna Loa on the Big Island—are alpine stone deserts. Within a few miles of each other on any of the main islands there may be tropical rain forests, low-lying drylands, sunstruck coastal dunes, and lightless lava tubes.

In these extravagantly varied habitats immigrant species adapted, and new species evolved, life forms never before seen on Earth. One kind of drosophilid fly became 800. Three hundred fifty kinds of immigrant insects evolved into over 10,000 native Hawaiian species. Twenty species of land snails became a thousand. Two hundred fifty flowering plants became 1,800. The silversword colonized from bog to cinder desert. The *'ohia lehua* found ways to live almost everywhere, from new lava to ancient bog, and in the process took on an abundance of different forms. And the native Hawaiian honeycreepers changed so much as they adapted to the wide range of Island habitats that they would have astonished Charles Darwin.

In the biological history of Hawaii these are the big, sweeping developments, landmarks of worldwide significance. Other native creatures developed more modestly, but no less remarkably. Crickets by the shore, so adapted to salt spray that away from it they cannot survive. In the rain forest, carnivorous green caterpillars. At the extreme freezing height of a stone desert summit, the *wekiu* bug, so finely adapted to cold that if you take it in your hand—blood heat 98.6 degrees Fahrenheit—its proteins cook.

All of this development and change occurred over millions of years. Plants and animals between them created soil, soil trapped moisture, moisture allowed more and more growth, until forests appeared which influenced climate. In all the different ecological zones of Hawaii, particular groups of interrelated species clustered together. These groups developed into something that was more than the sum of their parts. They were interrelated, interactive, interdependent, promoting each other's survival. They became, in other words, natural communities. And these elegant associations became numerous. In less than 6,500 square miles of land mass, there can be identified more than 150 kinds of natural communities, each community a small island of life harbored within the larger islands of life that are the Hawaiian Islands.

# Land of Gods

## MARTHA H. NOYES

*A.D. 150: Mokapu was where the gods created man, Waolani was where the gods lived, and Waikiki was where O'ahu's first mo'i built the heiau Helumoa.*

◆ In the time no longer remembered, but not quite yet forgotten, the first people were born in Hawai'i. Until that time only gods lived here.

No one knows for sure how long ago man was born in the Islands. Archaeologists have dated remains at Kahana on O'ahu to A.D. 150, and there are remains on the island of Nihoa that are older still. It is certain that the Islands were widely populated by the end of the fifth century. The waves of migration that came after that time, culminating in the Pa'ao migrations ending in about 1250, brought the population to perhaps 350,000.

## Mokapu: The Creation of Man

According to the *Kumu honua*, one of the two principal creation chants of Hawai'i, the very first man was made at Mokapu in Kane'ohe on O'ahu. The gods Ku, Lono, Kane, and Kanaloa determined that they would make a man. From the earth at Kahakahakea on the east side of the crater Mololani on Mokapu, the gods fashioned the first man.

*Kahakaha* means to draw lines. *Kea* means white or clear or a fair-complexioned person. Fair-complexioned people were often favorites in

---

First published February 1993.

a high chief's court. It can be said, then, that Kahakahakea was the place where the gods drew a favorite person.

There are some who use a different spelling for this place. To them it is *Kahakahakeea*, or *Kahakaha-ke-ea*. Spelled this way it is the place where the drawing of life—*ea*—was made, or the place where the drawing in the earth was made alive.

*Molo* means to interweave or interlace. *Lani* means heaven, heavenly, spiritual, exalted, or highborn. Together *molo* and *lani* can mean to be interwoven with the heavenly, the spiritual. It can also mean well kept, as a heavenly or highborn person would be.

Mokapu is a contraction of *Mokukapu*, or sacred district. Some say Mokapu was made sacred because it was the place where Kamehameha I met his chiefs. But others say that Mokapu was sacred long before the time of Kamehameha and that it was sacred because it was where the gods made the first man.

At Mokapu the gods blew the breath of life into man and man came alive. The gods gave man three special powers. In Hawaiian the expression is, *'Ekolu mea nui ma ka honua, o ka mana'o'i'o, mana'o lana, a me ke aloha*. Literally this means, "Three great things through the earth, thought in flesh, floating thought, and aloha." One could say those three things are the body and brain, the spirit or soul, and aloha.

At Keawanui on Mokapu, facing toward Kualoa, was a heiau. The last remnants of the heiau were destroyed by the U.S. Navy in 1941. It is believed to have been a heiau dedicated to agriculture. Some say the heiau was called Ulupa'u, and some say it was called Ku'au. Others say the name was forgotten long ago.

Near this heiau, toward the seaward point, was a *ko'a*—a fishing shrine. There was a small platform with one upright stone for Kane and another upright stone for Kanaloa. The stone for Kane was lighter in color than the stone for Kanaloa. The name of this *ko'a* is forgotten, but the legend is still remembered.

The legend says that there were two Hawaiian men, Keawanui and Keawaiki, who lived at Mokapu. One day two strangers came to visit. One of the strangers was light skinned. The two strangers built a fishpond which was called Pa'ohua. *Pa* means enclosure, and *'ohua* is a kind of fish. The 'ohua that entered Pa'ohua could not get out again, and the pond became full of fish. When the strangers were finished with their work and had enjoyed the hospitality of their two hosts, it came time for them to leave. Keawanui and Keawaiki watched as the two strangers walked away—over the water. That is how Keawanui and Keawaiki knew that their two visitors were Kanaloa, the dark-skinned one, and Kane, the light-skinned one. The two stones at the *koʻa* represent the two gods who came to visit and built the pond Paʻohua.

In the same area, there were two other stones near the beach. One was Ku, and the other was Hina. It is said that years ago a man named George Moa moved the stones and pushed them into the water. Shortly after pushing the stones into the water, George Moa went insane and died.

A long time ago Ku and Hina lived at Mokapu. The two stones commemorate their presence there. Hina gave birth to a son and a daughter. Later, the two gods left Mokapu to go to Kona on Hawaii. Their son went with them, but Kaʻau, their daughter, remained at Mokapu. She became Pohaku Hanau a Kuʻau, known as the disappearing stone of Kuʻau because she could only sometimes be seen above the surface of the waters.

The disappearing rock of Kuʻau is said to give birth to pebbles. *Pohaku* is stone or rock. *Hanau* means to give birth. This is how the disappearing stone of Kuʻau got its name, Pohaku Hanau a Kuʻau. The pebbles grow into large rocks, and in this way the sea is kept from washing away the land of Mokapu.

## Waolani: Birthplace of Wakea

In the ancient mists of time, Waolani in Nuʻuanu was the home of the gods. Kane and Kanaloa lived there. *Wao* means upland forest; it also means a place of mystery. Waolani was where the Oʻahu Country Club is now.

Lua-nuʻu is said to be the ancestor of the race of Mu people called the Nawao and of the Menehune people of Hawaiʻi. Both the Nawao and the Menehune were forest-dwelling peoples. Some say they were the original inhabitants of Hawaiʻi, here before the great migrations came.

The Menehune people of Waolani and the Menehune people of Nuʻuanu often fought each other over a particular stone called Pohaku a ʻUmeʻume. Along the edges of the stone are many small indentations, the marks of the Menehune fingers grasping it. Eventually the Waolani Menehune won control of the stone, and they carried it to Waolani.

The Menehune once warred against a giant king at Waolani. The Menehune king threw the stone Pohaku a 'Ume'ume at the giant king. The battle escalated, and Pohaku a 'Ume'ume was thrown back and forth many times. The Menehune were driven to Kupanihi, the cliff now known as Pacific Heights. From there they threw the stone back to Waolani, and it hit the giant king on the head and killed him.

In ancient times and into the time of kings and queens, there were many heiau in and associated with Waolani. It was at Waolani where the first heiau were built. Most of the sites are now unknown, but it is said that the first heiau was built on the top of the hill during the time of Wakea. Other heiau in Waolani were Kupuanu'u, Kupualani, Kapaka'alanalalo, and Kapaka'alanaluna.

Wakea was born at Waolani. He married Papa, and they lived for a time at Waolani. Before Papa and Wakea were united, the islands of Hawai'i were known by different names than they are now. The island of Hawai'i was called Lono-nui-akea. Maui was called Ihi-kapalaumaewa. Lana'i was called Nana'i or Lana'i-kaula. Kaho'olawe was called Kohe-malamalama or Kanaloa. O'ahu was called Lalo-i-mehani or Lalo-waia or Lalo-o-ho-aniani. Kaua'i was called Kamawaelua-lani.

Thus, when it is said that Papa and Wakea gave birth to the Islands, what is meant is that from their time the Islands were given new names, the names of the children of Papa and Wakea. In that sense, Papa and Wakea were the progenitors of a new ruling group which settled in the Hawaiian Islands.

Haumea is another name for Papa. Another name is Kameha'ikana. In her human form as Kameha'ikana, Papa/Haumea entered a tree and the tree became the breadfruit tree. This story has many versions, but several of them place the breadfruit tree body of Papa/Haumea in Nu'uanu near Waolani.

A child was brought to Waolani for Kane and Kanaloa to raise. He was called Ka-hanai-a-ke-akua—"Adopted by the Gods." The Mu and the Wa people were his servants.

With the priest Kahilona, Kahanaiakeakua had the heiau Kaheiki built on the ridge at Pacific Heights. It was at Kaheiki that the *mo'o kahuna* order of priesthood was begun. *Mo'o kahuna* were practitioners of *kilokilo*—they were seers, readers of omens, and readers of the signs of the stars, the clouds, and the earth. Together Kahanaiakeakua and Kahilona ruled the kingdom from Kaheiki until the government was overthrown by the cannibal dog Kaupe. Then, from his high perch at Kaheiki, Kaupe preyed upon the people, and Kahinaiakeakua and Kahilona went to ʻEwa. A chief from the island of Hawaiʻi came to Oʻahu to rescue his son from the cannibal dog. Kahilona taught the chief chants, which the chief used to outwit Kaupe. He saved his son, and the kingdom was restored.

Kawaluna was a luakini heiau at Waolani, consecrated by the chief Kualiʻi in the 1600s. Kawaluna was a puʻuhonua, a place of refuge for fugitives and for the sick and disabled.

It is probable that the heiau Kawaluna was at Waolani before the time of Kuialiʻi. The Oʻahu chiefs were not united under one rule. Koaliʻi was a chief of Kailua on Oʻahu. He sought to unite the chiefs of the island under his rule. He achieved the rank of *moʻi*, supreme chief of the island, but the chiefs of the Kona—Honolulu—region had not yet settled into the regime. It was the right of the *moʻi* to preside at the *luakini* service. Kualiʻi came over the pass from Kailua intending to claim his right. The Kona chiefs prepared to resist Kualiʻi. Kualiʻi assembled his warriors on the heights overlooking Waolani, then went down to Kawaluna and conducted the *luakini* service. When the service was successfully ended, Kualiʻi and his warriors battled the Kona chiefs. The Kona chiefs were subdued and submitted themselves to Kualiʻi, and the island of Oʻahu was united under one rule.

## Waikiki: Heiau for the Makahiki

Maʻlikukahi was the first Oʻahu chief to be consecrated as *moʻi*. He and his chiefs moved the seat of the government from ʻEwa and Waialua to Waikiki. Helumoa was in Waikiki, where the Moana and Royal Hawaiian hotels are today. At Helumoa, in about 1350, the *moʻi* Maʻilikukahi constructed a heiau which was also called Helumoa. Each year at makahiki, the annual harvest festival that begins at the time of the rising of the Pleiades, Oʻahu's celebration began at Helumoa.

From Helumoa the long god and the short god of the makahiki each began their journeys around the island. The long god was carried through ʻEwa to Kahuku and down the shoreline of Koʻolau Loa. The short god was carried through Makapuʻu and Waimanalo up the shoreline of Koʻolau Poko. Some say that is how the two regions, Koʻolau Loa and Koʻolau Poko, got their names—the long (*loa*) Koʻolau and the short (*poko*) Koʻolau.

At length, completing their circuit of the island, the long god and the short god met at Kualoa. From Kualoa the gods could look across Kaneʻohe Bay to Mokapu, the place where the first man was formed.

In this way, man and gods depended on each other. Without man, there could be no worship and respect for the gods, and without gods there would be no man. The lands were sacred because man nurtured the lands out of respect for the gods, and because of that respect the gods protected the people. All lands, and all life, are sacred. Lands which are especially sacred are those like Mokapu, Waolani, and Helumoa, where it is still remembered that acts of the gods, or acts of man in respect of the gods, occurred.

# II

♦

*Explorers and Exploiters*

# The Manila Galleons

## HERB KAWAINUI KANE

*Did the Spanish discover Hawai'i before Capt. Cook? The evidence includes a navigational chart and a stone image.*

◆ More than 200 years before the arrival of Capt. James Cook in Hawaii, Spanish galleons laden with gold and silver from the mines of Mexico (New Spain) were passing south of the Islands on 8,000-mile voyages to Manila in the Philippines. After delivering their treasure, the ships were loaded with spices, silks, porcelain, and other riches of the Far East. Then they sailed north until the prevailing west winds off Japan powered them back across the Pacific on the return voyage to Acapulco.

It seems improbable that Spanish mariners could have made several hundred trips, passing so near Hawaii, without becoming Hawaii's first European discoverers.

In 1743, two centuries after the Spanish began their exploration of the North Pacific, an English warship captured a Manila galleon equipped with a chart that showed islands at the latitude of Hawaii. When Cook entered the North Pacific 35 years later he carried a copy of that chart, and most of his officers and other navigators of that time believed that the Spanish had been in Hawaii before Cook. In addition to the evidence of the chart, the Hawaiians had several pieces of metal when Cook arrived, including what appeared to be the broken tip of a sword. Also, when the first American missionaries arrived decades

---

First published November 1982.

later, Hawaiians told them intriguing tales of strangers who had visited the Islands long before Cook and the English.

## The Spanish Explorers

Prevailing winds and ocean currents wheel through the North Pacific in a gigantic clockwise circuit. The discovery of this enormous system enabled the Spanish to follow that circle, sailing with the wind. But it was knowledge gained at a terrible sacrifice of ships and men, for no means of determining longitude had yet been invented for navigating and charting this awesome sea. The Pacific, greater in area than all the continents combined, covers one-third of the globe and spans nearly half the earth's circumference at the equator.

By treaty, Portugal and Spain divided the earth into spheres of influence. Portugal had already moved into India, China, and as far east as the Moluccas or Spice Islands (now Indonesia). Spain claimed most of the Americas and the entire Pacific as far west as the Philippines. Manila became Spain's port of contact with the wealth of the Orient.

Fernando Magellan (Fernao de Magalhaes), a Portuguese aristocrat in the service of the king of Spain, launched the first circumnavigation of the earth. He discovered the passage from the Atlantic through the southern tip of South America to the Pacific, made a fearsome 9,000-mile crossing of the Pacific in which famine killed most of his crew, and was himself killed in a battle with natives of the Philippines. Of his five ships, only *Victoria*, with 35 survivors, got through to Spain in 1522. Another ship, *Trinidad*, fell prey to the Portuguese.

Cortes sent a flotilla under Saavedra in 1527 to search for survivors of the Magellan expedition. The ships found the northeast trade winds and were carried across the Pacific just south of Hawaii, but upon reaching the Philippines they could not find westerlies for their return voyage.

In 1542 six ships commanded by Ruy Lopez de Villalobos left Acapulco and crossed the Pacific on a mission of discovery and conquest. An account by the Portuguese pilot Juan Gaetano briefly describes islands that may have been either Hawaii or the Marshalls, depending on how the conflicting data is interpreted. The islanders wore only loincloths, and "in these islands we found corals on the coasts, and

## The Manila Galleons

hens in the interior like those of Castile, and the fruits of the coconut and banana trees, but we did not see any gold, nor silver, nor other thing of consequence." Islands without gold or silver held no interest for the Spanish, so the expedition passed on.

In 1564 Miguel Lopez de Legaspi set out from Mexico with four ships, reached the Philippines and founded a Spanish settlement. He then tried to find a workable course back to Acapulco, and in 1565 he sent *San Pablo*, under Andre de Urdaneta, to make the attempt. Sailing north with the monsoon winds, Urdaneta cleared Japan, found the westerlies near 40 degrees north and rode them across the Pacific. Slanting southward, he made a landfall off Baja California, then followed the coast down to Acapulco. After 129 days at sea, Urdaneta had completed the first return voyage to the Mexico seaport.

The way was now open for the Manila galleons, also called the *tornaviaje* for their turn-around route. Each year for the next 250 years a galleon carried Mexican gold to the Philippines, then returned with riches from the Orient. These exotic cargoes were then packed on burros and hauled over the mountains of Mexico to Vera Cruz, and finally shipped across the Atlantic to enrich the Crown of Spain. Such goods were then sold in Europe at many times their cost.

## The Spanish Secrets

To protect their routes from English pirates and Dutch competitors, the Spanish cloaked their discoveries in the deepest secrecy. All knowledge gained by exploration was the property of the Crown, and Spanish charts could be acquired only by force.

But rumors of the Manila galleons leaked out, probably through English and Dutch adventurers who began their own explorations in the Pacific and Orient. The recently published novel *Shogun* is based on the experiences of the English sailor Will Adams, pilot of a storm-ruined Dutch expedition that landed in Japan in 1600 with only a few survivors. Tokugawa Ieyasu, the shogun of Japan, valued Adams' talents as a navigator and shipbuilder and gave him protection and patronage. Over the vociferous objections of Portuguese missionaries and traders, the shogun awarded Adams the status of a Japanese noble and enabled him to send letters to England and the Netherlands. Portuguese hostility toward Adams, whom they regarded as a heretic and interloper, aroused the shogun's desire to learn more about Europe's non-Catholic nations. He wanted to expand trade beyond the bounds of what he now perceived to be a Portuguese monopoly. Adams' letters soon brought about the establishment of English and Dutch trading stations in Japan.

In 1609 the Manila galleon *San Francisco*, carrying the governor of Manila to Mexico, was wrecked on the coast of Japan. The governor remained in Japan for a year, until a ship that Adams had built for the shogun was given to him for the completion of his voyage. Through such contacts the English and Dutch became aware of the Manila galleons.

## George Anson's Mission

A century later, with England and Spain at war, English Capt. George Anson persuaded his superiors to send him out after a Manila galleon. His superiors were not enthusiastic about such a hazardous mission; they gave him ships of doubtful seaworthiness, then forced him to lay in harbor for nine months, waiting for the men and supplies they promised him. His request for 500 "seasoned" troops was answered with a cruel joke; he was sent 500 old veterans from the military hospitals, most of whom were invalids more than 60 years old. Some had to be carried to the ships. About 200 deserted; most of the others died during the crossing of the Atlantic. None survived Anson's later difficulties in the Pacific.

After losing most of his ships, Anson finally arrived off Acapulco and took up station to intercept the treasure galleon. But the Spanish saw him and held their ship in port. He then decided to wait for the galleon at the other end of the route, and so he crossed the Pacific, suffering appalling manpower losses to scurvy. Only his flagship, *Centurion*, wracked by storms, completed the crossing. Desperate and faced with the threat of mutiny, Anson sailed to China where, after much wrangling, he was able to repair his ship. He then complemented his decimated crew with Chinese sailors (probably pirates), sailed back to the Philippines, and waited off Samar. The Spanish sent two galleons that year (1743) and the first got through. Anson surprised the second, *Nuestra Senora de Covadonga*, a "great galeon" with 36 guns and a crew of 150, and captured it after a brief but bloody battle.

The Manila Galleons

## The Spanish Chart

Along with more gold and silver than existed in the entire English treasury, Anson captured "a chart of all the ocean, between the Philippines and the coasts of Mexico, which was made use of by the galeon in her own navigation." On the chart was a cluster of islands in midocean. Of these, the island described as La Mesa is on the latitude of the Big Island of Hawaii. The term "mesa" accurately describes the long, massive shape of Mauna Loa as seen from sea, and this island is depicted on the chart with a southern coast similar to the southern coast of the Big Island.

La Mesa's longitude, however, is considerably east of Hawaii. Until the development of the chronometer in the mid-eighteenth century, longitude (degrees east-west) was impossible to establish; all charts made prior to the chronometer look grossly distorted for that reason. Latitude (degrees north-south) could be determined with relative accuracy by using a cross-staff or astrolabe (forerunners of the modern sextant) to measure degrees between the horizon and the sun or the fixed star Polaris. But longitude was only a rough guess based on time spent at sea multiplied by the ship's speed. Speed was measured with a log-line tossed over the stern, a method that did not take into account the force of the ocean current. On west-bound trips, this current carried navigators faster than they realized. Therefore any island they encountered was charted east of its true position.

Equipped with the first chronometer in the North Pacific, Capt. James Cook accurately determined the longitude of Hawaii. Later, when Lt. Roberts drew the map of Cook's voyages, he included the La Mesa group but depicted its position farther east. He did this, according to some critics, so that no one would dare dispute the English discovery of Hawaii.

James Burney, one of Cook's officers who later distinguished himself as a foremost expert on navigation and astronomy, calculated the longitudinal error in the Spanish chart at no more than 9 degrees, an error that could have been caused by the powerful North Equatorial Current. In his five-volume *A Chronological History of the Discoveries in the South Seas or Pacific Ocean*, published from 1803 to 1817, he concluded that the islands of the La Mesa group were indeed the islands that Cook found and named the Sandwich Islands. Burney's conclusion was shared by most of his contemporaries. The French explorer La Perouse wrote, "In the charts at the foot of this Archipelago, might be written: Sandwich Islands, surveyed in 1778, by Captain Cook, who named them, anciently discovered by the Spanish navigators."

## Why the Spanish Didn't Stay

There may be several reasons why the Spanish failed to establish a station in Hawaii. For one, the huge and unwieldy galleons required safe natural harbors. Such havens are notably absent in Hawaii. Honolulu's harbor, difficult to spot from out at sea, was not discovered until 12 years after Cook's arrival. Anson wrote: "By the concurrent testimony of all the Spanish Navigators, there is not one port, nor even a tolerable road as yet found out betwixt the *Philippine* Islands and the coast of *California* and *Mexico*."

Moreover, the Spanish had no need to stop for water. Whereas English water quickly went foul in wooden casks, the Spanish carried their water in ceramic jars to keep it potable. Anson wrote: "It is well known to those who are acquainted with the Spanish customs in the South Seas, that their water is preserved on shipboard not in casks but in earthen jars, which in some sort resemble the large oil jars we often see in Europe. When the Manila ship first puts to sea, they take on board a much greater quantity of water than can all be stowed between decks, and the jars which contain it are hung all about the shrouds and stays, so as to exhibit at a distance a very odd appearance."

It's possible that the Spanish may have been discouraged by circumstances similar to the fate suffered by Cook, who was killed at Kealakekua Bay while attempting to take the king hostage. Most moments of first contact between Polynesians and Europeans were marked by hostility, amicable diplomatic relations being established only after a demonstration of cannon fire. The Hawaiians were as warlike as the Europeans.

Early missionary William Ellis recorded Hawaiian tales of strange castaways who had come years ago. One story, told "by different persons at distant places" throughout Hawaii, concerned seven foreigners who landed eight generations earlier at Kealakekua Bay in a painted boat with an awning or canopy over the stern. They were dressed in clothing of white and yellow, and one wore a sword at his side and a feather in his hat. On landing, they kneeled down in prayer. The Hawaiians, most helpful to those who were most helpless, received them kindly. The strangers ultimately married into the families of chiefs, but their names could not be included in genealogies.

Another account told of a number of white-skinned strangers who landed on the southwest coast of Hawaii and retreated to the mountains where they made a dwelling. The Hawaiians gave them presents, but eventually the strangers sailed away. No description was given of their vessel, which may have been merely a boat from a storm-wrecked ship.

Once explorations were completed and the Acapulco-Manila route established, the captains of Manila galleons would have been under strict orders not to take any risks that might endanger their precious cargoes. They were on business trips. Ellis believed that the Spanish had sighted Hawaii and investigated its coasts but had not landed except as survivors of wrecked ships.

And since the Spanish were principally engaged in search of gold, silver, and precious stones, they may have simply lost interest after discovering that the Hawaiian Islands contained no such commodities. There were more than enough opportunities for conquests elsewhere.

## The Cook Legend

In other cultures Cook might have become a saint or a god after his death. In the English-speaking world of the nineteenth century, he became a hero of the British Empire. Though this honor may be richly deserved, the veneration of Cook may have been promoted to excess in generations of school books. He certainly deserves credit for making the first well-recorded discovery of Hawaii. He was a prudent navigator, but his celebrated accuracy was due in part to John Harrison, the Yorkshire carpenter who invented the chronometer that gave Cook an edge over his predecessors.

Cook's fame, Spanish secrecy, and centuries of enmity between England and Spain have all influenced writers in the English language to demean or completely overlook Spain's remarkable era of ocean exploration and trade. For example, the recently published *The Pacific Navigators* (Time-Life Books, 1980) does not mention the Spanish exploration of the North Pacific nor the Manila galleon trade route. Such omissions have become commonplace in English literature.

## If Not Cook, Then Who?

Somewhere in a dusty corner of a Spanish or Mexican archive may be ancient documents that await discovery. They may tell us who gave the names La Mesa, La Desgraciada, and Las Monjas to the islands on the chart of the Manila galleon. But if we don't have the navigator's name, we may have his visage. In the Museum Fur Volkerkunde in West Berlin is a stone image found in Hawaii shortly after Cook's visit. The museum's experts believe it is not a carving of an Englishman. The figure is wearing a cloak, with a full ruff around his neck. Spanish grandees dressed that way centuries ago.

# The Lost Hawaiian Island

VICTOR LIPMAN
in collaboration with
GEORGE BALAZS

*Two hundred years ago Capt. Cook's men heard numerous accounts of a small sandy island near Kaula. The island is gone today. What happened to it is a mystery.*

✦ On the afternoon of March 16, 1779, the two ships of Capt. Cook's third voyage, *Resolution* and *Discovery*, were about 18 miles southwest of Niihau. Capt. Cook was dead now, having been killed a month earlier on the Big Island. But the expedition, under the command of new captain Charles Clerke, had continued, and now, before leaving the Hawaiian Islands for good, had one final exploration to make.

They were looking for the one Hawaiian island they had heard about but not yet seen. Its name was Mokupapapa and, as best the Englishmen could judge from accounts they had gotten from natives, it was located somewhere in the area of Kaula, the mile-long, uninhabited, crescent-shaped rock 22 miles southwest of Niihau. Described as a small, low, sandy island, Mokupapapa was supposed to be visited by Hawaiians, who took turtle there.

In the late afternoon of March 16, in the open ocean, the *Discovery* encountered some Hawaiians in a canoe. The natives were on their way to Kaula, and then to Mokupapapa. In his journal, James Burney, *Discovery*'s first lieutenant, recorded the meeting this way:

---

First published November 1983.

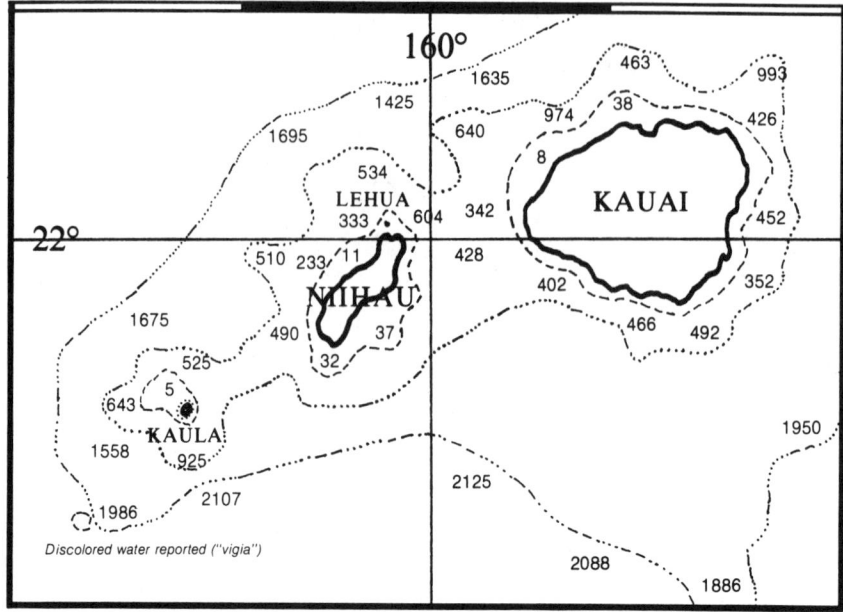

A map showing the location of Kaula in relation to Kauai and Niihau. Numbers indicate ocean depths in fathoms. Note the extremely shallow area just northwest of Kaula.

One canoe belonging to some Kauai chief staid with us till Sunset, and then went towards the Island Kaula which was 4 miles distant to the SE. Their business, they told us, was to catch red birds, and that next day they intended going to Mokupapapa for Turtle.

Apparently the English sailors (who, after all, had had so much practice finding islands throughout the vast reaches of the Pacific) were confident they could find Mokupapapa on their own, without being guided there by a small canoe. But they were wrong. They never found the island. For two days they sailed in a generally southwesterly direction, keeping a sharp watch out for what Capt. Clerke called "this good Sandy Isle." Finally, around 70 miles from Kaula, they gave up the search.

For the English sailors, this was their last contact with Hawaii. They headed north toward Arctic waters and one final look for the Northwest Passage. And for Mokupapapa, the small, sandy Hawaiian

## The Lost Hawaiian Island

island virtually unheard of today, this was the first and last time until 1983 anyone other than the old Hawaiians who kept no written records ever tried to find it.

Mokupapapa is gone *now*; there is no question of that. The waters within hundreds of miles of Hawaii are simply too heavily traveled for any island—even a tiny one—to go long undetected. But there is considerable evidence the island once existed.

At least seven men in Capt. Cook's voyages to Hawaii independently made reference to Mokupapapa in their journals. They were told about the island by natives from Niihau, Kauai, and Maui. The sailors' accounts were sometimes quite detailed. Capt. Clerke, for example, on March 16, 1779, the first day of their search for Mokupapapa, made this journal entry:

> At 8 haul'd our Wind and spent the Night upon our Tacks, with an intention in the Morning to look for an Isle which these People give an account of and call Mokupapapa. They describe it as a very low sandy Key to which they sometimes go to catch Turtle by which they say it is very much frequented, in their passage to it they lay a Night at Kaula and very easily paddle there in the course of the following day—by the best accounts I could get from the People at Niihau I conclude it to lay about swbw [southwest by west] from Kaula.

A day earlier, David Samwell, *Discovery*'s surgeon, had written this: "Light Winds and fair Wr. AM at 7 Weighd & Saild for the Island Kaula, to the SW of Which the Natives say there is a Small Sandy Isld with Plenty of Turtle on it called Mokupapapa."

Still earlier in the same month, *Resolution*'s first lieutenant, James King, in the course of a lengthy description summing up much that he had observed in six months in Hawaii, commented: "Molokini is too small to deserve the name of an Island, & that as well as Kaula are uninhabited. To the wsw of Kaula, they visit a low sandy Island for Sea birds and Turtle called Mokupapapa."

In fact, on December 1, 1778, King had heard mention of Mokupapapa all the way over on Maui—a significant point since it means knowledge of the island was not limited to nearby Niihau and Kauai but was widespread. While the *Resolution* was anchored off the east shore of Maui, about 10 or 12 natives came aboard. The meeting was a friendly one. King wrote:

We had now leisure to examine these people concerning the Number of Islands with their Knowledge. Hawaii for which we are now stearing & is the last Island to the East: to the Westward of which they mentioned Maui, Molokai, Lanai, Kahoolawe, Molokini, Oahu, Kauai, Niihau, Lehua, Kaula, Mokupapapa, of these they represent Hawaii as the largest.

Capt. Cook himself mentioned the island once, on February 2, 1778, at the conclusion of the voyage's first of two visits to Hawaii. At this point in his explorations here, Cook was familiar with only the five islands at the northern part of the chain: Kauai, Niihau, Lehua, Kaula, and Oahu. He noted: "Besides these five islands, we got some information of a low uninhabited island in the neighborhood of these, called Mokupapapa."

Cook of course would never get the chance to look for Mokupapapa, since on the return trip to Hawaii he would be killed at Kealakekua Bay. His successor, Capt. Clerke, would die at sea of consumption six months later. David Samwell would go on to a long career as ship's surgeon and become a prominent poet in London literary circles. But unlike the men, whose fame would live after them, Mokupapapa would be forgotten, a curious footnote to history.

Literally, the name "Mokupapapa" means low or flat island—"moku" meaning island in Hawaiian, and "papapa" meaning low or flat. Mary Kawena Pukui and Samuel Elbert's *Hawaiian Dictionary* even includes the word combination "moku papapa" together, defining it as a "low reef island."

Actually, the explorers did not always record the island neatly as Mokupapapa, although this is clearly the most probable rendering. The Englishmen were conversing with natives who spoke an unfamiliar tongue, one in which dialects could vary even from island to island. Kauai, for example, was referred to in sailors' logs as "A-Tou I" or "Tou'I" or "Koue I," among others. Kahoolawe could be "Kahowrowee" or "Tahowrowee," and Niihau could be "Neeheehow" or "Oneehow." Thus Mokupapapa, a complex and difficult word to pronounce in the first place, was sometimes rendered "Komodoo papapa" or "Tummata papapa," and so on. Still, once a reader has become accustomed to the language of the explorers' journals, and observes the context in which a name is being used, it is easy to tell what island is being referred to. When James King, for instance, writes: "To the WSW of Teura [Kaula],

## The Lost Hawaiian Island

they visit a low sandy island for Sea birds and Turtle called Modoo-papapa or Komodoo papapa," it is not hard to tell what island is being described.

John C. Beaglehole, the renowned historian and Cook biographer, was frankly puzzled by the Mokupapapa question. Here was an island that by all accounts should have been found but wasn't and never has been. In a footnote in his *Journals of Capt. James Cook: The Voyage of the Resolution and Discovery*, he comments:

> This 'low sandy Island' is quite baffling, though the name was picked up in both 1778 and 1779 . . . [*Ka*]*motu* or *moku papapa* is literally the low or flat and smooth island. Charlton, 15 March, renders the name Commevoopapappa, which at least is original; Burney, same date, Tomogoopapappa. There is a large isolated rock about four feet high, called Kuakamoku, standing near the middle of a shoal about $2^{1}/_{2}$ cables offshore of Niihau about a third of the way up its eastern coast, which has been suggested; but it fits none of the description, and though it might attract sea birds, would certainly not attract turtle. Dr. Emory suggests that, as Nihoa was known to the historic Hawaiians and frequently visited by them, Moku Papapa may have been an alternative name for this island. Although Nihoa is not low or flat, *papa* could have referred to the strata exposed in the great cliff walls. But then what becomes of our compass direction? Nihoa is certainly not WSW of Kaula, but a NW extension of the main Hawaiian chain.

So what are we to make of the situation? There are several possible explanations. One is that the island never existed, and that the Hawaiians who told the Englishmen about it were deliberately deceiving them or playing a joke on them. Yet this really does not seem likely; the name was picked up at different times in different places by different people; and most of the other geographical information the explorers received from natives was reliable. In short, it is extremely hard to imagine the entire Mokupapapa story as some sort of elaborate practical joke.

Another possibility is that the whole episode was an exercise in miscommunication—that the Hawaiians did in good faith describe a "moku papapa," but were not referring to a small island near Kaula. As Lee Motteler, geographer for Bishop Museum, responded when asked if there was much of a tradition for the natives deliberately deceiving the

Englishmen, "Well, there has been since, but usually at early or first contact it's more likely you have some kind of misunderstanding."

What then might the Hawaiians have been describing—if not a sandy island near Kaula? "If we could look at records," says Motteler, "and determine possibly the Hawaiians had said '*na*moku papapa,' that would make it plural—the low islands. Maybe they were referring collectively to all the low islands beyond Necker."

Could the Hawaiians have been referring to one or several of the Northwestern Hawaiian Islands like French Frigate Schoals—low, flat, sandy islands known to have plenty of turtle? There is a small amount of evidence that could conceivably be marshaled to support this theory. In their journals, two men do make reference to Mokupapapa as lying to the northwest of the other islands. In the upper left-hand corner of a map he drew of Kauai, Niihau, Lehua, and Kaula, Thomas Edgar, *Discovery*'s master per warrant, made a written note saying, "Tummata-papapa, an island that lays to the NW of these." And Charles Clerke, then *Discovery*'s commander, at the conclusion of his first visit to Hawaii, wrote: "This group of Isles consists of 5, which we saw; the Natives tell us of another, away to the NW, which they call Tummata-papappa; this however we have only their word for."

A year later though, when Clerke had become captain and presumably learned more from the natives about the islands they had knowledge of, he would lead the search for Mokupapapa toward Kaula, not the northwest.

In addition, there are several other factors that, taken together, weigh strongly against the likelihood of placing Mokupapapa in the northwestern end of the archipelago. First, there is no physical evidence of any kind to indicate that the ancient Hawaiians ever traveled beyond Necker. Second, the natives' main reason for visiting Mokupapapa was to catch turtles, who would presumably lay eggs or haul up on the sand and bask in the sun. Yet turtles were probably not scarce around the main Hawaiian islands at that time; the Na Pali Coast of Kauai, for example, has traditionally been a good turtle grounds. French Frigate Shoals, the nearest possible candidate for a "low, sandy island" to the northwest, is 400 miles from Kauai. It seems unreasonable to believe that anyone—even master navigators—would regularly undertake so long and potentially dangerous a journey for a food source available close to home. Lastly, how are we to explain the natives the explorers encountered in a canoe on their way to Kaula? The

## The Lost Hawaiian Island

natives indicated they were going to Kaula for red birds, and then on to Mokupapapa the next day. Kaula is 50 miles *southwest* of Kauai—certainly an odd route to take to the Northwestern Hawaiian Islands!

All of which brings us back to the point we started from: a speculative belief that Mokupapapa did exist, that it was near Kaula, and that it is gone today.

Capt. Cook's men were here 204 years ago. Mokupapapa was known about then. Yet it is not mentioned in any subsequent historic accounts. So if the island did exist, what happened to it?

As strange as this may sound, 200 years is enough time for an island to "disappear," or, more accurately, sink below the surface of the ocean. It's not common, but it's not impossible either. As John Sinton, professor of geology and geophysics at the University of Hawaii, explains, "If something was there 200 years ago, you can wear it away, no doubt about that, to where the thing might not be emergent anymore. Storms take some away; and once they go down, unless the sea level drops it's not likely they would come up, because in general everything is sinking."

The key factor is the contours of the island. It's totally absurd of course to think an island as large as Oahu today could sink below sea level in 200 years, but with a very low, small island that is barely above sea level to begin with—a description that fits Mokupapapa perfectly—the situation is quite different.

Violent storms, tsunamis, or earthquakes all could cause a tiny island to be worn away and covered over by ocean. A contributing factor could be the gradual cooling and contracting of the earth's plate; another factor is the day-to-day pounding by waves. If a feature is at sea level, says Michael Garcia, professor of geology and geophysics at the University of Hawaii, "waves will unmercifully attack it." In recent times there have been documented cases in Iceland and Tonga of small islands becoming submerged.

In the vast sweep of geologic time, islands are created and islands lost. Five million years ago Oahu was below the ocean's surface; in another five million years it may be gone again. Scientists are currently monitoring the activity of Loihi, a submarine volcano off the southeast coast of the Big Island. In time, perhaps thousands of years, it may become the next Hawaiian island. It is possible Mokupapapa was the last one.

One way to try to discover where Mokupapapa might have been was to consult bathymetric charts—detailed maps showing depths and contours of the ocean floor. Islands do not spring magically from nowhere; if an area were now very deep (say thousands of feet below sea level), it would be virtually impossible for that area to have been raised high enough to be emergent just 200 years ago.

A possible clue to the island's location was contained in Capt. Clerke's log. He wrote that to get to Mokupapapa, natives would "lay a night at Kaula and very easily paddle there in the course of the following day." How far could Hawaiians then paddle in a day? This was a hard figure to pin down, but according to historians and Polynesian Voyaging Society members, a reasonable estimate would be between 25 and 40 miles a day. Assuming that the visit to Mokupapapa would probably be a round trip, with the natives returning to Kaula before heading back to Niihau or Kauai, it seemed probable that the island was within 20 miles of Kaula.

One feature immediately stood out on nautical charts. About 20 miles southwest of Kaula—the direction of Mokupapapa, according to the sailors' journals—was a vigia, an area where something unexplained but potentially hazardous to navigation had been sighted in the water. It was represented by a dotted circle, with the words "Discolored Water Reported 1955."

Could this sighting somehow have been related to Mokupapapa? Unfortunately, the location of the vigia made this possibility highly unlikely. All around the discolored area the water depth is between 1,900 and 2,200 fathoms (one fathom equals six feet)—far too deep for an island to have settled into the ocean in this spot in the last 200 years. This discoloration was more likely caused by some sort of unusual biological phenomenon, such as a mass of floating plankton.

But the bathymetric charts also revealed a second, more promising feature. About three or four miles northwest of Kaula was an extremely shallow area—five fathoms. This was odd: Amid depths of hundreds and even thousands of fathoms within several miles, the figure "5" jumps right out at you when scanning the maps of the Kaula area. How shallow actually was the water there? How carefully had it been charted? How large was the shallow area, and what did it look like? True, it lay to the northwest of Kaula—not the southwest—but it seemed unusual enough to warrant further invetigation. And so was born the *Honolulu*-sponsored expedition in search of Mokupapapa.

## The Lost Hawaiian Island

We soon learned that a few local fishermen and scientists already knew about the five-fathom area. Although reports of its shape and size were vague, stories seemed to contain two similar elements: The shallow area did indeed "pop up" suddenly from greater depths all around it, and it was unusually swarming with sharks.

So, one day in early September, we, along with geophysicist John Sinton and diver/photographer Brad Tarr, reserved *Lady Ann*, a Kauai charter fishing boat with sophisticated navigation and depth-sounding equipment, and traveled to the area.

We found the spot we were looking for, that it was basically a small and most interesting flat-topped pinnacle, but that we could not conclusively say it was Mokupapapa.

Although it would be equally hard to prove this pinnacle was not the lost island, the main problem with believing the pinnacle had been Mokupapapa was its distance below the ocean's surface. Although previous mappings of the area had been inaccurate—greatly exaggerating the pinnacle's size—the five-fathom depth was essentially correct. And five fathoms, or 30 feet, is a long way for an island to have subsided, or sunk, in 200 years. According to John Sinton, the highest documented subsidence rate for islands is four millimeters a year, which over 200 years amounts to slightly less than three feet. Still, little is known about subsidence rates when islands are virtually at sea level to begin with.

Is it possible there are other, uncharted, even shallower regions within "an easy day's paddle" of Kaula?

In geologic terms, Kaula Island is a tuff cone rising from the southeast edge of a broad base that is a large, submerged shield volcano. what this means is that there is about a five-by-eight-mile area around Kaula where the water is not too deep—averaging 200 feet. Beyond this platform, depths drop off sharply.

Reviewing old marine charts recently, Sinton did notice that when the area was surveyed, sounding lines were spaced far enough apart for certain submarine features to still remain hidden. Although unlikely, it is not inconceivable other very shallow areas exist on the shield volcano platform. One way to investigate this would be to fly over the area thoroughly on a calm, clear day, since any submerged features rising to near the water's surface should be easy to see from the air.

While perusing old maps, Sinton uncovered one other interesting fact: A U.S. Coast and Geodetic Survey made in 1927 had given a name to the pinnacle we visited. No, it was not a Hawaiian name, not Mokupapapa. It was "Buoy Shoal." The name has never been used since.

The whole subject of names can become confusing. There is, for instance, a small, flat, basalt rock at the east end of Molokai named Mokupapapa. There is also a Mokupapa Point on the north shore of Maui, near Huelo. And in 1866, an emissary for King Kalakaua, James Harbottle Boyd, claimed Kure Atoll for the kingdom of Hawaii. His name for it? Moku Papapa.

None of these, however, are reasonable candidates for a low sandy island an easy day's paddle from Kaula. And so, for the present at least, the story of this lost Hawaiian island must remain a puzzle with a missing piece, an intriguing if somewhat frustrating real-life sea mystery. In retrospect, it just seems everything would have been a lot less complicated if, on that distant afternoon in March 1779 when the English explorers met the natives in that canoe bound for Kaula and then Mokupapapa, they had simply asked the Hawaiians to take them there.

# Capt. George Vancouver:
## The Forgotten Explorer

### HERB KAWAINUI KANE

*The extent of this British commander's involvement in Hawaiian history rivals that of his fellow explorer and contemporary, James Cook. Why is Capt. Cook today a household name and Capt. Vancouver a near obscurity?*

Sailing home to England in 1795, Capt. George Vancouver had earned a hero's welcome. A diplomatic mission to Spanish California had secured British commerce in the Pacific. The treaty he had worked out with Kamehameha, if ratified by Parliament, would bring Hawaii into the empire, giving British ships a safe and dependable source of provisions in the mid-Pacific. He had added more than 200 discoveries to the map of Australia and the Pacific Ocean. In all, his achievements in the North Pacific had far exceeded those of his mentor, Capt. James Cook. And for good measure, he had captured a Dutch ship on the way home.

What awaited George Vancouver, however, was not glory, but a furor that would destroy his career and force him into obscurity, and death, at age 40.

♦ It had been a wearing, dangerous voyage of more than four years. The largest ship in Vancouver's tiny squadron was his flagship, HMS *Discovery*, only 99 feet long, cramped with 100 men and the supplies

---

First published May 1985.

necessary for a voyage around the world. His ships had been wracked by storms and shoals. But despite the difficulties and the close quarters, discipline among the crew members had been preserved, and a new health record had been set under the care of physician-naturalist Archibald Menzies. Vancouver's own health, however, was failing, at 37, after 22 years of serving on the seas.

When he got back to England, Vancouver found his achievements overshadowed by controversy over the punishment he had dealt one of his officers during the voyage. He was charged with flogging a midshipman. The flogging of midshipmen, the "young gentlemen" officer trainees, was forbidden in the British navy. The accusation would not have been newsworthy, however, if young Thomas Pitt, the midshipman, had not been a cousin of the prime minister, Pitt the Younger, and a member of one of the most influential families in England.

By all accounts, Thomas Pitt was a youngster of impulsive and insubordinate behavior, who possessed an ungovernable temper. On the voyage he had become so troublesome that Vancouver had put him ashore in Hawaii. Pitt managed to find passage on a trading ship to the Orient, joined the crew of *Resistance* at Malacca, had trouble with its captain, and eventually reached England on another ship. On arriving home, he learned that his father had died, leaving him the title of Lord Camelford. He immediately brought the charge against Vancouver, and the press feasted on it.

He challenged Vancouver to a duel. Ill with what may have been tuberculosis, that scourge of so many of Cook's officers, Vancouver had retired to his brother's home in the country to assemble for publication the official account of the voyage. He responded to Lord Camelford's challenge by stating that any unpleasantness his lordship had experienced on the voyage had been brought upon himself by his lordship's own behavior and had been necessary for the preservation of the ship's discipline. He then accepted the duel on the condition that all the evidence be presented to any admiral of the navy, who would then determine whether or not Vancouver was liable, by the laws of honor, to be called upon. If such guilt were found, Vancouver declared, he would very cheerfully give his lordship satisfaction on the field of honor.

It was the proper response, but a bit too cold-blooded for Camelford, who rejected the condition. At a chance meeting on a London street, Camelford flew into a rage and attacked Vancouver with his cane until restrained by passersby. Continued persecution forced Vancouver to

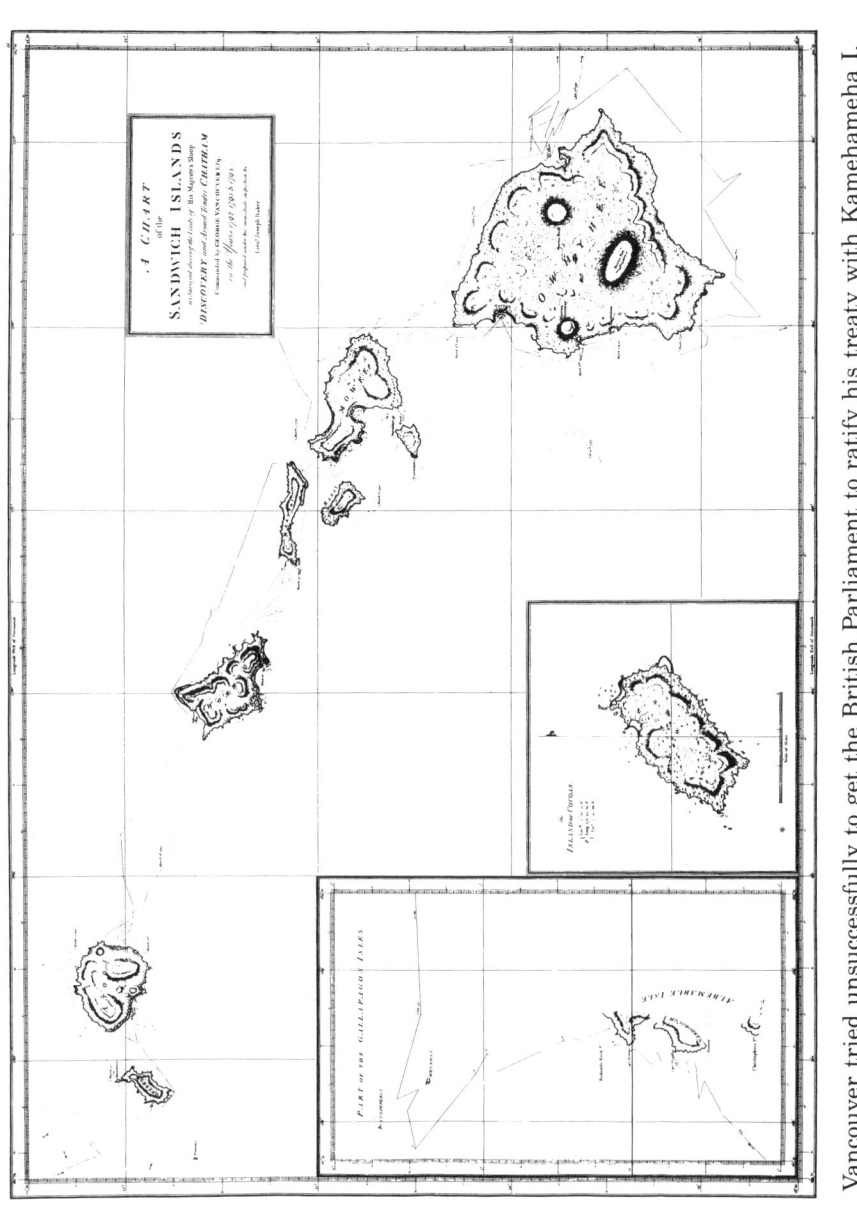

Vancouver tried unsuccessfully to get the British Parliament to ratify his treaty with Kamehameha I, which would have brought the Sandwich Islands into the empire.

appeal to the lord chancellor, Lord Loughborough, for protection. Loughborough sent for Camelford, who became so abusive that Loughborough ordered him to put up a large sum as bond to keep the peace.

Vancouver might have enjoyed vindication had he lived longer. In 1798, the year of Vancouver's death, Camelford was courtmartialed on the charge of murdering a fellow officer. He was acquitted in spite of the strong evidence. Thereafter, however, the navy repeatedly passed him over for promotion until he took the hint and resigned. Then, during a duel with a friend whom he suspected of having cast a slur on him, he was killed.

Vancouver's treaty with Kamehameha providing for the cession of Hawaii to the British Empire may have been a victim of the captain's troubles with Lord Camelford. Historians have suggested that Parliament's failure to ratify the treaty was due to its preoccupation with European problems. But the unpleasantness between Vancouver and the prime minister's annoying cousin must also have affected the outcome.

Back in Hawaii, Kamehameha had continued with his conquests, probably assuming that his alliance with King George was a fact, not having received any word to the contrary. Knowledge of the treaty may have done much to discourage his adversaries. He carried the flag Vancouver had given him, and the Union Jack became the dominant motif in the flag of the kingdom of Hawaii, named after the island under whose rule all the Islands had been united.

The opportunity which Britain failed to take advantage of was made possible by the extraordinary qualities of George Vancouver. Through his civility and diplomacy, he won for Britain the firm friendship of Kamehameha and other ruling chiefs of Hawaii.

Vancouver had first encountered Hawaiians as a young midshipman serving under Capt. Cook. He knew from personal experience the violence to which his hosts could be aroused; he had been severely beaten in a quarrel the day before Cook was killed. Thirteen years later, he was back in the Islands as captain of another expedition. Between 1792 and 1794 he made three visits to the Sandwich Islands, calling on chiefs in each of the "four kingdoms." Preaching peace and distributing new species of food plants and livestock, he adopted the role of a benefactor working on behalf of King George.

Hawaiians had seen few like him. Most foreigners brought trouble—rude seamen who deserted their ships and piratical sea captains who did little to conceal their disdain for the customs of their hosts. Even Cook, that most considerate of explorers, had arrived at Kealakekua Bay exhausted, ill, exhibiting tantrums that appalled his officers, and had made the rash and fatal attempt to take the king as hostage against the return of a stolen (or impounded) boat.

Shortly after Cook's death, British and American traders began buying furs on the Northwest American coast and selling them at great profit in China. On their trans-Pacific route, the newly discovered Sandwich Islands became an important stop for water and provisions. Firearms were traded. When some chiefs obtained muskets and cannon, it became a matter of survival for others to do the same, and the Hawaiian arms race was on.

These were uncertain and calamitous times. Beset by new diseases, awed by the technology and wealth of the Westerners, Hawaiians began to lose confidence in their own institutions. Hawaiians returning from travels overseas brought tales of continents swarming with humanity and nations competing for power. To Kamehameha it became clear that unless the Islands were brought under one rule and a favorable alliance made with a friendly nation, his world quickly would be devoured by outsiders.

Then came Vancouver, a pleasant representative of Britain, bringing a fervent wish for peace, seeds of a new prosperity and hope. Kamehameha welcomed the signals. The two became friends.

From his earlier meeting with Kamehameha on the Cook visit, Vancouver remembers him as a fierce-looking and impetuous young chief. Now he was astounded to find Kamehameha transformed into a man of impressive dignity, geniality, and diplomacy and as sharp in business as a London merchant.

Kamehameha had not lost his physical skills. In a demonstration, six spears were hurled at him at once, and he caught two, parried three, and dodged one. Modern warfare technology had captured the king's interest, but Vancouver refused to sell weapons to Kamehameha or his adversaries. Instead, he went among them, often at great risk, trying to dissuade them from fighting.

He was outraged at the conduct of certain traders, which was "not only infamously fraudulent but barbarous and inhuman ... Under a conviction of the importance of these islands to Great Britain, in the event of an extension of her commerce over the Pacific Ocean, I lost no opportunity for encouraging their friendly dispositions towards us."

Vancouver's initial proposal for cession was shrewdly parried by Kamehameha, who declined to consider it unless a British warship were stationed at Hawaii to assist in the defense of the island. While this impressed the naturalist Archibald Menzies as "a very strong and reasonable argument," it also suggests that Kamehameha may have been seeking a treaty of protection and military alliance rather than outright cession to Britain. Though his repeated requests for firearms were refused, Kamehameha played the negotiations until Vancouver built him a small schooner—providing a demonstration of shipbuilding techniques which, to the astonishment of the British, were quickly learned by the Hawaiians.

Persistent and eager to be of service, Vancouver on one occasion almost went too far. On his last visit to Hawaii, he involved himself in one of Kamehameha's domestic difficulties with the beautiful and willful Kaahumanu:

> I understood from the king's attendants, that the infidelity of the queen was by no means certain; and as I well knew the reciprocal affection of this royal pair, and as she was then residing with her father at, or in the neighborhood of Karakakooa [Kealakekua], I thought it a charitable office to make a tender of my endeavours for the purpose of bringing about a reconciliation. In reply to this obtrusion of my services, Tamaahmaah [Kamehameha] expressed his thanks; and assured me, that he should always be happy to receive my advice on state affairs, or any public matters, especially where peace or war may be concerned; but that such differences as might occur in, or respect, his domestic happiness, he considered to be totally out of my province. This rebuff I silently sustained.

The two men, however, eventually contrived a prank that demonstrates the extent of their friendship. Vancouver invited the queen and her party to his ship for an entertainment, then sent a message to Kamehameha, who came aboard acting as if he did not know Kaahumanu was present. As the two stood face to face, both burst into tears; and Vancouver, taking each by the hand, brought them together to the applause of all in the party.

At the end of Vancouver's final visit, Kamehameha called a meeting of the ruling chiefs of Hawaii at Kealakekua Bay. Lengthy discussions were held, and arguments for and against cession were offered, with Vancouver present to answer all questions. The matter was concluded in a formal meeting of the highest chiefs aboard *Discovery*. Kamehameha made a fine speech about the advantages of British protection. News of the cession was carried to the throng on shore and hailed with enthusiasm, followed by the planting of the flag at Kealakekua beach. The ships fired a cannon salute, and a copper plate was installed at Kamehameha's residence, inscribed:

> On the 25th of February, 1794, Tamaahmaah king of Owhyhee, in council with the principal chiefs of the island assembled on board His Britannic Majesty's sloop *Discovery*, in Karakakooa Bay, and in the presence of George Vancouver, commander of said sloop; Lieutenant Peter Puget, commander of his said Majesty's armed tender the *Chatham*; and other officers of the *Discovery*, after due consideration, unanimously ceded the said island of Owhyhee to His Britannic Majesty, and announced themselves to be subjects of Great Britain.

The strong friendship between the ruling chiefs of Hawaii and Britain lasted well into the nineteenth century, existing out of all proportion to the actual British presence, to the immense discomfort of American settlers. Still smarting from the humiliation of the War of 1812, and eager to gain influence, Americans made every effort to break this friendship and promote suspicion of Britain, including condemnation of Capt. Cook. The missionary Sheldon Dibble went so far as to fabricate a "history" that presented Cook as a blasphemer and philanderer. This campaign to discredit the British did not include Vancouver, however. He was simply ignored. His reputation in Hawaii fell into obscurity just as it had in Britain.

Capt. George Vancouver was one of the most outstanding of eighteenth-century explorers. Yet his life is one of the least documented. Vancouver's posthumous reputation today has currency only on the Northwest American coast, where his name is remembered in Vancouver Island; Vancouver, Washington; and Vancouver, British Columbia. In England, his portrait has been put in storage at the National Portrait Gallery because the curators are not certain that it is Vancouver's. His simple grave was forgotten and neglected for many years until the people of British Columbia took charge of its care.

Beginning in 1991, his reputation may at last be resurrected—that year will inaugurate the four-year bicentennial of his remarkable voyage. There may be observances in Britain, Australia, Hawaii, the U.S.

Pacific coast, Alaska, and Canada. It could all be quite splendid; Vancouver's ghost could at last bask in the attention it deserves.

But then again, recognition may not come to poor George Vancouver still. The attention of the world may be diverted to another observance, the 500-year celebration of another, more famous explorer, when the media and all our schoolchildren will be chanting: "In fourteen hundred ninety-two, Columbus sailed the ocean blue."

Had the British Parliament not been affected by Capt. George Vancouver's quarrel with Thomas Pitt, the prime minister's cousin, it might have ratified Vancouver's treaty with Kamehameha and made Hawaii part of the British Empire. In that case, these Islands would probably be very different today.

- Since the British name "Sandwich Islands" would undoubtedly have been kept for the new colony, the native People would not be called "Hawaiians" but "Sandwich Islands Maoli," to distinguish them from the Cook Islands Maori or the New Zealand Maori. "Maori," or the Hawaiian "Maoli," is the Polynesian term for Polynesians.
- Most of the land would still be under the control of the chiefly families. Today, throughout most of the Pacific islands, the land still remains under native ownership. Except for Hawaii, Guam, and New Zealand, land ownership is strictly limited. In some areas, land cannot be purchased at all; in others, land cannot be purchased by outsiders; and in others, land can be purchased only under severe restrictions.

The prevalent attitude in the Pacific islands toward land was expressed by Kamehameha III in his 1840 constitution. Referring to his father, he declared: "Kamehameha I was the founder of this kingdom, and to him belonged all the land from one end of the Islands to the other, though it was not his own property. It belonged to the chiefs and the people in common, of whom Kamehameha I was the head, and had the management of the landed property. Wherefor there was not formerly, and is not now, any person who could convey away the smallest portion of this land without the consent of the one who had, or has, the direction of the kingdom."

That consent came seven years later when private land ownership was introduced to Hawaii. Under strong pressure from American advisers, Kamehameha III was persuaded that land distribution would be of great benefit to his people. It was of greater benefit to Americans who were waiting to grab land from a people who had no concept of private land ownership, who believed that land, being immortal, could not be owned by mere mortals.

## Capt. George Vancouver

Unlike the Americans, however, British colonizers tampered very little with existing Pacific land tenure systems. Wherever they could find a local authority structure they could deal with, they were usually content to lease land as needed for plantations. (New Zealand was an exception; there the Maori were divided into numerous warring tribes and a central authority structure was absent.)

Had the Sandwich Islands developed along the same lines as the Fiji Islands, as a colony and later as an independent Commonwealth nation, the original land tenure system would have been largely preserved. In Fiji today, only 8 percent of the land is "freehold" and may be bought or sold. Ten percent is government land, and 83 percent remains under the ownership of "the chiefs and people in common," under the authority of the Grand Council of Chiefs sitting on the Native Land Trust Board.

All this may come as a shock to Americans who live in Hawaii but are unfamiliar with the rest of the Pacific islands. We seem to regard the opportunity to buy or sell land as universal.

- Immigration to the Sandwich Islands would have been so different from the immigration that actually took place that virtually none of the present locally born population would be here. Contract labor from India would have been preferred to Chinese and Japanese labor. For political reasons, Spanish and Portuguese immigration would have been unlikely. And without the "American connection," there would have been few immigrants from the United States, the Philippines, Puerto Rico, and Samoa. Immigration from the British Isles may have included convict labor from England, contract laborers from the poverty-stricken villages of Scotland, and refugees from the Irish potato famine.
- And World War II? Without a Hawaii, American interest in other Pacific dependencies may not have developed. Without a Pearl Harbor there may have been little reason for the United States to engage Japan during World War II.

✦ ✦ ✦

# The First Haole on Maui:
## La Perouse, the Humanitarian Explorer

### MIRKA KNASTER

*Two hundred years ago in May, on an expedition around the world, French navigator La Perouse became the first Westerner to visit Maui. This admirer of Capt. Cook was remarkable not only because of his accomplishments in world exploration but also because of his rare generosity of spirit.*

*At a time when oceanic exploration was associated with unbounded greed for new territory, wealth, and power, ruthless competition among neighbor nations, and callous indifference to the needs of both the common sailor and "uncivilized native," France's foremost navigator was a remarkable exception. Jean François de Galaup, count of La Perouse, was the first European to set foot on Maui, less than a decade after Capt. Cook's untimely death in 1779 on the Big Island. Had La Perouse been a man of less integrity, today we would probably need a passport and the ability to speak French in order to visit an island we might instead be calling Ile de La Perouse. But the great seaman and military officer, as benevolent to his enemies as to his crew, was a respectful visitor to foreign lands. In his career as world navigator, La Perouse demonstrated a humanity that was rare among explorers.*

---

First published May 1986.

✦ Although born a landed aristocrat in southern France in 1741, La Perouse chose sailing on the high seas over managing his family's estates. He joined the Royal French Navy when he was only 15. By 1778 he was a distinguished officer who was helping his country champion American independence. He provided valuable assistance along the Atlantic coast by supporting at sea the land maneuvers of Washington, Lafayette, and Rochambeau. He fought naval battles, relayed messages, and carried desperately needed money, supplies, arms and men.

Well respected for his outstanding navigational and military skills, La Perouse was also esteemed for his generous and noble character, even by those he fought. In 1782, he was ordered to destroy the English forts at Hudson Bay and confiscate their supplies. Concerned that the survivors would starve to death or be killed by the Indians, La Perouse left them arms and provisions. He had not forgotten how kindly he had been treated—even nursed back to health—when taken prisoner by the English during the Seven Years' War. Before long his reputation attracted the attention of Louis XVI and Marie Antoinette.

The king was eager to distract his people from the concerns of liberty and self-government which had been aroused by the American Revolution. Inspired by visions of glory for France, Louis planned a magnificent expedition to the Pacific. He chose La Perouse, his most experienced and trustworthy navigator, to direct what would be a long and perilous voyage.

La Perouse was given explicit instructions. The voyage was not to last more than four years and not to go beyond 60 degrees latitude north and south. As much as possible, he was not to follow in the wake of other explorers but was to trace new routes, chart undiscovered lands, and correct earlier findings. Louis also hoped La Perouse would locate the coveted passage from the Pacific to Hudson Bay that Capt. Cook had never found.

The French king also wanted political and economic information. How well defended were the far-flung Spanish, English, Russian, Dutch, and Portuguese settlements? What possibilities existed there for commerce and colonization? What did the Pacific islanders produce and how did they live and govern themselves? What effect had European contact had on them? Were Cook's gifts of grain and livestock thriving? Could France enter the North American fur market and trade with Japan and China for tea and silk?

La Perouse's voyage was also serving as a lavishly furnished scientific venture. An avid amateur geographer, Louis had consulted with

## The First Haole on Maui

the foremost specialists to transform two first-class frigates into veritable laboratories. The most up-to-date equipment was selected: microscopes, diving suits, chronometers to accurately determine longitude, and newly invented balloons to study upper air currents. Astronomers, botanists, zoologists, meteorologists, agronomists, geologists, and oceanographers were invited to go along to gather data and samples. Anthropologists were given the task of measuring the physical characteristics of different racial groups, observing native lifestyles, and collecting artifacts. Artists were engaged to illustrate everything from dwellings and ceremonies to faces and clothing.

For good-will purposes, Louis opened his coffers wide and provided an enormous quantity of goods to be used for gifts or barter. The varied cargo included jewelry, mirrors, beads, bells, dishes, tools, seeds, roots, textiles, and paper. The ships also carried four large German organs, 12 smaller ones, 2,000 combs, 2,000 hatchets, 1,000 scissors, 1 million assorted pins, and 9,000 fishhooks. Because the goods were regarded as essential in assuring the success of the voyage, La Perouse sacrificed part of his provisions in order to stow them all on board.

After two years of meticulous preparation, on August 1, 1785, the expedition finally set sail from Brittany, with *La Boussole* ("Compass") under La Perouse's command and *L'Astrolabe* ("Quadrant") under Capt. Paul-Antoine de Langle, who had been with him at Hudson Bay. The ships made their first stops at Madeira and Trinidad, then sailed around Cape Horn to replenish supplies in Chile.

Life at sea entailed extremely harsh conditions and the likelihood of disease. But La Perouse was an unusually considerate captain. He took precautions to keep his men well and in good spirits. He had them air their bedding in the sun, wash their shirts in rain water, and fumigate the quarters between decks. He alternated their four-hour watches with eight hours of sleep and gave them the best food and drink possible to prevent scurvy. He even set up a period of exercise from 8 to 10 in the evening, when the sailors would dance. (He also looked after their economic welfare. Later in the voyage, when furs obtained in North America were sold in Asia, he turned over all the profits to his crew, keeping nothing for himself and his officers.)

During the expedition's stop at Concepcion, a Spanish naval captain expressed surprise at the excellent health of La Perouse's crews. They were the first to round the Horn without sickness. (Two years later, a governor at Kamchatka, a Russian peninsula projecting into the Pacific, also remarked on the good condition of the French sailors.)

From South America, La Perouse sailed to Easter Island, where he completed an extensive scientific survey. According to his original instructions, at this point he should have directed his course toward Tahiti. Instead, he turned northward and headed for the Sandwich archipelago. En route he looked for Los Majos, La Mesa, and La Disgraciada, alleged islands mentioned in Spanish charts, plotted in the same latitude as the Hawaiian Islands, just 16 or 17 degrees to the east. But he cruised the area with no results. Remembering that the Spanish were notorious for falsifying maps in order to confuse other countries and that Cook had made no mention of the Spanish islands in his journal, La Perouse concluded the Spanish isles were none other than those Cook had discovered seven years earlier. Thus, 10 months after leaving France, La Perouse finally approached Hawaii.

On the twenty-eighth of May, 1786, he sighted the snow-capped mountains of the Big Island, then the lower peaks of Maui. He was still 20 to 30 miles away when night closed in. Early the next morning, he entered Alenuihaha Channel, where the winds funneling between the mountains of the two islands create the roughest seas in Hawaii. At nine o'clock the southern part of Maui came into view.

As the ships drew closer to the southeastern shore, the men were tantalized by what they beheld. Water cascaded from the mountains, running in streams to the sea. Greenery was everywhere: trees crowned the slopes and banana plants surrounded the numerous huts clustered for several miles along the Kipahulu coast. Charmed by this scenery, La Perouse wrote, "To get an idea of what we felt one has to be a seaman and be reduced, as we were in a burning climate, to a single bottle of water a day." Unfortunately, the French sailors could devour the bananas only with their eyes while the ocean battered the coast, preventing them from anchoring.

The winds grew stronger and the ships were unable to shorten sail to receive the 150 canoes coming out to greet them. The paddlers attempted to reach the ships anyway and managed to grab hold of the rope thrown out for them. But the canoes, swamped by the ships' wake, capsized and spilled their contents. Undaunted, the Mauians cheerfully recovered the hogs they had brought for trading, emptied their canoes of the water, and tried again. In the end these difficulties made it impossible for the expedition to obtain more than 15 animals and some fruit for the hungry crew.

La Perouse decided to move on, hoping to find shelter from the trade

## The First Haole on Maui

winds for the night. As he advanced along the Kaupo and Kanaio coasts, he noted the change in topography. What he saw made him regret leaving behind the lush countryside of Kipahulu: "The mountains seemed to withdraw farther within the interior of the island, which presented the form of an amphitheater of considerable dimension, and of a yellow green color. No cascades were to be seen, the trees were less crowded together in the plain, and the villages composed of 10 or 12 huts only were remote from each other."

He was having difficulty locating a well-sheltered anchorage. The best he could find was a spot along "a dismal coast, where torrents of lava had formerly flowed." Even here the situation was precarious. Clouds covering a large hill sent out violent squalls that churned up the water. The currents and the rocky bottom beneath the sand robbed them of a secure mooring. Ironically, this shallow inlet, now known as La Perouse Bay, would prove to be one of the safest and easiest stopping places in the journey.

Canoes laden with hogs, sweet potatoes, bananas, taro, and bark cloth rushed out to meet the French ships. The natives showed great interest in the old pieces of iron the expedition had brought along, but they bartered shrewdly. Refusing to trade wholesale, they sold each item separately for more profit. La Perouse found the Mauians "mild and attentive," unlike other islanders who had overrun foreign ships and stolen everything they could get their hands on. He had merely to say "kapu," and they "did not advance a step without . . . permission."

Fortunately, the night the ships spent in this less-than-desirable mooring was calm. At eight o'clock the following morning, May 30, the Frenchmen set off for shore, where about 120 men and women awaited the first haole visitors. La Perouse recorded the event: "The soldiers with their officers landed first. We marked the space we wished to reserve to ourselves, and the military having fixed their bayonets performed the same evolutions as if in the presence of an enemy." These precautions did not bother the Mauians. In fact, "The women showed by the most expressive gestures that there was no mark of kindness which they were not disposed to confer upon us, and the men in the most respectful attitude endeavored to discover the motive of our visit in order to anticipate our desires." The natives offered the foreigners a hog, and La Perouse in turn gave them medals, hatchets, and other pieces of iron.

La Perouse was impressed by the Mauians. Their courteous behavior dissolved the strong prejudices he had formed against Hawaiians because of their slaying of Capt. Cook, a man he greatly admired. Now he conceded that perhaps the Hawaiians had done no more than justly defend themselves against the Englishman's hasty and imprudent actions.

La Perouse and his men were back on board the ships by noon and ready to continue the expedition. Sailing west, they passed midway between the northwest point of Kahoolawe and the southwest point of Lanai. Without stopping, they headed for Kaiwi Channel between Molokai and Oahu and set a course due north.

"On the 1st of June at 6 in the evening," La Perouse wrote in his journal, "we were clear of all the islands. We had employed less than 48 hours in examining them and at most only 15 days to clear up a point of geography which appeared to me of the utmost importance, since it removes from the charts five or six islands which have no existence." (Later, on his way to the Mariana Islands from Monterey, California, he nearly wrecked his ships on the Northwestern Hawaiian Islands. He named the treacherous reefs Necker Island, French Frigate Shoals, and La Perouse Pinnacle.)

Although other European explorers routinely seized newly discovered territory in the name of their sovereigns, La Perouse did not think it appropriate to claim Maui for the king who had sent him to the Pacific. A man of the eighteenth century—the century of Enlightenment—La Perouse wrote: "The customs of Europeans on such occasions are completely ridiculous. Philosophers must doubtless lament to see that men, for no better reason than because they are in possession of firearms and bayonets ... consider as an object of conquest a land fertilized by the painful exertions of its inhabitants, and for many ages the tomb of their ancestors." He suggested that navigators would do better by helping native peoples to increase their food supply—through the distribution of livestock, the planting of trees, and the sowing of grains.

La Perouse was pleased that his visit to Maui was not marked by the kind of tragedy that had befallen Cook, the man he considered "the true Christopher Columbus of the South Sea." Louis XVI had instructed La Perouse to treat all "uncivilized or savage" people with kindness and courtesy. Force was to be used only as a last resort, in absolute self-defense. "One of the happiest events of the expedition," the king had said, "would be if it were accomplished without costing the life of a single individual." Firmly in agreement with this progressive attitude, La Perouse had no trouble carrying out his orders on Maui.

After Hawaii, La Perouse explored the North American coast from Alaska to Mexico, where he checked, corrected, and completed Cook's discoveries. He remained convinced that there was no northwest passage south of the Arctic ice.

From America he headed back across the Pacific. He stopped at Macao and Manila for necessary provisions and repairs, then continued northward through waters never before sailed by European ships. His discovery of a pass to the Sea of Okhotsk between Sakhalin Island and Hokkaido in northern Japan, now called La Perouse Strait, became his major contribution to world exploration.

Elated over his find, he wrote, "We have been so fortunate as . . . to resolve at length the only geographical problem that remained perhaps to be determined concerning the globe."

During a stopover at Kamchatka Peninsula, La Perouse received word of his promotion to the rank of commodore. The friendly Russians joined the crew in celebrating the good news. It was the last warm reception the expedition would enjoy. Before leaving the outpost, La Perouse entrusted Barthelemy de Lesseps, his young Russian interpreter and the son of the French consul-general in St. Petersburg, with carrying his journal, notes, plans, and maps overland to France. (De Lesseps' nephew, Ferdinand, later became famous for building the Suez Canal.) La Perouse's foresight was fortuitous. Were it not for de Lesseps' year-long trek along primitive roads through fierce weather conditions, we would know very little about La Perouse's voyage, including his stop at Maui.

The South Pacific was the ships' next destination. La Perouse still had many details to clear up in the discoveries made by Cook, de Surville, and Bougainville. It was during this exploration of tropical waters that he lost his friend and captain, de Langle—along with his romantic illusions about the "noble savage."

In the Samoan islands, the natives turned out to be aggressive thieves around European goods, "very unruly and only slightly under the control of their chiefs." At Tutuila, when a party of Frenchmen led by de Langle tried to obtain fresh water from a stream, they were suddenly overwhelmed by a crowd of natives who were upset that others had received gifts of beads and they hadn't. The mob, whose ranks quickly swelled from 200 to 1,000, threw stones and tried to keep the visitors from leaving the cove. De Langle ordered shots fired into the air. Instead of being scared off, the natives massacred the Frenchmen.

The crew was enraged and wanted revenge. As hundreds of natives surrounded the ships, La Perouse was faced with a difficult decision. He realized that reprisal would only expose innocent men to harm. He decided not to retaliate. He wrote, "I am a thousand times more angry with the philosophers who praise the savages than with the savages themselves."

Greatly saddened, he headed for Australia. From there he sent his latest journals home on a British ship. At Botany Bay, on February 7, 1788, he wrote his last letter to France. He indicated he would return home after visiting the Tongan islands, New Caledonia, the Louisiade group, and the Solomon Islands. He was never heard from again. After spending nearly three years at sea exploring the world, La Perouse and his ships had mysteriously vanished.

In 1791, although France was in the throes of revolution, mounting concern for her favorite explorer led the French National Assembly to dispatch a special search expedition under d'Entrecasteaux. But the ships unknowingly passed the island where some survivors of La Perouse's voyage might have been found.

Navigators of other nations, constantly plying the oceans, were also put on the alert. But they too were unable to provide any news of La Perouse's whereabouts. It was not until 1826, 38 years after his disappearance, that evidence began to surface.

That year Peter Dillon, an Irishman, called at the island of Tikopia in the Santa Cruz group. Through trade, Dillon obtained the silver guard of a sword that was obviously of French origin. When he inspected it closely, he discovered La Perouse's engraved initials. Along with other objects, the silver piece had been taken from the wreckage of two large ships that had sunk in a reef at nearby Vanikoro during a hurricane.

Unable to make a detailed investigation at the time, Dillon returned the following year. The natives had much to tell him, but each had a different story. Dillon pieced together what he thought must have occurred:

One ship ran onto the reefs near Vanu and was totally destroyed. The men who were able to escape were either lost to the sharks or slain when they reached land. Their skulls, offered to the deity in a temple, remained on display for many years. The second ship, wrecked at Paiu, floated off the coral and drifted. Because it did not sink immediately, the men had a chance to save enough materials to build a two-masted ship. Many of the islanders were hostile, except for a few who were friendly toward them during the shipbuilding. Months later, having anxiously fended off the aggressive natives, all but two of the Frenchmen attempted their getaway. They were never seen again.

Dillon retrieved a multitude of relics from the coral surrounding Vanikoro. He brought them to France, where the aging de Lesseps, La Perouse's faithful journal bearer, tearfully identified them. King Charles X knighted Dillon with a cross of the Legion of Honor and endowed him with a life pension. More than a hundred years later, in 1957, a group of French divers discovered further proof of the tragic shipwreck. From underneath the coral they dug out lead ballasts, anchors, copper spikes, and other parts of the ship.

Still, in spite of all this evidence, no one knows what happened to La Perouse. Did he escape from the wreck, reach land, only to be killed by natives? Was he able to make his way to the second ship, help his men keep the natives at bay while the boat was being built, and finally sail away? Did the rough seas swallow up the makeshift vessel? On the odd chance that it did manage to reach another island, were the survivors able to avoid the kind of massacre that de Langle and his men had suffered at Tutuila?

It was an unfortunate end to an exemplary life. The courage, generosity, kindness, and integrity displayed throughout his career had set La Perouse apart from his fellow explorers. His final voyage had been undertaken to carry out the grandiose plans of his king. The expedition that brought him to the Sandwich Islands and gave him the distinction of being the first Westerner to set foot on Maui also delivered him to an uncertain fate we are still wondering about today.

# The Rape of the Fragrant Trees

## JOHN P. WAGNER

*In the early nineteenth century, Hawaii's most important resource was sandalwood. But greed for the highly valued tree brought the Islands economic and environmental disaster.*

✦ In the soft hush of a warm Hawaiian evening in March 1790, the American merchant brig *Eleanora*, outbound from Boston, lay at anchor in the blue waters of Kealakekua Bay. The *Eleanora* was China-bound with a cargo of furs from the Pacific Northwest to trade on the Canton market.

All day the members of the crew had toiled, stocking the ship with firewood, water, fruit, vegetables, and fresh pork for their upcoming voyage to the Orient. Now they were relaxing—bathing in the clear water, idling on deck, and watching towering cumulus clouds glow in the sunset.

Meanwhile, in the galley the brig's cook went about his duties preparing the evening meal. With some choice logs gathered earlier from the forests, he built his fire in the galley stove and went on with his culinary chores in a routine fashion.

The wood was most extraordinary. Its smoke gave off a strange, exotic fragrance. During dinner the aroma had a dramatic effect, especially in the officers' quarters where Capt. Simon Metcalfe and his mates celebrated a historic discovery. Their cook was burning precious sandalwood.

The next day, the *Eleanora* delayed her departure. Instead, the crew

---

First published November 1986.

went back to shore to gather more sandalwood to add to a cargo of furs for trade on the Canton market.

In the town of Kealakekua, where sailors came to replenish their ships' stores, Capt. Metcalfe's discovery soon became a poorly kept secret. In the months that followed, American seamen blazed trails through all of the Hawaiian Islands. And many found what they were looking for: vast forests of sandalwood.

At that time, Hawaiian sandalwood seemed to be an inexhaustible natural resource. Yet, in 30 short years, the forests were recklessly plundered and destroyed in a period of greed known as the "Sandalwood Bonanza."

For thousands of years, sandalwood has been highly valued. The fragrant wood has been associated with the ancient civilizations of India and China, and Baghdad and the fabled city of Tyre.

Sandalwood is mentioned frequently in ancient Hindu literature. There is even a saying: "Sandalwood teaches us to love our enemies for it perfumes the very axe which destroys it."

Today, sandalwood is still a valued forest product. Because of its sweet fragrance, the dried heartwood is important in Buddhist religious rites. Sandalwood incense and joss sticks burn in their temples.

Since 500 B.C. sandalwood has been used in China, Burma, and India for making boxes. The tree is a hardwood, and the wood is close-grained with an even texture which takes an exceptionally fine polish. It saws easily, seasons slowly but well, and is highly rated for durability.

Its exotic aroma comes from an oil contained in the heartwood which is distilled from shavings. Even now, it is used in medicines, perfumes, and cosmetics. Sometimes it is burned in lamps to keep away insects. And it is best known for the carvings and inlaid wood found in the delicate furniture pieces and statuettes made by skilled Chinese artisans.

The Hawaiian sandalwood discovery came at a convenient time. Forests were being depleted in India, Java, Timor, and other islands in the East Indies.

Although Capt. Metcalfe and his crew on the *Eleanora* discovered sandalwood on the island of Hawaii in 1790, some historians give the honor to Capt. John Kendrick, skipper of the American sloop *Lady Washington*. Six months after Metcalfe's discovery, Kendrick left three men on Kauai to collect sandalwood logs while he sailed to Boston with the news.

## The Rape of the Fragrant Trees

Unfortunately, the sailors were stranded, and Kendrick met a bizarre, unfortunate fate. He died soon afterwards in Honolulu Harbor, the victim of a wad from a cannon fired in salute by the British vessel *Jackal*. Incredibly, the wad passed through a porthole of the *Lady Washington*, killing the captain at his dinner table.

In Boston, the blow of Kendrick's death was softened by the news of his Kauai discovery. For American commerce, this was a bonanza—a great new trade opportunity coming at a time when the 13 colonies had only recently won their independence.

From the beginning, the sandalwood trade was an outgrowth of the Pacific Northwest fur trade. Cargoes of seal skins, pelts of beaver, mink, and other fur-bearing animals reaped handsome profits in China. Hawaii was squarely in the path of the fur-laden ships, and the Islands became a way station at which sailors could replenish supplies.

To the Hawaiians, sandalwood had little importance. Their polytheistic religion had no special place for it. The tree was called *iliahi*; because of its sweet aroma, the wood was known as *laau ala*, or fragrant wood. It was used chiefly as a powder or mixed with coconut oil to perfume tapa cloth. It was also—and commonly—used as firewood.

When the sandalwood era came to Hawaii, the forests were so abundant that little or no thought was given to conservation. What gold was to California half a century later, sandalwood became to Hawaii: its first major export commodity.

By 1805 the trade was so promising that numerous ships were dealing exclusively in sandalwood. Taken to Canton, the wood was bartered or sold for tea, silks, spices, and other exotic goods. In China, the Hawaiian archipelago even acquired a new name: *Tahn Heung Shan*, the Sandalwood Islands.

The advent of the sandalwood trade coincided with the reign of Hawaii's most powerful king, Kamehameha I. As ruler, Kamehameha encouraged agriculture and industry. He reinforced the age-old customs and beliefs of his people, specifically the kapu system and the land tenure arrangement which established royal control over the trade activities of the sandalwood merchants.

Under a Hawaiian sort of feudalism, the land was owned by the chief in each district and apportioned among lesser chiefs. They in turn permitted the common people to live on the land, taking in exchange a good portion of the crops raised by the tenants.

When Kamehameha ascended the throne in 1795, he allowed the chiefs to retain local control over the land and its people. Sandalwood was collected in the name of the king, and the chiefs became his agents. Thus, the wealth from the land flowed upward to the royal coffers.

Kamehameha was uncommonly shrewd in dealing with American and European merchants. He personally directed all trading transactions with the hundreds of sailing ships plying Hawaiian waters. With absolute control over the sandalwood resources, he barred other chiefs from any share in the profits as long as he lived.

Kamehameha's chief desire during the sandalwood bonanza was to acquire ships, and before his death he purchased six vessels to compete with the Yankee and British seamen on the China run. He paid for these with varying amounts of sandalwood.

The king also desired personal articles. When one of his captains, Alexander Adams, returned from China, he delighted the king with chests of rare and fragrant tea, 20 tubs of sugar candy, four boxes of hats for the queen, 100 pairs of shoes, and a large quantity of rum for his chiefs. Another ship brought with it 16 more kegs of rum, a box of tea, and $8,000 worth of guns and ammunition.

By 1815, Honolulu's waterfront bustled with the activities of officers and men from the ships in the harbor. No port in the Pacific could surpass its safe and commodious anchorage.

During Kamehameha's reign, the sandalwood forests were so vast that in some places they extended down to the sea. Yet the densest areas were in the mountains where the lack of roads and pack animals made transportation difficult and arduous.

Stripped of bark and cut into sections three or four feet long and two to eight inches in diameter, the logs were strapped on to the heads and shoulders of men, women, and children so they could be carried down the rough terrain to warehouses along the coast. Even the king himself joined in the sandalwood harvest. At such times, thousands of natives would gather in the forests and make the occasion a ceremony of feasting, dancing, and song.

An eyewitness account of a sandalwood festival was written by a British sailor in a magazine called the *Old Quarter Master*:

> I asked and obtained leave to ascend the hill in the evening; the ascent was painful and fatiguing, but it fully repaid me by the pleasing sight that met my eyes; there stood a vast number of men assembled, each with a torch made from sandalwood, which burns bright and clear.

## The Rape of the Fragrant Trees

At a certain signal they dispersed; each taking his own way to cut his load, accompanying his labour with a song, to which the whole band within hearing distance join in the chorus ... After the labour of two or three hours, the wood is collected together, each chief inspecting his own lot, judging the quality by the colour and weight. It was taken to the water's edge and piled on end ready for the boats to take away; the people then returned to their homes.

Throughout the bonanza years, the picul, roughly 133 pounds, was the standard unit of measure—one picul being the maximum weight a man could carry handily on his back. Sandalwood values fluctuated widely during this era, ranging between $3 and $18 a picul. In one year alone more than $400,000 found its way into the Hawaiian treasury, and for some years, the logs replaced money, owing to a scarcity of coins.

The death of Kamehameha in May 1819 closed out a quarter of a century of peace and prosperity for the Hawaiian people and brought on the last act in the sandalwood drama. With Kamehameha's passing came an end to the royal monopoly over the sandalwood forests. King Liholiho ascended the throne by right of inheritance. Still, he could gain the support of his chiefs only by allowing them to share in the sandalwood profits.

Kamehameha had paid cash for his purchases, but Liholiho and his followers turned to credit, giving promissory notes payable in sandalwood. During the decade that followed, the Hawaiian aristocracy went on a buying spree that damaged the economy for many years to come.

The chiefs purchased nearly everything the traders could bring them. Stores were filled with the latest in London clothing styles. For the men, stove-pipe hats became the rage. For the women, silk creations were in demand. One chief paid $8,000 for a full-length mirror so he could admire his new cutaway coat and hat.

Most irresistible of all were sailing ships. In Liholiho's reign, owning a brig was the fashion of the day. Within three years, he and his retinue bought eight vessels at a cost of more than $300,000.

These were indeed "bonanza days"—but mostly for the traders. Profits ranged from $3 to $4 a picul when the wood was sold in China. Since the traders rarely paid cash for sandalwood, but dealt in goods which were overvalued, the merchants made two profits on a single transaction, at the expense of Liholiho and his chiefs.

When it came to buying ships, the Hawaiians paid for them with sandalwood logs piled into an open rectangular pit, the same size as the hull of a ship with respect to length, breadth, and depth. One such pit still exists today on the Kapalama-Nuuanu Ridge above Honolulu. Another is located in the Molokai Forest Reserve.

The peak year of the sandalwood era was 1821, when 30,000 piculs of logs (more than 2,000 tons) were shipped to China. By the end of that year, Liholiho and his chiefs had piled up a national debt of 22,000 piculs valued at $222,000. Three years later the debt was $300,000; and pressure for payment was coming in from all sides.

For the average Polynesian, the situation became intolerable. His fields and taro patches were being neglected to satisfy the greed of the chiefs. When the easily reached sandalwood groves had been cut away, the people had to climb higher into the mountain forests. Some died of exposure in the cold higher altitudes, and for the first time in centuries famine stalked the paradise islands.

By 1827 the economy was in critical shape. The sandalwood logs were poor in quality and harder to find. Only 13,000 piculs were shipped that year. Moreover, the trade fell off because of competition from newly discovered sandalwood forests in the East Indies.

In an attempt to alleviate the economic crisis, Liholiho turned to special taxation. He issued a royal decree: "Every man is required to deliver half a picul of good sandalwood or in lieu thereof, to pay four dollars on or before September 1, 1828, and every woman to furnish a woven mat, a piece of tapa, or pay one Spanish dollar."

Liholiho's order did little to improve the situation. Two years later the shipments consisted only of small crooked sticks which brought $1.50 a picul—effectively ending the sandalwood trade in Hawaii.

Yet, the royal debt still remained.

In desperation, Boki, governor of Oahu, organized an expedition to the New Hebrides, where sandalwood was said to be abundant. Under Boki's command, the brigs *Kamehameha* and *Becket* left Honolulu in December 1829, with 500 men to search for the fragrant wood.

Both vessels made their first port of call at Rotuma in Fiji. From there, Boki, in the *Kamehameha*, set sail for the island of Erromanga in the New Hebrides. Ten days later, the *Becket* docked at Erromanga. But Boki never arrived—and nothing was ever seen or heard of him again.

In August 1830 the *Becket* returned to Honolulu with only 20 of her crew alive. Famine and scurvy had taken the rest.

## The Rape of the Fragrant Trees

Boki's fiasco broke the patience of the Hawaiian people, who turned to an orgy of destruction. They burned and destroyed nearly all of the remaining sandalwood trees "so that the despotism of their chiefs could not be extended to their descendants."

Still, this act of collective vandalism did not have an irreversible ecological effect. According to the U.S. Forest Service, plenty of sandalwood can be found in Hawaii today. In the past 150 years, rejuvenation has taken place, and sandalwood can be found near mountain trails on all of the islands. Some even grows along roadsides. Despite the abundance of native trees, considerable effort has been made to increase sandalwood growth here. Some 20,000 to 30,000 trees have been imported from India and planted in the various forest reserves.

Will sandalwood ever regain its historic position as a major Hawaiian resource? Forest researchers say it's not likely. Besides the difficulty in establishing the tree, its growth is extremely slow; it takes 40 to 60 years for a sandalwood to reach maturity. Also, the world markets today are satisfied by Australian and Indian varieties.

Nevertheless, reforestation continues. The largest known sandalwood tree in Hawaii is located above Honomalino on the Kona Coast. At 75 feet high and 39 inches in diameter, it is a true survivor of the sandalwood era.

# The Life, Death, and Rebirth of an Island

VICTOR LIPMAN

*Laysan Island, in the northwestern reaches of the Hawaiian archipelago, has undergone some strange, radical changes in the last 100 years.*

◆ On May 1, 1857, Capt. John Paty of the schooner *Manuokawai* landed at Laysan Island to annex it to the Hawaiian kingdom. He found a small island, about two miles long, covered with beach grass, shrubbery, and a few palm trees, with a lagoon in the middle. But the main thing he noticed was birds: The island was "literally covered" with them. "The birds were so tame and plentiful," Paty wrote, "that it was difficult to walk about the island without stepping upon them."

Sixty-six years later, on April 8, 1923, the Tanager Expedition landed at Laysan Island. The expedition was made up mostly of scientists and naturalists who surveyed the island and examined its wildlife. They found a much different island from the one Capt. Paty had visited.

There was still a lagoon in the middle, but there were far fewer birds. And the vegetation was gone. The once-green island had become a desert.

Today, on the surface, Laysan Island looks much as it did more than 100 years ago. It has grass once again and abundant birdlife. But the island is not quite the same as it was either. Gone forever from Laysan are three species of birds—the Laysan rail, the Laysan millerbird, and

First published November 1984.

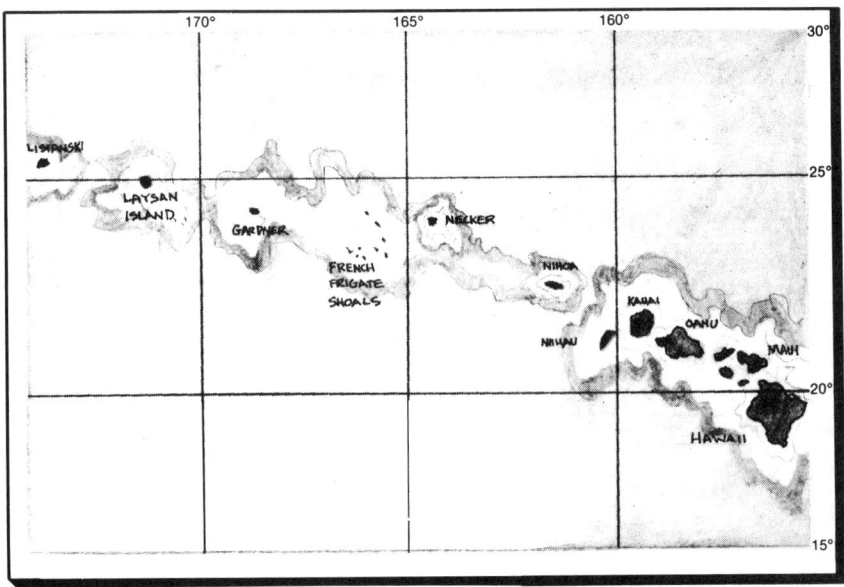

A map showing the location of Laysan Island. The nearest land, Lisiansky Island, is 115 miles away.

the Laysan honeycreeper—that were found nowhere else in the world. Gone also are several species of plants that were found only on Laysan. Located in the northwestern reaches of the Hawaiian archipelago, Laysan Island is near nothing in particular. Gardner Pinnacles lies 202 miles to the east and Lisiansky Island is 115 miles west; Honolulu is 709 miles to the southeast. No humans live on Laysan now, just as no humans lived on it for most of its thousands of years of existence. But for about 25 years—from 1890 to 1915—it was inhabited, and what happened during those years makes an unusual story involving guano mining, feather poaching, murder, and rabbits. Oddly enough, it was the rabbits that nearly brought about the ruin of the island.

It's generally believed that Laysan Island was discovered early in the nineteenth century by an American ship, but details are unavailable. The earliest recorded visit took place in 1828 by the Russian ship *Moller*. Unaware that the island had already been discovered and called Laysan, the Russian captain named the island "Moller." It is unclear where the name Laysan comes from.

## The Life, Death, and Rebirth of an Island

The story of Laysan Island, at least insofar as its story concerns man, and not just the ceaseless and unchanging rhythms of the natural world, is a classic example of the fragility of the environment and the disastrous consequences that man—even unintentionally—can have upon it. The chain of events that eventually would almost ruin Laysan Island were set in motion innocently in 1890 when an Englishman named George Freeth convinced the Honolulu firm of Hackfeld and Co. (a forerunner of Amfac) to finance a guano mining operation on Laysan. Guano, the accumulated bird droppings of centuries, was valued as fertilizer. The company was named the North Pacific Phosphate and Fertilizer Co.

When some of the members of the company visited Laysan in July 1890 to examine the guano deposits, one of the people in the party, a Mr. A. B. Lyons, made some observations of the trip. Approaching Laysan from the ocean, Lyons noted,

> there rests over the land perpetually a cloud of sea fowl, and these you can see at a glance hold undisputed possession of the island . . .
>
> The soil of the island consists of a peculiar kind of white sand, made up partly of fragments of sea shells, but largely of bits of egg shells and the bones of sea birds. A rough calculation puts the bird population of the island at about 800,000; it may reach 1,000,000. They have not yet learned to fear man excessively, and are in fact no more shy than barn door fowl, so that it is very easy to study their habits.

In short, Laysan Island was an ornithologist's dream. Birds were everywhere: in the sky, on the ground—their bones were even mingled with the sand.

According to the Atoll Research Bulletin, *The Natural History of Laysan Island*, written by Charles Ely and Roger Clapp and published by the Smithsonian Institution, the guano mining operation proceeded like this: "Laborers mined the guano, consisting mostly of a hard, conglomerated phosphate of lime, with picks, crowbars, shovels, and sledges. This material was placed on cars on a narrow gauge railway and pulled by mules to storage sheds where the guano was kept until a ship arrived."

In return for the rights to mine Laysan Island's guano, the North Pacific Phosphate and Fertilizer Co. agreed to pay a royalty of 50 cents per ton to the Hawaiian government. In April 1891 the first shipment of guano, 80 tons that sold for $15 a ton, was removed from the island. In 1894 the company's name was changed to the Pacific Guano and Fertilizer Co. And in 1896 a man named Max Schlemmer became superintendent of operations on Laysan. This is an important name: For years to come Max Schlemmer would be virtually synonymous with events of Laysan Island.

Another name associated with Laysan Island is Kosten. (Actually, the exact spelling of the name is unknown, but Kosten is thought to be a close approximation.) Kosten was a caretaker of Laysan Island. Since guano was shipped from Laysan only during spring and summer, each winter a caretaker was left on the island to watch over the company's facilities. It must have been a strange, solitary way to spend six or seven months. At any rate, when the island was revisited in the spring of 1904, Kosten the caretaker was found dead. He was still seated at the table where he had been working on his journal.

Labor unrest in the guano mining era was felt on Laysan Island, just as it was on Hawaii's plantations. Probably the most noteworthy incident took place in August 1900, when a confrontation between labor and management resulted in a shooting that left two workers dead and three injured.

A newspaper account of the incident in the *Pacific Commercial Advertiser* gave a markedly sensational version of events. Its headline was "Laysan Island's Story of Blood." The article began this way: "War has been declared, waged, and ended on Laysan Island . . . four against forty—those were the odds, four white men fighting desperately against forty infuriated Japanese. And the white men conquered."

Without going into the reasons for the confrontation, the article depicted the Japanese laborers as "determined to annihilate all the white people and run things to suit themselves." It said the Japanese were armed with "knives, clubs, stones, and cutlasses made of hoop iron sharpened." It said they charged the white men, who then fired into the crowd: "Though they moved quickly, Capt. Spencer's trigger fingers moved quicker. Eight times his revolver spoke to the point. Pistols in the hands of the other white men also had something to say." After the shooting, both sides retreated to their quarters. The next day the Japanese laborers were rounded up at gunpoint, put aboard a ship, and taken to Honolulu.

This newspaper article probably says more about race relations at

## The Life, Death, and Rebirth of an Island

the turn of the century than it does about actual events on Laysan Island. Eventually, Capt. Spencer, the guano mine manager, was tried in Honolulu for murder. After a 10-day trial with much conflicting testimony, all charges against him were dropped.

It may never be known what really happened that day on Laysan Island. It seems the Japanese laborers were making demands for more food and higher pay, and the situation possibly was aggravated by the fact that the interpreter—the only person who spoke both English and Japanese—had recently been demoted from luna to common laborer. There was a confrontation; some workers did press forward (it is unclear whether they were armed); shots were fired, men were killed. Regardless of who was to blame, the incident comprises an obscure chapter in the history of Hawaii's labor and race relations.

By 1904 most of the guano on Laysan Island was gone, and the Pacific Guano and Fertilizer Co. sold everything on the island "excepting houses" to Max Schlemmer for $1,750. Schlemmer hoped to continue to live on Laysan, plant a thousand coconut trees a year, and make a coconut plantation out of the island. Meanwhile, a little guano mining was still being done.

It was around this time that Schlemmer brought rabbits to Laysan. The rabbits were mainly a food source for Schlemmer, his family, and his workers. There had never been rabbits on the island before, and they encountered no natural enemies. There is also speculation that Schlemmer, who was something of an entrepreneur, planned to can or smoke the rabbits and sell them in Honolulu.

Whatever the reasons for introducing the rabbits, the results were disastrous. As time went on, the rabbits began to run freely over the island, multiplying rapidly and consuming vegetation. As Rob Shallenberger, a refuge manager for the U.S. Fish and Wildlife Service, explains, the pattern is not an uncommon one. "Rabbits have been introduced all over the world," he says, "that same species. And every time they are, there's always some idea about the potential for the commercial value of it. But with virtually every introduction the rabbits tend to explode, eat themselves out of house and home, and kill themselves off."

On Laysan Island, the rabbits didn't kill themselves off quickly. They continued to eat the grass and shrubbery for around 20 years. By then they had almost transformed Laysan into a new and different island.

As the rabbits were slowly eating their way into oblivion, events involving humans on Laysan were taking place as well. In December 1908 Max Schlemmer entered into an agreement with a Japanese man named Genkichi Yamanouchi to remove and sell phosphate, guano, and "products of whatever nature" from Laysan Island. By now the island's guano deposits were nearly gone, and the hoped-for coconut plantation had not materialized either. So the "products of whatever nature" were birds' feathers, a highly marketable item in the millinery trade—the women's hat business. In return for allowing the Japanese to use the island, Schlemmer would receive $150 a month in gold.

Unfortunately for Schlemmer, an executive order from President Theodore Roosevelt on February 3, 1909, had set aside much of the Leeward Islands as a protected bird reserve. Thus the Japanese feather gatherers were feather poachers. When rumors filtered back to Honolulu that poachers were raiding the northwestern Hawaiian islands, a U.S. ship was sent to the area.

In January 1910 investigators arrived at Laysan to find 15 Japanese on the island and many dead birds on the beaches. The old guano mining buildings were being used as storehouses for more than two tons of feathers and 300,000 birds' wings—materials worth around $130,000.

The Japanese were arrested and returned to Honolulu. Max Schlemmer was charged with poaching on a federal bird reservation and with two counts of illegally importing contract laborers. One of the Japanese was also charged. Eventually, however, Schlemmer was tried and found not guilty, and the feather gatherers were given free passage back to Japan.

Max Schlemmer and Laysan Island were still not through with each other; one final adventure remained. This one took place five years later and *The Natural History of Laysan Island* recounts the story this way: "Despite his earlier financial and legal difficulties over Laysan, Max Schlemmer had by no means given up his desire to live there. Early in 1915 he applied for a position as permanent warden of the Hawaiian Islands Reservation, stipulating that he wished to reside on Laysan with his two sons, a daughter, and two assistants."

No such job was ever created for him, but Schlemmer ended up going to Laysan anyway in July 1915 with his son Eric, then 12, and a young sailor named Harold Brandt. Life passed uneventfully on Laysan until one September afternoon when a schooner was sighted nearby. It turned out that the boat, with a captain and crew of nine, was on its

## The Life, Death, and Rebirth of an Island

way to San Francisco but had been damaged on a reef. Schlemmer generously offered the stranded crew the use of his yacht *Helene* to sail to Midway—leaving himself and the two boys on the island with no way to get off it.

A month passed with no sign of any return vessel. Schlemmer's diary reflects their plight:

> Nov. 4—This day we had great hopes of seeing the U.S. Coast Guard Cutter *Thetis* arrive but all in vain. We have a pretty hard time of it and we have to live on water and flour only for the last two weeks. This is pretty tough on the boys, but as for myself, I keep up good courage and hope for the best.

> Dec. 1—It is becoming very hard on the boys' nerves as they are not used to this kind of living we have had here for the past three months. It takes all I can do to keep up their courage. I told them, however, not to be discouraged and that they should pray to God... so they said their prayers.

A day later a ship came for them. It turned out *Helene* had been wrecked at Midway in a storm, so the USS *Nereus* had been sent by the Department of Agriculture. Five days later Schlemmer and the boys were back in Honolulu. But even this trip was not without incident. This was 1915—wartime—and Max Schlemmer, who had been born in Germany, was accused by authorities of being a German spy and using Laysan Island for espionage purposes. It was an unfounded accusation but it hurt Schlemmer, who was proud of being an American. "That damn near broke his heart," recalls his son Eric. "He never wanted to go back to the sea again after that."

Between 1915 and 1923 times were quiet on Laysan. There was no more guano mining, no more dreams of coconut plantations, no more attempts to live there; the island lay as isolated and forgotten as it had been for nearly all of its existence. But now the rabbits were running wild, and it was during these years that their destructiveness reached its height.

The Tanager Expedition arrived at Laysan in April 1923 and found two coconut trees and three bushes near the old guano mining houses, but otherwise the island was a sandy wasteland. Sea birds, such as terns, boobies, and shearwaters, were still around, but for three of Laysan's five rare land bird species, it was too late. Sometime between

1915 and 1923 the Laysan millerbird, a friendly, fearless bird that relied on "millers"—a type of moth—for food, had become extinct. And members of the Tanager Expedition found only two Laysan rails, a flightless bird that had once been plentiful on the island, and three Laysan honeycreepers.

A sandstorm finished them. From April 23 to 27, during a harsh four-day gale that sent sand swirling across the island, the last three Laysan honeycreepers passed out of existence. It was perhaps the only time in history that man has been present to document precisely the time and place of an extinction. The two Laysan rails also died in the storm, but the species was not yet extinct, since it had earlier been introduced to Midway. Unfortunately, rats were later introduced to Midway, which resulted in the Laysan rail's extinction in 1944. Laysan's two other endemic bird species, the Laysan teal and the Laysan finch, have survived to this day.

Before leaving Laysan, the members of the Tanager Expedition killed the remaining rabbits with poison, rifles, and stones. In a sense, the siege of Laysan Island was over.

In the years that followed, vegetation returned to Laysan. The island was visited once in a while by survey parties and wildlife researchers, but it was protected by federal law and the days of commercial ventures there were over. Today the island has no buildings on it, just the remnants of railroad tracks that used to carry the cars of guano, and a few crosses to mark old graves. And the island is green once again. Has Laysan Island recovered? "Recovered," says Rob Shallenberger of the U.S. Fish and Wildlife Service, "is not the correct word for it. It's certainly fully vegetated. But the rats almost certainly caused the extinction of some endemic plants that were found only on Laysan. So what you've got now is different from what you had before."

Sea birds abound there now. The island's estimated breeding population is just under a million pairs, or two million birds. Yet the three lost bird species can never return. Would they probably still survive if rabbits had not been introduced? "Absolutely," Shallenberger says. "There's no reason to expect the habitat would have changed. It was clearly a habitat-related problem. There have never been any other rodents or predators on the island. The extinct species were tied to the vegetation, either for nectar, for insects, for cover or for nest sites and so on."

## The Life, Death, and Rebirth of an Island

Guano mining. Feather poaching. Murder. Rabbits. Extinctions. A lovely tropical island becomes denuded and then recovers. Sort of. If there's a moral to the strange story of Laysan Island, maybe it's this: In the face of all sorts of unforeseen obstacles, life endures, but we often lose a few things along the way.

# III

♦

*Travelers and Their Tales*

# The Inevitable Visiting Writer

## TOM HORTON

*Each time a writer sets into port, Hawai'i is dissected anew—but how much better it was done when at the hands of masters.*

◆ "Nothing had prepared me for Honolulu," wrote W. Somerset Maugham. "It is a typical western city."

"I find Honolulu a beastly climate after Tahiti," complained Robert Louis Stevenson, who also groused, "The Sandwich Islands do not interest us very much; we live here, oppressed with civilization, and look for good things in the future."

"Here," wrote Herman Melville, "as in every case where Civilization has in any way been introduced among those whom we call savages, she has scattered her vices, and withheld her blessings."

"Hawaii is a Paradise—and I can never cease proclaiming it; but I must append one word of qualification: *Hawaii is a paradise for the well-to-do*," warned Jack London.

"It's a great place, Honolulu. We're certainly lifting its face for it. Give us another year and we'll make it look like Pittsburgh," brayed Admiral Henry D. Smedley, a character in a World War II short story, "Lunch at Honolulu," by J. P. Marquand.

Of the illustrious names in literature who called on Hawaii with notebooks at the ready in the second half of the nineteenth century and the first half of the twentieth, it might seem that only the visiting writer who called himself Mark Twain took an instant delight in what he found. After his first stroll through town in 1866, Twain declared, "I

---

First published November 1980.

had rather smell Honolulu at sunset than the old police courtroom in San Francisco." As first impressions of the Islands go, especially among those with the critical writer's eye, Twain was one of the few to give Honolulu the best of it at first blush.

This is not to deceive the reader into the notion that celebrated men of letters have for the most part taken instant dislikes to Hawaii. On the contrary, they have mostly been charmed and invariably fascinated by these islands and proved as much by paying Hawaii more than passing literary attention. Robert Louis Stevenson and Jack London each spent considerable time in Hawaii, the frail Stevenson for health reasons and the adventurous London as a sailing forerunner of today's jet-setters who become known as FIV's, *Frequent Isle Visitors*; and each wrote extensively and with enthusiasm about Hawaii, as well as drawing on Island experiences and characters to enliven additional works of fiction. R. L. S., as the famed author from Scotland was known wherever books were being read, and Jack London traveled throughout the Pacific at the height of their literary fame. For Twain, it was the opposite; his *Letters from the Sandwich Islands* and subsequent public lectures on nineteenth-century Hawaii were a major turning point in the rise of an itinerant newspaperman to the status of literary lion. Mostly they wrote as traveling observers, setting down their impressions of the Islands in the form of long essays or fictional short stories, sometimes in the casual style of a traveler at leisure, and at other times with the passion of skilled artists who had achieved their lofty reputations by effectively portraying the foibles and also the evils of man. Some, such as Stevenson and Twain, aspired to write epic novels with Hawaii as a setting and the imperfections of forcing civilization upon the so-called uncivilized as a theme, but in both instances the authors' aspirations exceeded their reach. Regardless of the amount of their time spent in Hawaii and the volume of their literary output, most all of those who came were challenged by what Maugham called "the incongruity of Honolulu," which he pronounced "its most striking characteristic."

Was it not ever thus? To this day, doesn't Hawaii suffer anew each time a visiting writer sets into port, goes forth upon the fabled land, and judges it to be below whatever standards he has raised for his personal vision of the ideal Island Paradise? Hasn't there been an endless succession of 201 years of scornful writing about Hawaii, or ever since James Burney, who sailed with Capt. Cook, published the

# The Inevitable Visiting Writer

*Journal of Jas. Burney, H.M.S. Discovery 1776–1779*, in which he wrote about the second trip to Hawaii with Cook not being nearly as much fun as the first? "Our launch watering on shore this afternoon was much disturbed by the Indians, who threw stones and played other mischievous tricks, which made it necessary to have a guard when she was next sent," is an example of Burney writing about Hawaii in 1779, perhaps the first printed case of a repeat visitor complaining about the aloha spirit going to hell.

With increasing frequency ever since, writers both gifted with insight and prejudiced with malice aforethought have been calling on Hawaii and attempting to expose wounds old and new for the reader's examination and judgment. Mostly, dissatisfaction stems from one of two reasons: Hawaii isn't what it used to be or what it should have become. Quite often there is a cover-up at work here, a visiting writer's way of saying, without admitting to it, *Hawaii is not what I desired it to be*.

A tempting target, isolated and compact, Hawaii has thus been attracting writers eager to tell the rest of the world what's wrong with Hawaii, as noted earlier, for roughly 201 years—but, oh how much better the dissection was done when it was at the hands of masters. When the critical visitor with pen in hand was a Melville, a Maugham, a Stevenson. Abandon your newspapers and your magazines; visit your nearest library and you'll discover endless rows of works containing all manner of commentary on one of the most enduring themes in literature or journalism, *Trouble in Paradise*; but the difference between reading the selected prose of nineteenth- and early-twentieth-century writers and the contemporary reports of the jet-age journalists of today is that you will be rewarded with some smashing good reads.

You want to read a critical view of Honolulu? I give you Herman Melville and his South Seas novel *Typee* (1846):

> Behold the glorious result! The abominations of Paganism have given way to the pure rites of the Christian worship—the ignorant savage has been supplanted by the refined European! Look at Honolulu, the metropolis of the Sandwich Islands! A community of disinterested merchants, and devoted self-exiled heralds of the Cross, located on the very spot that twenty years ago was defiled by the presence of idolatry. What a subject for an eloquent Bible-meeting orator! Nor has such an opportunity for a display of missionary rhetoric been

allowed to pass by unimproved! But when these philanthropists send us such glowing accounts of one-half of their labors, why does their modesty restrain them from publishing the other half of the good they have wrought? Not until I visited Honolulu was I aware of the fact that the small remnant of the natives had been civilized into draft horses, and evangelized into beasts of burden. But so it is. They have been literally broken into the traces, and are harnessed to the vehicles of their spiritual instructors like so many dumb brutes!

How long have writers, haoles all, been blaming their own kind for the destruction of Hawaii? Again, Melville in 1846:

There is something decidedly wrong in the practical operations of the Sandwich Island missions. Those who from pure religious motives contribute to the support of this enterprise, should take care to ascertain that their donations, flowing through many devious channels, at last effect their legitimate object, the conversion of the Hawaiians. I urge this not because I doubt the moral probity of those who disburse these funds, but because I know that they are not rightly applied. To read pathetic accounts of missionary hardships, and glowing descriptions of conversions, and baptisms taking place beneath palm trees, is one thing; and to go to the Sandwich Islands and see the missionaries dwelling in picturesque and prettily furnished coral-rock villas, whilst the miserable natives are committing all sorts of immoralities around them, is quite another.

In justice to the missionaries, however, I will willingly admit, that whatever evils may have resulted from their collective mismanagement of the business of the mission, and from the want of vital piety evinced by some of their number, still the present deplorable condition of the Sandwich Islands is by no means wholly chargeable against them. The demoralizing influence of a dissolute foreign population and the frequent visits of all descriptions of vessels have tended not a little to increase the evils alluded to. In a word, here, as in every case where Civilization has in any way been introduced among those whom we call savages, she has scattered her vices, and withheld her blessings.

Melville may seem to soften his heavy blows against the missionaries by concessions to their purity of motive and even an element of ultimate good. Don't be misled. Joe Gores, who included Melville's work in a 1974 paperback collection of noted authors writing on Hawaii

## The Inevitable Visiting Writer

and the South Seas (*Honolulu: Port of Call*, Ballantine Books), prefaces Melville's piece, titled *The White Man in Hawaii*, with these remarks: "As here abstracted, they make the most vitriolic, and most accurate, contemporary portrait of Hawaii under missionary control that we have—despite perfunctory lip service to Christian ideals which the publishing practices of the day demanded."

Vitriolic is a nice word to describe the way the man who wrote *Moby Dick* described Hawaii. Melville's depiction of Hawaiian royalty in general and King Kamehameha III in particular is so mean I dare not repeat it here for fear of being banned forever from all places once royal. Likewise, Melville's view of those who came to civilize the Islands is as strong a broadside as you're likely to read; to wit:

> Among the islands of Polynesia, no sooner are the images overturned, the temples demolished, and the idolaters converted into nominal Christians, then disease, vice, and premature death make their appearance. The depopulated land is then recruited from the rapacious hordes of enlightened individuals who settle themselves within its borders, and clamorously announce the progress of the Truth. Neat villas, trim gardens, shaven lawns, spires, and cupolas arise, while the poor savage soon finds himself an interloper in the country of his fathers, and that too on the very site of the hut where he was born. The spontaneous fruits of the earth, which God in his wisdom had ordained for the support of the indolent natives, remorselessly seized upon and appropriated by the stranger, are devoured before the eyes of the starving inhabitants or sent on board the numerous vessels which now touch at their shores.
>
> When the famished wretches are cut off in this manner from their natural supplies, they are told by their benefactors to work and earn their support by the sweat of their brows! But to no fine gentleman born to hereditary opulence does manual labor come more unkindly than to the luxurious Indian when thus robbed of the bounty of Heaven. Habituated to a life of indolence, he cannot and will not exert himself, and want, disease, and vice, all evils of foreign growth, soon terminate his miserable existence.

Surely you can see why no one has ever called Herman Melville what A. Grove Day calls Robert Louis Stevenson: "The foreign author most beloved by the people of Hawaii." Day is the resident expert on Hawaii and other Pacific Islands literature. The former senior professor of English at the University of Hawaii has written and edited an impressive number of books, including Mark Twain's *Letters from the Sandwich Islands*, Robert Louis Stevenson's *Travels in Hawaii*, and *A Hawaiian Reader*; the latter, it might be noted, omitting any contribution from Melville while containing the writings of Stevenson, Twain, London, Maugham, Marquand, and even the Rev. Abraham Akaka.

As so often seems to be the case with authors who have achieved lasting literary fame, their Hawaii works are usually little more than footnotes to their more widely recognized achievements, James Michener's *Hawaii* novel notwithstanding. Few readers beyond Hawaii who recognize Robert Louis Stevenson as the author of *Treasure Island*, *Kidnapped*, and *The Strange Case of Dr. Jekyll and Mr. Hyde* know that he spent the last six years of his life in the South Seas, including five months in Hawaii in 1889, residing at Sans Souci on Waikiki Beach, and another five weeks in 1893. "Stevenson's writings about Hawaii are more considerable than most readers would expect," says Day in the preface to his Stevenson collection. "These writings, for several reasons, have not been widely circulated."

Among the best known of the Stevenson works from his Hawaii period are two short stories, "The Bottle Imp" and "The Isle of Voices," and "Letter to the Reverend Dr. Hyde," in which R. L. S. passionately defended Father Damien against posthumous criticism of the "martyr of Molokai" made in a published letter by Dr. C. A. Hyde of Honolulu. The Stevenson letter was so brutal, even Stevenson admitted seven months later that his attack was "barbarously harsh." Which is why, I suppose, you hear less of the enraged Stevenson letter in defense of Father Damien than you do the little Stevenson poem in honor of Princess Kaiulani upon her sailing for school in Great Britain—"Forth from her land to mine she goes." Alas, even among the literary lions, some of their mush outlives their mustard.

As a visiting writer in 1889, Stevenson proved to be ahead of his time: He preferred the Neighbor Islands and damned Honolulu. Stevenson expressed a preference for the Kona Coast over "vile" Honolulu with its "beastly climate." And there was another reason, he wrote, that put him off about Honolulu: "beastly haoles." In a letter to his lifelong friend, business and literary agent in Britain, Charles Baxter, Stevenson wrote:

> I have just been a week away alone on the lee coast of Hawaii; the only white creature in many miles, riding five and a half hours one

## The Inevitable Visiting Writer

day, living with a native, seeing poor lepers shipped off to Molokai, hearing native causes and giving my opinion as *amicus curiae* as to the interpretation of a statute in English: a lovely week among God's best—at least God's sweetest—works, Polynesians. It has bettered me greatly. If I could only stay there the time that remains, I would get my work done and be happy; but the care of a large, costly and no' just preceesely forrit-gaun family keeps me in vile Honolulu, where I am always out of sorts, amidst heat and cold and cesspools and beastly haoles. What is a haole? You are one, and so, I am sorry to say, am I. After so long a dose of whites, it was a blessing to get among Polynesians again, even for a week.

Stevenson had a few choice words for the missionaries, of course, especially for the Rev. Hiram Bingham, leader of the first group of missionaries to arrive on *Thaddeus* in 1820. James Michener, who modeled one of his principal characters in *Hawaii* after Bingham, has written that Bingham's "self-righteous, unyielding rectitude gave Hawaii its formative character." Stevenson, in the journal of his visit to the Kona Coast, took note of Bingham's writings, *A Residence of Twenty-One Years in the Sandwich Islands*, which R. L. S. perceived as "testifying to a degree of prejudice that would utterly unfit a man to be a missionary to angels." In this vein, Stevenson continued:

he [Bingham] thinks all the heathen go to Hell, he testifies it in a hundred places; I will trouble you for the glad tidings! When he and his brethren saw the Polynesians in their own attire—"much of their skins bare," says he, more honest than most missionaries who I am sorry to say continually use the expression naked about people clothed with perfect tropical decency—and again he describes the king as "destitute" think of it! "of hat, gloves, shoes, stockings and pants" an exact description of my own attire in warm weather, and of that of the Tahitians today, and of most Highlanders till yesterday, all quite as decent people as Bingham. Well, when they saw them, "the appearance . . . was appalling. Some of our number, with gushing tears, turned away from the spectacle. Others with firmer nerve continued their gaze, but were ready to exclaim, Can these be human beings?" Even so, O Bingham! and a blessed sight better these two than you or your excellent spouse with "the large projecting fore-parts of her bonnet in the fashion of 1819," which awoke so much mirth and earned your party a nickname in Hawaii! And these . . . were the missionaries of civilization and of Christianity, and Bingham was a fine fellow and had talent, which is the richest of the joke. Think of me goaded to pick quarrels with this devoted pioneer of better things. But I trust no one supposed I would not sooner be Bingham with all his degrading superstitions, and . . . vulgarities in the religious "fashion of 1819," than myself in the glories of 1889. The superiority I claim is that I can see him.

The civilizing of Hawaii is, as you must notice, a recurrent theme for the visiting author. And more often than not it is that which stands, supposedly, as the most civilized, Honolulu, which draws the heaviest fire. W. Somerset Maugham, who fashioned from his South Seas travels many memorable stories, such as "Rain," and his novel, *The Moon and Sixpence*, passed through Hawaii in 1916 and left with these impressions, recorded in his short story, "Honolulu":

Nothing had prepared me for Honolulu. It is so far away from Europe, it is reached after so long a journey from San Francisco, so strange and so charming associations are attached to the name, that at first I could hardly believe my eyes. I do not know that I had formed in my mind any very exact picture of what I expected, but what I found caused me a great surprise. It is a typical western city. Shacks are cheek by jowl with stone mansions; dilapidated frame houses stand next door to smart stores with plate-glass windows; electric cars rumble noisily along the streets; and motors, Fords, Buicks, Packards, line the pavement. The shops are filled with all the necessities of American civilization. Every third house is a bank and every fifth the agency of a steamship company.

Along the streets crowd an unimaginable assortment of people. The Americans, ignoring the climate, wear black coats and high, starched collars, straw hats, soft hats, and bowlers. The Kanakas, pale brown, with crisp hair, have nothing on but a shirt and a pair of trousers; but the half-breeds are very smart with flaring ties and patent-leather boots. The Japanese, with their obsequious smile, are neat and trim in white duck, while their women walk a step or two behind them, in native dress, with a baby on their backs . . .

It is the meeting place of East and West. The very new rubs shoulders with the immeasurably old. And if you have not found the romance you expected you have come upon something singularly intriguing. All these strange people live close to each other, with different languages and different thoughts; they believe in different gods and they have different values; two passions alone they share,

## The Inevitable Visiting Writer

love and hunger. And somehow as you watch them you have an impression of extraordinary vitality. Though the air is so soft and the sky so blue, you have, I know not why, a feeling of something hotly passionate that beats like a throbbing pulse through the crowd. Though the native policeman at the corner, standing on a platform, with a white club to direct the traffic, gives the scene an air of respectability, you cannot but feel that it is a respectability only of the surface; a little below there is darkness and mystery. It gives you just that thrill, with a little catch at the heart, that you have when at night in the forest the silence trembles on a sudden with the low, insistent beating of a drum. You are all expectant of I know not what.

One is left with the feeling that W. Somerset Maugham had a definite passion for Honolulu, and perhaps more compassion than many, and might have fashioned from it even more, finer pieces of literature had he spent more time in Honolulu. There was another author of note in Honolulu at the time of Maugham's passing through in 1916, one who did spend a great amount of time living and writing in Hawaii. Jack London had sailed into Pearl Harbor on his 43-foot ketch *Snark* in 1907, found the surroundings to his liking, and returned in 1915 to live in Honolulu for a year. London could become absolutely gushy in writing of his love for the Hawaiian Islands, declaring that of all the honors, accolades, and degrees he had received in life, it was his fondest desire to someday be called *kamaaina*. In *My Hawaiian Aloha*, three articles written in 1916, London gushed:

> Nearly a quarter of a century ago—to be precise, twenty-four years ago—I first saw these fair islands rise out of the sea. I have been back here numerous times. As the years pass, I return with increasing frequency and for longer stays. Some day, some one of Hawaii may slap me on the shoulder and say, "Hello, old *kamaaina*." And some other day I may chance to overhear some one else of Hawaii speaking of me and saying, "Oh, he's a *kamaaina*." And this may grow and grow until I am generally so spoken of and until I may at last say of myself. "I am a *kamaaina*. I belong." And this is my Hawaiian Aloha: *Aloha nui oe, Hawaii Nei!*

For this Jack London was called a bigot? Not for his praise of the *kamaaina* as a superior being, but because of the manner in which he wrote of those who then, as now, were never qualified to be called old *kamaainas*, London was indeed branded a racist. But before he delved so deeply into the racial pot in the manner which blackened his name in some scholarly quarters, London did his best to discourage others from catching the next boat to Hawaii in the dream of becoming, like writer Jack, an old *kamaaina* virtually overnight. London issued a warning, one which essentially hasn't changed during the following 64 years: Bring money. Or a capacity for low-paying jobs. Wrote London:

> Hawaii is a Paradise—and I can never cease proclaiming it; but I must append one word of qualification: Hawaii is a paradise for the well-to-do. It is not a paradise for the unskilled laborer from the mainland, nor for the person without capital from the mainland. The one great industry of the islands is sugar. The unskilled labor for the plantations is already here. Also, the white unskilled laborer, with a higher standard of living, cannot compete with coolie labor, and, further, the white laborer cannot and will not work in the canefields.
>
> For the person without capital, dreaming to start on a shoestring and become a capitalist, Hawaii is the last place in the world. The shoestring days are past. The land and industries of Hawaii are owned by old families and large corporations, and Hawaii is only so large.

Was Jack London a racist writer? Some have accused him of being just that, citing such Hawaii stories as "The Inevitable White Man" and "Chun Ah Chun" as evidence. The latter is a piece of fiction built upon the true-to-life example of one Chun Ah Fong, who arrived in Hawaii in 1849, married a local girl with royal blood, and made a fortune in business. London's fictional character Chun Ah Chun might strike some as an amusing rascal devoted to the realities of the American dollar as the god, in Hawaii as elsewhere, which can best deliver the goods. London did not endear himself to believers in the myth of Hawaii as the happy melting pot of the Pacific with his profile of Ah Chun: "He was rather undersized, as Chinese go . . . shrewd little eyes, black and beady . . . His beady black eyes saw bargains where other men saw bankruptcy." There is a revealing view of the philosophy of Ah Chun during a discussion with his Hawaiian-English-American-Italian-Portuguese wife on why their 12 beautiful daughters—a mixture of "one thirty-second Polynesian, one-sixteenth Italian, one-sixteenth Portuguese, one-half Chinese and eleven thirty-seconds English and American"—had distinguished suitors but no marriage proposals.

## The Inevitable Visiting Writer

Mrs. Ah Chun suggested it was because their daughters' young gentlemen callers were from prominent haole families with a reluctance to have their sons marry any but "an American girl." It is during this discussion that Ah Chun asks his wife:

"What is greater than God, then? I will tell you. It is money. In my time I have had dealings with Jews and Christians, Mohammedans and Buddhists, and with little black men from the Solomons and New Guinea who carried their god about them, wrapped in oiled paper. They possessed various gods, these men, but they all worshipped money."

Ah Chun promptly arranges for word to leak that his eldest daughter, when wed, will bring a dowry of $300,000. And a Capt. Higginson, who had hoped to become an admiral, promptly decides instead to rise above the conventions of white society and marry Ah Chun's oldest daughter. The remaining 11 daughters, graced by similar-size dowries, are in turn married off to respectable haoles. To make a short story shorter, Ah Chun then takes a hike with all his loot to Macao to enjoy his golden years and leaves his three sons, twelve daughters, and dozen disillusioned sons-in-law holding the bag of family greed.

Funny story, I thought. Left me with a certain fondness for old Ah Chun. James Michener thought it clearly revealed Jack London to be a race supremacist. In his introduction to A. Grove Day and Carl Stroven's *A Hawaiian Reader* (Appleton-Century-Crofts, Inc., 1959), Michener attempts to lay London low:

> Jack London, while writing on the mainland of America, had built for himself a solid reputation as a socialist defender of the underdog, and his works had worldwide acceptance; but when he came to Hawaii and saw at firsthand a population—the Chinese—which had many of the characteristics he had espoused in mainland America, he was completely unable to understand what he saw. In "Chun Ah Chun," reprinted here, and in other stories he not only failed to comprehend what was happening in the Pacific; he actually denigrated an entire body of people, largely on racist grounds. The story, as Day and Stroven properly point out, was founded upon events occurring within a real Chinese family, but is, I fear, a pathetic misreading both of the Chinese and of the spirit that activates Hawaii. I have never understood how Jack London could be one man in California, and such a different man in Hawaii. I still cannot understand how he could be a practicing socialist on the one hand and a race supremacist on the other. Yet the story *Chun Ah Chun* does have a sly warmth and

much wit and remains one of the focal works in the London repertoire.

Such charges do not go unanswered by Jack London followers. Joe Gores, who edited the 1974 anthology *Honolulu: Port of Call*, dedicated the book to Jack London and included two of London's stories, "The Inevitable White Man" and a piece from London's 1921 book of short stories, *The House of Pride*. Gores prefaces "The Inevitable White Man" with these remarks:

> English department types [a reference perhaps to A. Grove Day, among others] delight in citing "The Inevitable White Man" as proof of their contention that Jack London was a closet bigot, a liberal at home but a racist in the islands. "Bang, bang, bang, bang, went his rifle, and thud, thud, thud, thud, went the niggers to the deck. It was amazing to see them go down." The trouble is, it just ain't true. London was a storyteller and incidental (they all seem to have a hard time accepting this) ironist. He wrote of the Pacific world as he found it, not as he might have wished it to be, or as it should have been. He spent countless hours listening to old-timers yarn about black-birders and cannibals and headhunters, and recreated such stories as "The Inevitable White Man" out of this native idiom.

Since so much is being made of London's story, "The Inevitable White Man," an excerpt would seem to be in order, such as this, the commentary of a fictional South Seas pub owner:

> Tell the white man there's pearl-shell in some lagoon infested by ten thousand howling cannibals, and he'll head there all by his lonely, with half a dozen kanaka divers and a tin alarm clock for chronometer, all packed like sardines on a commodious, five-ton ketch. Whisper that there's a gold strike at the North Pole, and that same inevitable white-skinned creature will set out at once, armed with pick and shovel, a side of bacon, and the latest patent rocker—and what's more, he'll get there. Tip it off to him that there's diamonds on the red-hot ramparts of hell, and Mr. White Man will storm the ramparts and set old Satan himself to pick-and-shovel work. That's what comes of being stupid and inevitable.

And so it goes with *The Inevitable Visiting Writer*. Let him sniff the winds of discontent from a seeming Paradise set upon by those who plunder until it seems less a Paradise and more a part of Civilization, and *The Inevitable Visiting Writer* will come flying to bay at the heels of the scoundrels, armed with a mighty rage at the greed of the invaders and a sorrowful compassion for the plight of the invaded. It has been this way for two hundred and one years and will surely carry forward two hundred and one more, or as long as *The Inevitable Visiting Writer* persists in tampering with his ideals of Hawaii as Paradise by exposing himself to the realities of Hawaii as Civilization, with her vices scattered and her blessings withheld, instead of heeding the advice of W. Somerset Maugham, who said flat out in the opening line of his short story, "Honolulu": "The wise traveler travels only in imagination."

# Mark Twain in the Sandwich Islands

## TOM HORTON

*Looking back on 124 days of his travel through the Kingdom of Hawai'i as a turning point to great American literature for all times, while touching upon the mystery of his unfinished Hawai'i novel and the tragedy of his uncompleted voyage back to his beloved isles.*

◆ Riverboats. Hannibal, Missouri. *Life on the Mississippi, Tom Sawyer*, and *Huckleberry Finn. The Celebrated Jumping Frog of Calaveras County, The Prince and the Pauper*, and *A Connecticut Yankee in King Arthur's Court.* There are the life and works of Mark Twain best known to the casual reader, the high school graduate or the average American who doesn't read ancient books written by men no longer alive but who of course has heard of old Mark Twain and knows that he was a famous writer who wrote funny stories and always wore white suits to match his shaggy white mustache. Most people even know that Mark Twain was not his real name, which was Sam Something.

How many know that the single most important turning point in the career of Samuel Langhorne Clemens, that catalyst which seized an itinerant young newspaper correspondent of limited reputation and fired his ascension to literary greatness until he soon became what Rudyard Kipling would call "beyond question the largest man of his time" and an American author of books for all time and all ages, came

---

First published November 1979.

in Hawaii? More accurately, perhaps, the turning point did not come *in* Hawaii so much as it came *because* of Hawaii.

What Mark Twain did during a meager four months and one day in Hawaii is not nearly so significant as what immediately followed. A remarkable, rewarding chain of events was ignited by this 31-year-old character's romp through the Sandwich Islands which contributed little of substance to his eventual claim on literary posterity but was distinctly meaningful to him in so many other ways.

Since he spent no more time in Hawaii than today's wealthy travelers on winter vacations, it is a source of wonderment and something of a mystery that these Pacific islands played such a decisive role in the development of a brilliant writer and humorist more widely known for the influence of his adolescent days spent as *Life on the Mississippi*, his bawdy times *Roughing It* out West and his illuminating world travels as *The Innocents Abroad*. He wrote hilarious, vividly descriptive letters about Hawaii but when tallied against the complete ledger of works of a creative genius William Dean Howells praised as "the Lincoln of our literature," the Hawaii letters barely leave a mark. His later lectures—"Our Fellow Savages of the Sandwich Islands"—delivered from San Francisco to New York and London were vastly more important to his recognition as a public literary figure, and not inconsequentially to his woeful pocketbook, than the 25 letters he wrote for the *Sacramento Union* at the rate of $20 per letter.

But then the power of the story of Mark Twain in Hawaii is just that: what happened to him *after* Hawaii, but in no small measure *because* of Hawaii. The flattering mystery is how these islands, which this great force of literary energy called "paradise for an indolent man," could exert such a powerful influence on his career and clamp an eternal hold on his affections and his monumental imagination despite the fact that he would never return except for one tragic voyage which brought him within sight of a romance he had long dreamed of reliving and then turned him away. So it was that after spending 124 days in Hawaii, Twain spent the remaining 44 years of his life expressing a haunting passion for these islands, even an intense longing to come back and live out his life here, without ever once again actually setting foot on Hawaiian soil. Certainly the demands on his time as an international literary force, compounded by his financial disasters and other personal travails, made the long voyage to Hawaii for reasons other than commerce a luxury that even a man of Twain's stature could not so easily afford. It's a tantalizing mystery nevertheless, but perhaps one which out of charity to a popularly pleasing romance between a revered man of American literature and a dreamy Pacific paradise should be left alone and not reduced to speculation that, just perhaps, Mark Twain's natural gift of exaggeration was at work when in later years he wrote and talked so sentimentally of how these islands forever called to him—without his actually ever doing a damn thing about it except talk it to death in such a beautiful, melancholy way.

Walter Francis Frear, lawyer and distinguished Honolulu citizen who had married Mary Dillingham, devoted years of research and personal enthusiasm to the brief but telling episode of Mark Twain's time in Hawaii. In 1947 the Lakeside Press of Chicago published 1,000 copies of a private printing of Frear's *Mark Twain and Hawaii*. With its exhaustive and meticulous historical documentation, Frear's work is the single best source of accurate information on this tiny yet revealing slice out of a literary life which has been scrutinized as thoroughly as that of any in the history of American letters. In the foreword to his book, which runs to 500 pages including reprints of the Sandwich Islands letters, lectures, and other Island-related appendixes, Frear summed up the impact of that period from March 18 to July 19, 1866, in the life of Samuel Langhorne Clemens, a.k.a. Mark Twain:

> The visit marked the most significant turning point of Mark Twain's life—the interstice between the thirty years of preparation in the extraordinary rough school of his early experiences and the forty-five years of his phenomenal career as writer, lecturer and personality. (1) It was an oasis in his life ever refreshing as a "golden memory"; (2) it marked the transition between his cruder and briefer previous writings and his more refined and elaborate subsequent ones; (3) it gave him a new and, at times afterward sorely needed, lucrative profession, that of lecturer.

Frear's assessment of the weight of the Hawaii visit on Twain's future does not suffer from the bias of a Honolulu viewpoint. Others who have studied Twain across the entirety of his 75 years usually agree. Albert Bigelow Paine, Twain's designated biographer who collected and edited his letters, unpublished works, dictations, and notebooks, dismissed the letters from Hawaii as having popular newspaper reader appeal but no enduring literary value, but he observed:

That the same man who wrote the Hawaiian letters in 1866 (he was then over thirty years old) could, two years later, have written that marvelous book, *The Innocents Abroad*, is a phenomenon in literary development. The Hawaiian letters, however, do show the transition stage between the rough, elemental humor of the Comstock and the refined and subtle style which flowered in *The Innocents Abroad*. Certainly Mark Twain's genius was finding itself, and his association with the refined and cultured personality of Anson Burlingame undoubtedly aided in that discovery . . . They [the letters] do, however, reveal a sort of transition stage between the riotous florescence of the Comstock and the mellowness of his later style. He was learning to see things with better eyes, from a better point of view. It is not difficult to believe that this literary change of heart was in no small measure due to the influence of Anson Burlingame.

Anson Burlingame was on the way to his post as United States Minister to China when he encountered Twain in Hawaii. Twain said in this fourteenth letter to the *Union*, "Burlingame is a man who would be esteemed, respected and popular anywhere, no matter whether he were among Christians or cannibals." The refined, eloquent diplomat, such a cultured contrast to the roughnecks Twain had been associating with in Nevada and California, had a profound influence on Twain, a rather ramshackle character himself at the time, and that influence lasted a lifetime.

Karma was not a word in vogue in the last half of the nineteenth century as it is today to describe, however loosely, the inevitability of one's predestined fate on earth. If it had been, Twain might have been given to reflect that it was his karma and not just the steamer, *Ajax*, which brought him from San Francisco to the Sandwich Islands that eventful spring of 1866. As it was he expressed a personal philosophy in his later years about one's inability to control one's own fate against the stronger forces of circumstance and temperament. Near the end of his life he was invited along with other celebrated writers of the time to reflect on "The Turning Point of My Life" for *Harper's Bazaar*. Twain's contribution appeared in February 1910, months before he died. He submitted that there are numerous turning points in a person's life, each a link in a long chain and each link seeming more crucial than its immediate predecessor. Recounting the links, or turning points, that led to his career as a journalist, he came to one that led him from a journalist's occupation to the higher calling of a literary career. That

## Mark Twain in the Sandwich Islands

link, he said, was forged by *circumstance*, which had sent him to the Sandwich Islands.

So Hawaii's place in the literary development of Mark Twain is well set in history, even if still not as popularly acknowledged as his Missouri/Mississippi roots, his days out West, and his maturing years as a beloved, internationally acclaimed writer, humorist, and speaker at residence in Connecticut. As it is, Hawaii can be thankful that after his first venture outside the United States, Mark Twain went home flat broke. For it is entirely probable that Twain's association with Hawaii would not have flourished as long and as passionately as it did, if not for another of those links, another appearance of circumstance, which took hold of the man immediately upon his return to San Francisco: Circumstance in the shape of the Sandwich Islands made Mark Twain a lecturer.

Without the lectures, the letters from Hawaii might have been forgotten as quickly as most newspaper correspondence. The lectures made him a presence. In the era of the lecture he became its brightest star. It all began when he got off the boat which brought him back from Hawaii.

Five years later, in a piece for *The American Publisher* that was to later appear in *Roughing It*, Twain humorously recreated that magical night of October 2, 1866, in San Francisco in Maguire's Academy of Music, which he had rented from his old Virginia City pal Tom Mcguire at half price, $50, and despite being "the most distressed and frightened creature on the Pacific coast" he took to the stage to lecture on the Sandwich Islands and become what today we would call an overnight star. There are few examples in literary history where the personality and performance of the author were as much attraction as his books, as became the case with Twain, a born performer even if he came to the role grudgingly. As a lecturer Twain was, said Stephen Leacock, "Unrivaled except by . . . his senior contemporary, Charles Dickens." Said Twain biographer Paine, "His Sandwich Islands letters to the *Sacramento Union* had been nothing remarkable, but the lecture he was persuaded to deliver a few months after his return indicates a mental awakening, a growth in vigor and poetic utterance that cannot be measured by comparison with his earlier writings, because it is not of the same realm." With all due respect to poetic utterance, Twain himself valued the lectures for one earthly reason: money. Says Frear, "The Sandwich Islands lecture was practically his sole dependence on the platform for a year and a half and a chief standby for over seven years—in the West, Middle-West, East and in England. It nearly gave him an even wider reputation than did the letters to the Union, and the two together not only furnished the necessary pecuniary means, but led directly to the *Alta* letters, the *Quaker City* excursion and *The Innocents Abroad*, and thus gave him, after his long period of preparation in the rough school of Western life, a good flying start on his phenomenal world career as writer, speaker and personality."

It was a good swap, what the Sandwich Islands were doing for a relative unknown and what he proceeded to do for them. As one writer expressed it, Twain "put the tiny remote monarchy on the map and, in fair exchange, the islands put Mark Twain on the map, too—map of literary America." The sadness of it is that Hawaii never became quite as large a part of that map to Mark Twain's literary life as he first set out to make it.

So it was nevertheless that a man whose creative instincts were so powerful San Francisco papers wouldn't trust him as a working reporter, a man who was sent to Hawaii to write about sugar and by his own proud confession "threw in a good deal of extraneous matter," and who was in Hawaii a sum total of 124 days, was looked to for several years thereafter as one of America's foremost authorities on the mysterious Kingdom of Hawaii. Certainly Mark Twain did as much as anyone since Captain Cook 88 years before him to make the remote islands known to the rest of the world. It was a splendid arrangement, satisfactory to both parties: the world was sufficiently titillated by the exotic and, many assumed, uncivilized islands to make Hawaii a marketable topic, and Twain never lost his enthusiasm for Hawaii as a literary subject. His appetite for the lecture circuit, it should be noted, was less hearty. For all his success on the lecture platform he dreaded the thing. He kept swearing off lectures the way a tout swears off the horses, only to keep returning out of economic need (and sometimes for charitable causes). He delivered several "farewell" lectures, but after the one that actually was his last, a benefit lecture in 1906 in Carnegie Music Hall—"for two hours last night Mark Twain had as big an audience as ever gathered in Carnegie Music Hall roaring with laughter," reported one paper—he told his audience at the end, "I shall never again talk for a fee unless I'm driven to it by bread and butter necessity. And I hope I won't live long enough to feel that."

Never in his lifetime did he allow time or distance to diminish his affection for and his interest in that "dreamy, beautiful, charming land." Circumstance would not permit it. Even as his original Sandwich Islands exploits would begin to dim as greater achievements overtook him, there would be something new, some new spark, to draw his mind back to "that peaceful land, that beautiful land, that far off home of profound repose, and soft indolence, and dreamy solitude, where life is one long slumberless Sabbath, the climate one long delicious summer day, and the good that die experience no change, for they but fall asleep in one heaven and wake up in another." Twain's *The Gilded Age* appeared in 1873, seven years after his Hawaii voyage, and yet he found himself once again turning his pen toward the Islands. Kamehameha V had died December 11, 1872, and it revived America's interest in Hawaii and, in turn, Twain's. In response to their request he wrote two long letters for the *New York Tribune*, the first of which was headlined, "The Sandwich Islands, Schemes of Annexation," followed by "*Views of Mark Twain*, a Characteristic Letter from the Humorist." He advocated annexation by the United States for reasons both sound and satirical—"We *must* annex those people. We can afflict them with our wise and beneficent governments." Whenever the subject of Hawaii came up during the last 34 years of the nineteenth century and even into the first decade of the twentieth, the American whose views were most popularly solicited continued to be this 124-day visitor of 1866.

No travel writer, or any visitor for that matter, has ever done so much for Hawaii on the strength of such a short stay. Twain's relationship with Hawaii was simply unending. It began so deceptively offhandedly with the first of the 25 letters to the *Sacramento Union*, then the most important paper on the West Coast. To appreciate what the name Mark Twain meant before Hawaii, consider that his first letter from the Sandwich Islands appeared in the *Union* with only this editorial preface: "We publish letters from special correspondents at Boston, New York, Washington and Honolulu." Mark Twain's letter ran last. His correspondence soon gathered momentum and some landed on page one. Paine, unimpressed as the biographer was with the letters' literary quality, describes them as "convincing, informing, tersely— even eloquently—descriptive, with a vein of humor adapted to their audience" and said they "added greatly to his prestige on the Pacific coast." Frear gives the letters higher marks: "The Sandwich Islands letters were comprehensive and intrinsically interesting in subject matter. They covered not only the sugar and whaling industries and transportation problems, the primary purpose of his reportorial errand, but, to a far greater extent, and largely on his own initiative, scenic beauty and grandeur, social, political and religious conditions, personalities, history and legends, reciprocity and annexation, and a host of other matters, to present all of which his penetrating powers of observation and unflagging industry eminently fitted him. International rivalries in the Pacific, the westward outlook of developing California, novel conditions in Hawaii, such as the full-fledged, independent monarchy with all its regalia, the recent graduation from the field of missions, and rapid progress along American lines, not to mention the physical attractiveness of the islands and the salubrity of the climate, all accentuated the interest. It was Twain's first reportorial task of consequence and he spared no effort to make it a success." Stephen Leacock agreed: "His Sandwich Islands letters attracted great attention in California. They well deserved it. Apart from any incidental humor, they reveal that power of vivid description, that marvelous facility in conveying the sights and sounds of nature, which henceforth constitutes one of the distinctive charms of Mark Twain's work. He returned to San Francisco in a blaze of glory."

Most important of the letters, perhaps as important to his career as the other 24 put together, was the fifteenth, in which Twain reported his famous scoop on the burning of the clipper ship *Hornet* and the incredible survival of its captain, 12 members of the crew, and two passengers after 43 days of drifting at sea in an open longboat before reaching land at Laupahoehoe (which Twain reported as "Sanpohoihoi") on the Big Island of Hawaii. It was a brilliant piece of reporting and accomplished in a fashion that pained him sorely at the time but, in the end, must have sat well with Twain's flair for dramatics. When the first Hornet survivors arrived in Honolulu, Twain was flat on his back and suffering miserably from a horseback trip he had taken around the Big Island where, in addition to copious notes on the island's fabulous volcanic terrain, he collected a wealth of backside saddle boils which left him embarrassingly debilitated. But this was not a man to let a great story get away. With help from no less than two U.S. diplomats he had himself carried on a cot from his lodgings to the hospital where the *Hornet* survivors were recovering and where he interviewed them at length. Then he worked furiously on the story through the night in order to finish it by morning, stuff it into a large envelope and literally throw his scoop from the wharf onto the deck of the schooner

## Mark Twain in the Sandwich Islands

*Milton Badger* as it was making sail that morning for California. Twain's newsbeat made page one of the *Union* and ran to three and a half columns. Upon his return he shocked the *Union* owners by billing them an extra $100 per column for the *Hornet* story. Twain later reported on their response: "They only laughed in their jolly fashion, and said it was robbery, but no matter; it was a 'good scoop' (the bill or my *Hornet* report, I didn't known which)." A footnote provided in 1910 by Bailey Millard illustrates the journalism fraternity's bemusement with Twain's notorious disregard for facts in favor of fancy: "This occasion (the *Hornet* story) was really the only one on which Mark Twain distinguished himself as a newsgatherer, and some of the old timers in California are still wondering how he did it."

During his 25-day return voyage to San Francisco his shipmates included the captain of the *Hornet* and the two surviving passengers and Twain took full advantage of this good fortune by transcribing from their diaries of the disaster and by personally interviewing them. Circumstance presented him a bonus in research time since the return voyage was doubly long because of prolonged Pacific calms. Twain saw his *Hornet* story as his entree to the Eastern literary circles, a step he considered critical to his advancement as a humorous writer to be taken seriously. He set out to expand and rewrite his *Hornet* story and to get it published in *Harper's New Monthly Magazine* and he succeeded. It was a serious turning point which he described with typical humor 33 years later in *My Debut as a Literary Person*.

If Mark Twain's unfulfilled dream to return to the Islands that represented a watershed in his career was a personal disappointment to him, his failure to produce a Hawaii novel which he nourished in his imagination for nearly half a century was a literary misfortune for Hawaii. How grand it would be today to have a story of nineteenth-century Hawaii among the classics penned by Mark Twain. Circumstance in this instance did not work to his or Hawaii's favor. Procrastination is a thief which can rob the best of writers and even the prolific Twain, who worried as a young man that he leaned toward laziness, procrastinated too long on Hawaii as a theme for fiction. As a consequence Hawaii may have been robbed of a larger literary inheritance from the mighty pen of Mark Twain than even that left in his letters, his lectures, and his prosaic salutations. *It wasn't my fault*, he might cry today if given a chance to defend himself on the matter—it was that scoundrel Circumstance!

His first project, after placing the *Hornet* story in *Harper's*, was to bring out a book based on his Sandwich Islands letters. There is conjecture aplenty on why this never happened. George Wharton James, writing in *The Pacific Monthly*, in 1910, the year of Twain's death, blamed it on that damnable fact of publishing life, timing, and the publication of Charles Warren Stoddard's *South Sea Idylls*. Said James, "It is a singular thing that his great friend, Charles Warren Stoddard, and himself should both have been sent to the Sandwich Islands in the early part of their literary careers, and I am under the impression that if Stoddard had never published his *South Sea Idylls*, Mark Twain's correspondence from the Islands would have been edited and put into book form long ago." Frear is more convincing in dismissing that reason, noting that *Idylls* did not appear until seven years after Twain's Hawaii trip, and even a year after *Roughing It*, which contained material from Hawaii, and wouldn't have been judged a competitive book anyway.

It could have been that it was no easier in 1866 to sell New York publishers on a book about Hawaii than it is today, James Michener's success notwithstanding. A few months after his return from the Islands Twain was talking of getting an "illustrated book on the Sandwich Islands in the hands of the printers" but by May of 1867 he complained to his family in a letter, "I hardly think that Dick & Fitzgerald [New York publishers] will accept the Sandwich Island book." A month later he seemed to have given up, remarking cynically, "I have withdrawn the Sandwich Island book—it would be useless to publish it in these dull publishing times." But this was still the same man who had covered the *Hornet* story while bedridden with saddle boils and he did not give up quite so easily. As late as 1870 he wrote to A. F. Judd, later chief justice of Hawaii, "I am under contract to write two more books the size of *Innocents Abroad* and after that I am going to do the Islands and Harris. They have kept 4 years and I guess they will keep 2 or 3 longer." (The Harris referred to by Twain was C. C. Harris, Prime Minister of Hawaii at the time of Twain's visit, a man he much detested and delighted in saying so, calling Harris "all jaw, vanity, bombast, and ignorance, a lawyer of 'shyster' caliber, a fraud by nature.")

Frear, who tried to deal with Twain and Hawaii in the lawyer's fashion of reliance on fact and evidence to the exclusion of unsubstantiated conjecture, probably has it right, however unromantic, when he says of the nondelivery of Twain's Sandwich Islands book, "The real effective reason was that the book was crowded out by the rush and press of other matters—lectures, travels, other correspondence, books, etc., so fast did things pile up on him after his Sandwich Islands visit."

As it turned out Twain needed some extra copy to fill out *Roughing It*, published in 1872, so he resurrected his Sandwich Islands letters, notes, and lectures and out of them built the final 18 chapters of *Roughing It*, thereby making the autobiography of his Western years thick enough to qualify as a subscription book. It's unsatisfying from a Hawaii standpoint to have had his island episode end up this way, an addition to another book for reasons of length, and Frear notes with a hint of sadness, " . . . these eighteen chapters of *Roughing It* must be regarded as the final outcome of his long contemplated plan to produce a book on that subject." Of course there have been numerous modern collections of the letters in book form but they cannot substitute for a Sandwich Islands book that might have been produced by the legend himself.

Fortunately, Twain would continue to add bits and pieces to the Hawaii story, some written, some delivered as lecturer and after-dinner speaker. He was bedeviled by recurrent dreams and tried to deal with them in literary form. He struggled with one particular dream for several years, wrote a story built around it, and, difficult as it is to believe today with the perspective of history, had the dream story rejected by a magazine. It was finally published two years after his death and titled "My Platonic Sweetheart." One of the dream story's most beautiful scenes is set in Iao Valley on Maui. Other published writings based on his Hawaii experiences included stories titled "Remarkable Instances of Presence of Mind" and "A Strange Dream," the former being about the *Ajax*'s first voyage to Hawaii (Twain missed it; he took the second sailing) and the latter a fictional tale about searching for Kamehameha's bones, with spiritual guidance, at the Kilauea Volcano.

We will never know how close Hawaii came to being the subject of a Mark Twain novel. What we know is that it was in his head to write one. He started the story. He had a theme. He had the central character. He got some of it, including the opening of a first chapter, down on paper. Some say he never finished the story, others think he did. But only pieces of the story have survived and the matter of Mark Twain's unfinished, or at least unpublished, novel of Hawaii is itself a haunting mystery. In 1884, 18 years after he had been in Hawaii and when his literary fame was well in place, he would write to his good friend W. D. Howells telling him how he had "saturated myself with knowledge of that unimaginably beautiful land and that most strange and fascinating people." In words that held such meaningful promise when they came from the pen of Mark Twain, he told Howells, "And I have begun a story."

The story never came. Twain's biographer Paine, with full access to all his letters and notes and unpublished writings, said he never finished the Hawaii story. Frear counters with the evidence of an 1884 letter to a Mrs. Fairbanks in which Twain said he had finished it and was to give it a "most painstaking revision." Perhaps it perished in the revising. But in another letter of 1884, says Frear, Twain asks Howells if he has yet blocked out the Sandwich Islands play, which Frear submits as an indication that Twain "had sent the story to (Howells) for that purpose." If it was ever finished, it remained unpublished, a victim perhaps of—what else but circumstance?

We come inevitably to the final scene, the final link in a bittersweet tale: why he never came back. He was not so different in this regard, really, from all the others who had come before him and the many millions who have come after him, who experienced a memorable visit in the Islands while filled with the spirit of youth and adventure, and then gone home or moved on to other parts of the world to spend their remaining years embellishing the memory of a long trip to paradise and vowing, someday, to return. It is and always has been a part of the mystique of any island paradise. How many travelers across the years have paused in these enchanting islands for an even shorter time than four months and a day and gone away with dreams of someday returning to stay forever? On the matter of Mark Twain's undying love for Hawaii even his biographer Paine was touched. He wrote, "Mark Twain immediately fell in love with Hawaii and remained in love with it his life long." And, "The languorous life of the islands exactly suited Mark Twain. All his life he remembered them—always planning to return some day, to stay there until he died." Seven years after his visit Twain said in a letter written for the *New York Tribune*, "if I could have my way about it, I would go back there and remain the rest of my days." Even later, in 1881, he would write to Charles Warren Stoddard, who was then in Hawaii,

## Mark Twain in the Sandwich Islands

The house is full of carpenters and decorators; whereas, what we really need here, is an incendiary. If the house would only burn down, we would pack up the cubs and fly to the isles of the blest, and shut ourselves up in the healing solitudes of Haleakala and get a good rest; for the mails do not intrude there, nor yet the telephone and the telegraph. And after resting, we would come down the mountain a piece and board with a godly, breech-clouted native, and eat poi and dirt and give thanks to whom all thanks belong, for these privileges, and never housekeep any more . . . Maybe you think I am not happy; the very thing that gravels me is that I am. I don't want to be happy when I can't work; I am resolved that hereafter I won't be. What I have always longed for was the privilege of living forever away up on one of those mountains in the Sandwich Islands overlooking the sea.

Finally in 1895 after 29 long years of fantasizing, Mark Twain prepared to return to Hawaii, to a turning point in his life. Sentiment had nothing to do with it. He had set off on a world lecture and reading tour to earn money to pay off debts of some $100,000, owing to a dismal pile of business disasters that included his own printing machine invention scheme and extended to bad management by his publishers. But sentiment quickly took hold of him as the *Warrimoo* steamed to within sight of Diamond Head and "a paradise which I had been longing all these years to see again." As the ship lay anchored in darkness and lingered overnight off the port of Honolulu, within shadowy sight but still tormentingly removed from the land he had been itching to put his feet upon since the voyage began, Twain was understandably overcome with memories: "pictures—pictures—pictures—an enchanting procession of them! I was impatient for the morning to come."

Morning came and with it tragedy. It is almost too melodramatic to be real. It is the stuff of cheap novels. It is heartbreak. There had been a plague of cholera in Honolulu and because of it no one was allowed to leave the ship. Impossible! One can hardly keep a dry eye looking back across 84 years of time to the sight of Mark Twain standing alone on the deck of that ship just outside Honolulu harbor and looking longingly toward the shore. *Pictures—pictures—pictures—an enchanting procession of them!* Circumstance be damned! —how could this happen? Later he would write simply, "Thus suddenly did my dream of twenty-nine years go to ruin." But in his notebook at the time he wrote, "If I might I would go ashore and never leave."

Perhaps it was better that way. Twain had changed. He was no longer 31 and in reckless pursuit of his destiny. He was 60 and world famous and deeply in debt. He had suffered great personal tragedies. And his Sandwich Islands had changed too. Since their discovery by the so-called civilized world, has anyone ever visited these *isles of the blest* and returned after 29 years to anything except disappointment in the changes? Perhaps it was providence that Mark Twain returned and saw Hawaii again only from a distance. He had submitted during his first visit that some works of nature are so overpowering they can only be fully appreciated from a distance. Better perhaps that he did not come ashore and record the changes. Better that when he stood on the deck of the ship that painful morning and when for the remaining 15 years of his life he would think of the Sandwich Islands, he would still see them through the eyes of a wisecracking free spirit filled with wanderlust, whose untamed head of rich reddish-brown hair and boisterous mustache made his presence as strongly felt as the powerful cigars he was forever smoking, who shocked some of the puritanical islanders with his mock profanity and left others convinced he was constantly drunk because of the Missouri drawl that marked his speech and the exaggerated awkwardness with which he slouched about, but who amused them all with the outrageous tales he had to tell and who impressed just about the whole blasted Kingdom of Hawaii by demanding to see everything, go everywhere, talk to everyone, hear all the gossip, know all there was to know about these islands, and then to write it all down and throw in a good deal of extraneous matter of his own to make it all worth reading and to make the experiences of four months and a day last forever.

He was a great writer, perhaps America's greatest, yet nothing he published about Hawaii would be remembered as well as what he would say about Hawaii in the reminiscences of his later years. In 1908 when he was building his new home in Redding, Connecticut, which he called "Stormfield," the Hawaii Promotion Committee sent him a house gift: a mantelpiece of hard curly koa wood with columns that bore carvings depicting plants and flowers of hau, ilima, taro, and fern, with letters in the panel that said "Aloha"; and for mounting above the koa mantelpiece, a breadfruit plaque. In grateful response he wrote a letter saying Hawaii's gift would be a daily reminder to him of "the loveliest fleet of islands that lies anchored in any ocean." It was some years earlier at a baseball dinner at Delmonico's in New York on April 8, 1889, a dinner to honor two touring American baseball teams that had stopped briefly in Honolulu (where they were rained out and never played), that he delivered himself of an even more memorable homage to Hawaii. By then he was so identified with Hawaii, the master of ceremonies introduced him in all seriousness as "a native of the Sandwich Islands." What he said that night came to be known as the "prose poem" and it stands as the best epitaph to Mark Twain and Hawaii:

> No alien land in all the world has any deep, strong charm for me but that one; no other land could so longingly and so beseechingly haunt me sleeping and waking, through half a lifetime, as that one has done. Other things leave me, but it abides; other things change, but it remains the same. For me its balmy airs are always blowing, its summer seas flashing in the sun, the pulsing of its surf-beat is in my ear; I can see its garlanded crags, its leaping cascades, its plumy palms drowsing by the shore, its remote summits floating like islands above the cloud rack; I can feel the spirit of its woodland solitudes, I can hear the plash of its brooks; in my nostrils still lives the breath of flowers that perished twenty years ago.

How strange that Mark Twain could never return and Hawaii could never leave him. Circumstance.

# Jack London and Hawaii

## A. GROVE DAY

*Writer Jack London first visited Hawai'i at the age of 17 and came back again and again. Most people associate London's work with the Alaskan gold rush; not many know he wrote extensively about Hawai'i.*

◆ In the spring of 1907, Jack London, his wife, and a crew of four arrived off Diamond Head in the author's yacht *Snark*, designed by him and navigated from San Francisco to Hawaii during a month of near disasters.

The men of the customhouse tug hailed the visitors and reported that, since the yacht had not been heard from, they had assumed that the ketch had gone down with all hands.

After mooring safely at Pearl Harbor on May 21, London and his second wife, Charmian, divided their time between the cottage of Thomas W. Hobron at the harbor and a tent on the grounds of the Seaside Hotel in Waikiki.

At the beach, later the site of the Royal Hawaiian Hotel, the Londons chatted with bronzed Hawaiian swimmers and became fascinated with the art of riding a surfboard. Under the tutelage of several experts, London tried the new sport for four hours, and suffered such a painful, skin-peeling case of tropical sunburn that he was out of action for days. A happier result was his celebrated essay, "A Royal Sport: Surfing at Waikiki," in which he described his first big wave:

> I saw it coming, turned my back on it, and paddled for dear life. Faster and faster my board went, till it seemed my arms would drop

First published November 1984.

off. What was happening behind me I could not tell. One cannot look behind and paddle the windmill stroke. I heard the crest of the wave hissing and churning, and then my board was lifted and flung forward. I scarcely knew what happened the first half-minute. Though I kept my eyes open, I could not see anything, for I was buried in the rushing white of the crest. But I did not mind. I was chiefly conscious of ecstatic bliss at having caught the wave. At the end of the half-minute, however, I began to see things, and to breathe. I saw that three feet of the nose of my board was clear out of water and riding on the air. I shifted my weight forward, and made the nose come down. Then I lay, quite at rest in the midst of the wild movement, and watched the shore and the bathers on the beach grow distinct.

Recovered, the writer and his wife attended a reception for visiting congressmen at the home of Prince Jonah Kuhio Kalanianaole. There they were privileged with an appearance by the deposed Queen Liliuokalani, who emerged from her seclusion to greet the visitors.

Later, the Londons climbed Diamond Head and viewed the interior of this extinct volcano. They waved farewell to a transport steamer at the wharf while wearing flower leis and listening to the strains of the Royal Hawaiian Band. They had breakfast with Sanford B. Dole who, for a decade, had been the political leader of the Islands. There the theoretical socialist revolutionist (London) talked with the head of a real, if bloodless, revolution that had deposed the old Hawaiian monarchy. At Ainahau, the visitors were welcomed by A. S. Cleghorn, father of the late heiress apparent, Princess Kaiulani, who had died in 1899 at the age of 23. London included this anecdote about Cleghorn in his piece "My Hawaiian Aloha":

> The sailor boy, Archibald Scott Cleghorn, had no intention of leaving his ship; but he looked upon the Princess Likelike, the Princess Likelike looked on him, and he remained to become the father of the Princess Kaiulani and to dignify a place of honor through long years. He was not the first sailor boy to leave his ship, nor the last.

During a five-day visit to the leper settlement at Kalaupapa on the island of Molokai, the Londons viewed a Fourth of July parade among the isolated patients and decided that fun and humanity could be found even among grim surroundings. The couple left the peninsula by ascending the almost vertical 2,300-foot cliff trail and departed for Honolulu from the port of Kaunakakai.

Soon after, the Londons visited the island of Maui and rode with the Polish adventurer Louis von Teinpsky on a cattle ranch on the slopes of the gigantic crater of dormant Haleakala. London was impressed with the former bank cashier from New Zealand who had stopped—and stayed—in Hawaii on his way to California. "Today," said London of von Tempsky, "his sons and daughters about him, he looks down on half a world and all of Maui from the rolling grasslands of the Haleakala Ranch."

The exploring party, which included publisher Lorrin A. Thurston and his wife, was led by von Tempsky and accompanied by his two daughters, Armine, 14, and Gwen, 15. Guided by two paniolos, they descended the world's largest crater and camped among the brightly colored cinder cones. After several days in "The House of the Sun," they emerged through the Kaupo Gap. The return trip took the riders by way of beautiful Hana and through the sugar lands of the torrential Nahiku Ditch country, where even the bravest cowboy sheepishly dismounted and led his horse across narrow wooden flumes spanning hair-raising gorges. During the journey, Armine von Tempsky talked with London about the craft of the writer and apparently was encouraged enough to eventually produce her girlhood autobiography, *Born in Paradise*, as well as half-a-dozen novels.

*Snark*, refitted and supplied with a new crew except for the faithful Martin Johnson, who later became a famed African explorer, sailed the Londons to the Big Island of Hawaii. The couple disembarked on the Kona Coast, later to rejoin the yacht at the eastern port of Hilo. "My Hawaiian Aloha" contains this lyric description of Kona:

> It is the land of the morning calm, the afternoon shower, and the evening tranquillity. Harsh winds never blow. Once in a year or two a stiff wind of twenty-four to forty-eight hours will blow from the south. This is the Kona wind. Otherwise there is no wind, at least no airdrafts of sufficient force to be so dignified. They are not even breezes. They are air-fans, alternating by day and by night between the sea and the land. Under the sun, the land warms and draws to it the mild sea air. In the night, the land radiating its heat more quickly, the sea remains the warmer and draws to it the mountain air faintly drenched with the perfume of flowers.

Going over land, London had a chance to ride the range of the Parker Ranch and to visit the sugar plantations of the Hamakua Coast, where the tourists experienced a mild earthquake. Up from Hilo, they ascended the seismic region of Kilauea and stopped at the Volcano House, hosted by the genial Greek innkeeper, George Lycurgus. They gazed into the bubbling fire pit of Halemaumau, which London admiringly called "a hell of a hole." On the way back to Hilo, the manager of the Waipalia Sugar Mill invited the party to a thrilling ride down the steep water flumes on mats of sugar cane stalks.

On October 7 the Londons' pleasant sojourn ended. They sailed, regretfully, for the Marquesas Islands and other Pacific adventures that would take two years and result in half-a-dozen books on the South Seas. But they were destined to return.

Jack London was born in San Francisco in the centennial year of 1876. He worked variously as a newsboy, oyster pirate, sailor, jailed hobo, and prospector in Alaska. His 1907 visit to Hawaii was not his first. At the age of 17, from the deck of a sealing ship, he had viewed the fiery glow of Kilauea. He had set foot in Honolulu in January 1904 on his way to Asia to serve as a correspondent during the Russo-Japanese War and had stopped over briefly on his return to California six months later.

During all his travels, London managed as a professional writer to turn out 1,000 words of printable prose each day. Even while learning to navigate *Snark* in mid-Pacific in 1907, he wrote chapters of his best novel, *Martin Eden*. While sitting in tropical Pearl Harbor, he managed to compose a famous short story, "To Build a Fire," about a man who freezes to death in Alaska.

Jack London's prodigious output included many pieces on Hawaii. Three stories in his 1912 collection, *The House of Pride*, dealt with the dread disease leprosy, which had been introduced into the Islands from China. During London's time leprosy was controlled by isolating the sufferers from the sound populace. Like Robert Louis Stevenson before and James A. Michener after him, London was accused by residents of exploiting in his stories a minor feature of the Hawaiian scene in order to terrify prospective visitors. However, "Koolau the Leper," one of the best tales in the collection, drew as much upon local history as legend for its core.

London probably first heard of the exploits of Koolau from his young Stanford crewman, Herbert Stolz, on *Snark*'s pitching deck. Stolz had been born on the island of Kauai, the setting of the story, and his father had been the deputy sheriff who was shot while attempting single-handedly to capture the outlaw.

The facts behind the Koolau legend: During the unsettled year of 1893, right after the overthrow of Queen Liliuokalani, the provisional government ordered that all known lepers should be sent to Molokai. The 31-year-old cowboy Koolau helped to round up those on Kauai. When he himself was stricken, he agreed to go to Molokai provided his healthy wife, Piilani, could go along to attend him. At the last minute she was held ashore on a baseless charge, and Koolau leaped overboard and swam back.

Koolau became the leader of a defiant leper band hiding in the precipitous Kalalau Valley. He killed deputy sheriff Louis H. Stolz and withstood a company of National Guardsmen armed with a Krupp cannon. For three years Koolau, his wife, and their young son hid in the valley. Then the child, who had been infected with leprosy, died and was buried by the grieving couple. Two months later Koolau died. He was buried in a grave overlooking the valley of his exploits, a grave hacked out beneath a cliff by Piilani, using only a small knife. The outlaw was dead, but his legend had just begun.

Although the Koolau of London's story varies from the man of history, he is true in spirit to the Koolau who felt that his cause was just and who never gave in to death. London infused his Koolau with dignity:

> At last the shells ceased. This, he reasoned, was because the soldiers were drawing near. They crept along the trail in single file, and he tried to count them until he lost track. At any rate, there were a hundred or so of them—all come after Koolau the leper. He felt a fleeting prod of pride. With war guns and rifles, police and soldiers, they came for him, and he was only one man, a crippled wreck of a man at that. They offered a thousand dollars for him, dead or alive. In all his life he had never possessed that much money. The thought was a bitter one. Kapahei had been right. He, Koolau, had done no wrong. Because the haoles wanted labor with which to work the stolen land, they had brought in the Chinese coolies, and with them had come the sickness. And now, because he had caught the sickness, he was worth a thousand dollars—but not to himself. It was his worthless carcass, rotten with disease or dead from a bursting shell, that was worth all that money.

Another story in *The House of Pride*, "Chun Ah Chun," was also loosely based on a local legend, that of the Ah Fong family. Chun Ah Fong had arrived in the Islands in 1849, married a part-Hawaiian, part-Caucasian woman, and fathered 16 children—four boys and 12 girls. All but one of the children lived to be adults. Most of them married well, with dowries and legacies from the family fortune; many of the girls married leaders of haole society. In "Chun Ah Chun," London again featured a man of strong character who single-mindedly pursues his purpose:

> Ah Chun was observant. He perceived little details that not one man in a thousand ever noticed. Three years he worked in the field, at the end of which time he knew more about cane-growing than the overseers or even the superintendent, while the superintendent would have been astounded at the knowledge the wizened little coolie possessed of the reduction processes in the mill. But Ah Chun did not study only sugar processes. He studied to find out how men came to be owners of sugar mills and plantations. One judgment he achieved early, namely, that men did not become rich from the labor of their own hands. He knew, for he had labored for a score of years himself. The men who grew rich did so from the labor of the hands of others. That man was richest who had the greatest number of his fellow creatures toiling for him.

During the two years before America entered World War I, the Londons returned to Hawaii for several more visits. By then Jack London was the author of half-a-hundred books—the best-known, highest-paid, and most popular writer in the world.

In March 1915 Jack and Charmian arrived in Honolulu on *Matsonia*. On this visit, after a day ashore they went on a circle cruise of the Big Island and witnessed an eruption of the Halemaumau fire pit.

Later that year, they took a six-week jaunt around the landmarks of the Big Island again. Back in Waikiki, they relaxed and swam with Duke Kahanamoku, who in 1912 had broken the 100-yard record at the Stockholm Olympics. "I'm glad we're here now," Jack commented, lying in the shade of the Outrigger Canoe Club veranda, "for someday Waikiki Beach is going to be the scene of one long hotel." The couple returned to California in July but were back again just before Christmas. They found a comfortable cottage at 2201 Kalia Road, and there London wrote most of the stories reprinted in his collection *On the Makaloa Mat* (1919).

On July 26, 1916, after giving a dinner for 40 people at their cottage, the Londons departed the Islands for the last time. The following November 22, Jack London died from uremic poisoning at Glen Ellen, California. Buried with him was a withered ilima lei given to him in Hawaii by Col. Samuel Parker.

Perhaps London's most touching epitaph came from a Hawaiian lad: "Better than anyone, he knew us Hawaiians ... The news came to Honolulu—and people, they seemed to have lost a great friend—auwe ... I tell you this: Better than anyone, he knew us Hawaiians."

# The Mauna Kea Killing

## JOSEPH THEROUX

*Was world famous botanist David Douglas murdered on the slopes of Mauna Kea? There's new evidence about the man who may have killed him.*

◆ When the torn and battered body of David Douglas—the world famous botanist, discoverer of the Douglas fir tree—was carried into Hilo on that humid July morning in 1834, none of the missionaries suspected foul play. They engaged a man to dig a grave beneath a breadfruit tree and proposed a quiet but moving rite for the man who had visited them only a few months before. But the gravedigger—a man named Charles Hall—looked at the body and heard the story of how Douglas had fallen into a camouflaged bullock pit and been trampled to death.

Hall was troubled by the story. A native of Virginia, he was a tough and experienced cattle hunter. He had heard that Douglas was no mincing scientist, that he was able to hike a good 50 miles a day with a 60-pound pack on his back, often in his bare feet. He asked around and found that Douglas had disembarked from his ship at Kohala, to make one last trek over the island collecting specimens before his departure for England. His path would take him past the house of Ned Gurney, a cattle hunter whom Hall distrusted, for it was rumored that Gurney was an escaped convict from Port Jackson (now Sydney, Australia).

Hall took his suspicions to the missionaries who were horrified at his idea. Nevertheless, they halted plans for a burial and directed Hall to go into the hills to collect evidence. He returned with his suspicions

---

First published November 1989.

confirmed. He held up a bull's head with old and blunted horns. These, he said, could never have caused the injuries to the botanist.

Hall believed that early on the morning of July 12, Douglas had come to the convict's hut on the slopes of Mauna Kea. He had been given a breakfast of fried potatoes and beefsteak. He had asked Gurney to point out the way to Hilo. The man accompanied him part of the way and then was abruptly dismissed by the botanist. They argued, and the convict, in a fit of passion, fractured Douglas's skull, killing him. Gurney dumped the body in one of the many bullock pits he had dug to trap the beast. He then called some nearby Hawaiians to witness the discovery and asked them to deliver the body to Hilo. At least that was how Hall had reconstructed the crime.

The body was washed—washing away evidence—and the abdominal cavity was packed with salt. It was sent, along with the bullock head and horns, to Honolulu, where an autopsy was performed by doctors Thomas C. B. Rooke and Gerrit P. Judd. Their conclusions, however, supported the story that the Hawaiians had relayed from the convict. Douglas was buried at KawaiaHaʻo Churchyard on August 4, 1834.

Hall returned to the Big Island convinced of the convict's guilt but unable to prove it. He believed that Gurney had killed another man the same morning, a missionary's servant named John, who had followed Douglas from the ship. Hall died at Kainaliu in 1880.

Over the years, there have been various theories advanced about Douglas's death, including murder, suicide, and accident. Those who believed in the accident theory noted that David Douglas had poor eyesight—indeed, on occasion he suffered from ophthalmorrhagia, which meant that he bled from his eyes. Always curious about nature, the theory runs, he crept to the edge of the bullock pit to peer in. He leaned over too far and toppled to his death. Another theory says that it was his nearsightedness that prevented him from focusing in on the pit that lay alongside the path to Hilo.

Others point to Douglas's growing disappointment with his lack of scientific fame, arguing that in a lonely moment of despair he hurled himself to certain death into a remote bullock pit. Still others are convinced that Charles Hall was right: the convict, Ned Gurney, murdered Douglas for a sack of gold Douglas supposedly carried, cleverly disposing of the body.

It had always troubled me that historians have been too quick to accept the story, that no work has been done to track down Gurney's origins, to discover if he was indeed an escaped convict or if he was capable of murder. I set out to learn the answers to these questions. I was convinced that if I could learn his history, I could solve this 150-year-old mystery.

I had only a handful of facts. Edward "Ned" Gurney, according to early missionary Sarah Joiner Lyman, was "an Englishman who resides on the mountain for the purpose of killing beef for the Gov. [and] is a convict from Botany Bay, who has resided at these islands several years."

So, if this was all true, Gurney had been a convict some time in the 1820s. I wrote to the archives office of New South Wales and received the following:

CONVICT RECORDS
Name of Convict: EDWARD GURNEY
Convict Ship: Canada (5) [That is, its fifth voyage.]
Port and date of departure:
    London 23rd April 1819
Date of arrival: 1 Sept. 1819
Age: 19
Native Place: London
Trade or Calling: Servant
Offence: Larceny
Where tried: Middlesex Gaol Delivery
When tried: 13th January 1819
Sentence: 7 years
Height: 5$^1$/$_2$
Complexion: Florid
Hair colour: Flax
Eye color: Grey

The section of the data sheet marked "How disposed of" was blank. Gurney had not been pardoned, given a "Ticket of Leave" or a "Certificate of Freedom." How had he escaped Port Jackson? I wrote back and received a pile of poorly photocopied documents, which strained my eyesight to decipher. One was a long letter to a certain Capt. John R. Kent dated October 2, 1821. It gave orders for him "to proceed . . . in the

Cutter Mermaid under your command to the Sandwich Islands taking under your charge the Prince Regent Schooner."

Back in 1793, George Vancouver (who had first introduced cattle to the Islands) promised a schooner to Kamehameha the Great. The *Prince Regent* was the long delayed fulfillment of that promise.

According to historian Ralph Kuykendall, in his book *The Hawaiian Kingdom*: "In 1822 upon the arrival from New South Wales of a small schooner, the *Prince Regent*, armed with six guns, built at Sydney by direction of the British government for presentation to Kamehameha in fulfillment of Vancouver's promise. The schooner was delivered to Liholiho at Honolulu, May 1, 1822, by Captain J. R. Kent of the cutter *Mermaid*."

But what was Gurney's connection to all this? There was another document in the packet from New South Wales. It was dated "Sydney 10th October 1821" and superscribed

List of three male
convicts embarked on board
His majesty's Cutter Mermaid—
Kent Master for government
purposes at Owhyhee—

The three were Will Thompson, Dan Ashton, and "Edw. Gurney," now listed as 20 years of age (he had been in Australia for just over two years). His trade was now listed as "Laborer." The document concluded with "Remarks: To assist in taking the schooner Prince Regent to Owhyhee and to then return again with Master of the Mermaid Cutter—." It was signed by the superintendent, William Huchinson.

But Ned Gurney never returned. He crewed on the schooner as the superintendent had directed. The *Mermaid* and the *Prince Regent* stopped over for refreshments at Huahine in the Marquesas. There they picked up the missionary William Ellis and brought him to Hawaii. In Hawaii Ellis kept an interesting journal and later wrote his famous *Polynesian Researches*.

How ironic, that one of the most obscure men of the time and one of the best known both arrived at Hawai'i on the same little schooner.

But what had brought Ned Gurney to Port Jackson? What was the "larceny" that he had been convicted of on January 13, 1819, at Middlesex near London?

## The Mauna Kea Killing

To find that out, you must search out the dusty Guildhall Library on Gresham Street near Moorgate. You ask for nineteenth-century court records and are directed to the Proceedings of the Old Bailey Sessions Papers. The 1819 volume is removed from the gray wooden shelf and put in your hands. The date given for Gurney's trial in the Australian archives turns out to be wrong, but the Sessions Papers are indexed, so that Case No. 302, January 23, is on page 123. The name "Edward Gurney" appears and sends icy fingers down your spine.

He had been arrested on December 29, 1818, carrying a knife and a pack of cards. He had been in league with some "lifters," or petty thieves. They specialized in ripping lead sheets off the roofs of houses and selling them to ironmongers. The thieves had gotten a key to an empty house in Fitzroy Square and copied it at William Hills' locksmith shop. On the twenty-ninth, they made their way into the house and up to the roof. Gurney's friend, Salmon, had a pair of pincers which he used to pull out the nails. They removed the lead sheets in the darkness, Salmon pulling the nails and Gurney folding them to carry. Then they made their way across the roof, walking across the gutter, and began drawing out more nails. About 5:30 a.m. they heard knocking at the front door. They peered over the gutter and were spotted by some men on the street. An outcry arose. Gurney and Salmon jumped up and dashed back across the roof and down the stairs. They were chased through the alleys of Fitzroy Square, but were soon grabbed and turned over to Constable Richard Coates, who took the pincers from Salmon and the knife and pack of cards from Gurney.

Gurney was charged with two counts of stealing. The two thieves had removed 17 pounds of lead, worth three shillings. Coates, the constable, and Hills, the locksmith, testified against them, as did several witnesses. To all this, Gurney only replied, "I ran with the rest, and was taken."

He was found guilty and sentenced: "Transported for seven years." Was it a harsh sentence? The day before one Henry Nichols, aged 14, also got seven years. His crime? He had stolen five shillings worth of pins. Transportation was the popular sentence in the face of overcrowded prisons.

Had Gurney's two years at Port Jackson so hardened him that he was capable of murder? For a man who rips the lead off of roofs is not necessarily a murderer.

Gurney was a convicted thief. But was he also a killer?

If Douglas was indeed carrying a sack of money or gold to pay his guides and his ship passage—as the Hilo missionaries believed—it is possible that Gurney robbed him. He was certainly capable of it. After all, on Mauna Kea's slopes he and Douglas were in the middle of nowhere. Gurney must have found it a safer place to bring off a crime than in Fitzroy Square, St. Marylebone, London. And how was he to know that Douglas was not as anonymous as himself? He may have considered that by killing Douglas, he could cover up his robbery. And by dumping the body in a bullock pit, he could conceal signs of a stabbing. He carried a knife in the Fitzroy Square job. Did he ever use it? Charles Hall believed that Douglas's wounds could not have been inflicted by the blunt horns of the bull's head as Gurney claimed.

But the questions remain. If Gurney was grudgingly surviving on the mountain, and if he *had* seen Douglas's money, or if they *had* quarreled . . .

What sort of man lived on a mountain in Hawai'i?

For an answer we go back to the missionary journal of Sarah Joiner Lyman. In June 1838, four years after the death of Douglas, she wrote to her sister that the family—her husband David, little Henry, and some Hilo students—had been traveling and "at sunset arrived at a beef establishment at the foot of Mauna Kea, where an Englishman resides, who is employed by the Governor to catch wild cattle for their hides and tallow. He resides in a small house, has two wives, two children—a few servants and about 70 dogs."

Seventy dogs? It suggests a fortress mentality, as if he lived in fear of Hall's accusations or felt guilty about his actions on the mountain. He also had a large protective door. Little Henry recalled years later:

> At nightfall we reached the mountain-house of "Ned the bullock-hunter." This worthy was said to have been an escaped convict from Sydney, who had found his way to Hawai'i, where he pursued the wild cattle among the mountains, above the upper border of the black forest that covered the lower slopes of the island. . . . Ned's house was a large native structure, thatched with mountain grass, floored with mats, and provided with a wooden door of dimensions more ample and convenient than those of the ordinary Hawaiian dwelling.

He lived there as late as December 2, 1839. On that date he wrote to "His Majesty Tamehameha III," requesting a land grant at "Kohalla," land he claimed he had turned from "a complete Barren place" to a productive garden. He also asserted that he had fought with Billy Pitt Kalanimoku on Kauaʻi during the 1824 civil war there. He wrote: "I went with Mr. Pitt to Attoi [Kauaʻi] [and] I was promised a land on my return. I was not in want of it at that time for I had no Family but now I got children to provide a home for. I am constantly in the Mountain myself and I want some place for them. I hope you will please to take those things into consideration." The letter was signed "your most obd. Humble Servant, Edward Gurney."

Was he granted the land? Had he fought on Kauaʻi? Did he keep his family together?

A few years later members of a U.S. Naval exploring expedition commanded by Charles Wilkes investigated Douglas's death. They visited Gurney's establishment, interviewed people and drew maps of the site, complete with the Hilo trail and the bullock pits. But they noted on January 15, 1841: "Ned's house is now deserted."

The site was visited again 10 years later, in January 1851, by Henry Lyman, who was surveying in the area. He had been there as a four-year-old with his mother and father in 1838. He wrote:

"One of the guides brought up a handful of potatoes from a deserted plantation, once cultivated by Ned, the notorious bullock-hunter, long since summoned to his last assize, and now troubling the earth no more."

No one now knows where Ned lies, nor if he sleeps peacefully. David Douglas's gravesite at KawaiaHaʻo in Honolulu is likewise unknown, but a plaque there describes him as a *victima scientiae*, a victim of science. It is known that he died a violent death, perhaps at Ned's hands.

My own travels in their footsteps did not yield any answers. Douglas's birthplace at Scone, where there is a monument to him, tells us little. It is a chilly Scottish town which he was glad to leave. Sydney may have been a hospitable port to a willing immigrant, sunny and optimistic, but not to an angry convict. But on the slopes of Mauna Kea is a country beautiful enough for poets, lively enough for hunters, peculiar enough for scientists. It is there, at Kaluakauka ("The Doctor's Pit") that I stood recently. The pit has been filled in and majestic Douglas fir trees now guard the place. It is quiet and lovely and eerie, with Mauna Kea on one side, and the blue Pacific on the other. There are no answers there either.

# Life and Death at the End of the Chain

## BRIAN NICOL

> Kure Atoll, more than 1,300 miles northwest
> of Honolulu, is a refuge for endangered wildlife
> and a home for 23 Coast Guard men and women.
> But it has also been a deadly nemesis
> to decades of seafarers.

✦ As the Coast Guard C-130 Hercules dips and banks into its final approach to Kure Atoll, one of the crewmen reaches into his pocket and pulls out a lacy, blue-and-white garter. He sniffs it, then slips it onto his right arm, over his sleeve and all the way up to his bicep. The plane continues its descent; the crewman peers out the large scanner window on the side of the fuselage. A few seconds later the wheels touch down with a bump, the entire plane vibrates, the propeller engines roar into reverse, straining to stop the rolling aircraft before the end of the 4,000-foot coral runway. The crewman turns toward the passengers, smiles, and hollers, "No bird!" He then slips the garter down off his arm and tucks it back into his pocket.

Our C-130 has landed at Kure without hitting a gooney bird. The short runway at the small atoll 1,367 statute miles northwest of Honolulu International Airport is difficult enough for a pilot and his aircraft, but the numerous gooneys make touch down even more nerve wracking. Many times C-130 propellers splatter the unfortunate birds, bending prop blades, and, of course, risking the lives of crew and pas-

---

First published January 1986.

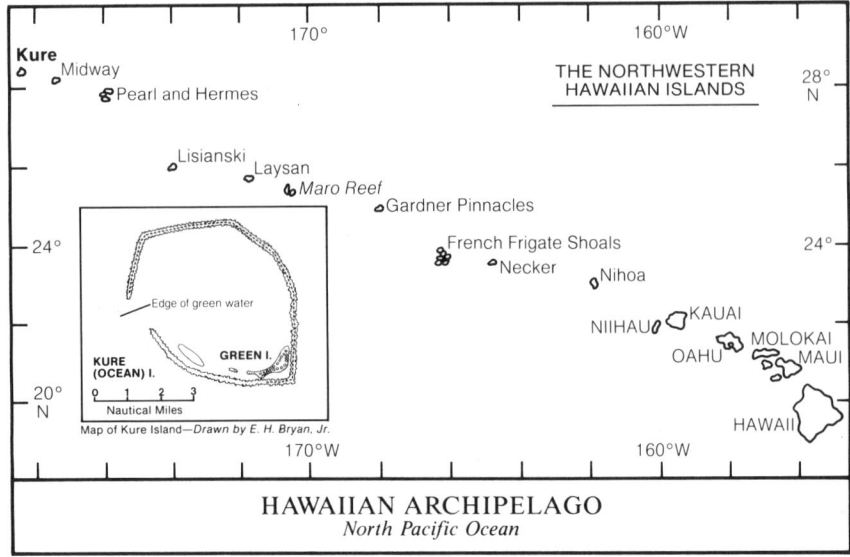

A map of the Hawaiian chain, with an inset of Kure Atoll.

sengers. When a prop is bent, a replacement must be flown out from Barbers Point Naval Air Station, a five-hour flight away. The resulting wait and maintenance time usually strands an aircraft and crew for at least a day.

But there are worse places to be stranded.

Kure is an oval-shaped atoll five miles across at its widest. Within its coral reef, along the southern edge, sits Green Island, the only permanent land here at the farthest end of the chain of atolls, rocks, islands, and shoals known as the Northwestern Hawaiian Islands. Green Island is the oldest Hawaiian Island; it is more than 1,500 miles northwest of the Big Island, the youngest Hawaiian Island. Sometimes called Ocean Island, Green Island is 1½ miles long and a half-mile wide. Its highest point is a sand dune 26 feet above sea level. It is almost completely covered by green, waist-high vegetation called Scaevola. It is completely surrounded by a pristine lagoon teeming with ocean life. Its inhabitants include an assortment of birds, hundreds of small Polynesian rats, an occasional monk seal or sea turtle hauled up onto the sand, and 23 men and women of the United States Coast Guard.

## Life and Death at the End of the Chain

A C-130 lands at Kure every two weeks or so, bringing provisions, mail, replacement personnel, scientists, and occasionally, like on this July afternoon, "VIPs." Honolulu City Council members Leigh-Wai Doo, Marilyn Bornhorst, and Tony Narvaes, accompanied by council staffers, department heads, scientists, and seven of us from the media, are here to stake Honolulu's claim for this tiny island in the middle of a lagoon in the middle of an ocean.

Kure is a fragile, austere place, under the protection of a variety of state and federal agencies and departments. But the city and county of Honolulu, because state law assigned to it "any island not included in any other county," also has jurisdiction here. The city recently formalized its claim for Kure and the rest of the Northwestern Hawaiian Islands (except Midway, which remains federal territory) by including them in the city's general plan and development plans. The islands are zoned "conservation."

All these layers of government bureaucracy could prove to be a blessing. Although a destination resort is not about to sprout up on Kure or any other of these faraway islands, there have been plans for undersea exploration for manganese nodules and a proposal for a fishery at Tern Island in French Frigate Shoals. Such commercial projects could upset the delicate balance between the environment and the land and sea creatures.

Any development proposal must be cleared by the federal government, the state, and, now, the city and county. "If a project passes through all that, it probably deserves to happen," says Councilman Doo. "The city is providing another overlay of protection."

The three council members and the rest of us have only a few hours to tour Kure's Coast Guard facilities, marvel at the island wildlife, and take a refreshing swim in the lagoon. Our stay on Kure will be brief and according to schedule. But it has not always been that way for visitors to these shores.

## Greater Love

During the early morning darkness of October 9, 1870, Capt. Montgomery Sicard steered USS *Saginaw* slowly and cautiously toward Kure. The atoll, named for a Russian navigator decades earlier, had already earned a reputation as a shipwreck isle. In July 1837, the

British ship *Gledstanes* had smashed onto Kure's windward reef, and five years later a similar fate befell the American whaling ship *Parker*. In both cases, the crews swam ashore to Green Island and survived for months on seals, turtles, and birds. And in both cases, rescue came only after a contingent of survivors challenged the open sea and sailed in small boats to Kauai to summon help.

So, in October 1870, Capt. Sicard approached Kure with care. He was sailing from Midway, 58 miles to the east, after having picked up an eight-man engineering party that had been working for months dredging a passage through Midway's reef. But now money for the project had run out and *Saginaw* was sent from California to bring the men home. But before sailing back to San Francisco, Capt. Sicard decided to steam west to Kure, circle the atoll once, looking for any shipwrecked sailors, and then turn toward home. It was the kind of gesture expected of seagoing men, no matter what flag they flew.

Sicard didn't want to be near Kure's reef until well past dawn, when the sky would be bright and the dangerous coral visible. And so the ship steamed slowly. But apparently a quiet current caught the vessel and swept it too quickly toward the atoll.

Suddenly from the darkness, the lookout heard the ominous rumble of waves on a reef. Capt. Sicard ordered reverse engines, but a boiler blew and *Saginaw* was pushed to its fate. George Read, the ship's paymaster, writing in 1912 in *The Last Cruise of the Saginaw*, described the next few moments:

> Just before I reached the top of the wardroom ladder, I felt the ship strike something and supposed we were in collision with another vessel. The shock was an easy one at first, but was followed immediately by others of increasing force, and, as my feet touched the deck, by two severe shocks that caused the ship to tremble in every timber. The long easy swell that had been lifting us gently along in the open sea was now transformed into heavy breakers as it reached and swept over the coral reef, each wave lifting and dropping the quaking ship with a frightful thud.

*Saginaw* was quickly breaking up, but no one panicked. Capt. Sicard directed a swift evacuation into the calmer waters on the lagoon side of the coral. All 93 men—crew and engineering personnel from Midway—reached Green Island safely. The men managed to salvage some of the ship's stores and a gig, a long, light boat equipped with oars and sails.

## Life and Death at the End of the Chain

At dawn, the captain organized work details to construct a makeshift camp and to forage the island for food sources. The men also erected a small lookout tower and flagstaff on the island's highest dune. The 93 had soon settled in for a long wait, but they were not content to merely sit and hope a ship would pass and spot the flag. Someone must go for help.

From the many volunteers, the captain chose four of the most able-bodied of the men and one of his best officers. The five would sail the small gig to Kauai, more than a thousand miles away.

On Friday, November 18, Peter Francis, John Andrews, James Muir, William Halford, and Lt. John Talbot set sail on a voyage that, if successful, would take about a month and would sorely test their physical prowess and navigational skills. George Read described their sendoff:

> The hour set for the boat's departure [four o'clock] arrived and we were all mustered upon the beach. Prayers were read by the captain, after which farewells were said and the brave men who were to peril their lives for us waded off to the gig and climbed on board. They quickly stepped the little masts, spread the miniature sails, raised their anchor, and slowly gaining headway stood off for the western channel through the reef. With full hearts and with many in tears, we gave them three rousing cheers and a tiger, which were responded to with spirit, and we watched them until the boat faded from sight on the horizon to the northward.

Read and the others still on the island would learn later just how much the five needed those prayers. Along the way three different gales pounded the gig and blew much of the rigging and the oars overboard. Their food was spoiled by salt water; they lived off flying fish that flopped on board and a sea bird that Halford caught with his bare hands. Four of the five men suffered from extreme diarrhea throughout the voyage. The strong winds continually hampered their progress and blew them off course frequently. At one point, Peter Francis was swept overboard but managed to grab the trailing fishing line and was pulled back onto the deck.

Despite all that, they hit their mark. Exactly one month after setting sail from Kure, they spotted Kauai. The five of them, exhausted and weakened by sickness, tried to keep the gig outside the reef at Hanalei until the light of day when they could navigate safely into the bay. But high seas pushed their craft onto the coral. Breakers capsized the gig and spun it crazily over the reef. Francis, Andrews, and Lt. Talbot were tossed overboard into the churning water. Halford and Muir managed to swim into the calmer bay and eventually made it to shore. Muir was babbling incoherently and died within a few minutes, his face turning immediately black. Lt. Talbot's body washed ashore that morning; John Andrews', the next day. Peter Francis was never found. William Halford, the lone survivor, informed the authorities of the wreck of *Saginaw*. King Kalakaua immediately dispatched the royal steamer *Kilauea* to Kure to rescue the remaining 88.

About 3:30 in the afternoon of January 3, 1871, *Kilauea* was spotted on the horizon by the men on Green Island. "I witnessed such a scene as never will be forgotten," wrote George Read. "Rough-looking men—many of them having faced shocks of storm and battle—all of them having passed through our recent misfortunes without a murmur of complaint—were embracing each other with tears of joy running down their cheeks, while laughing, singing, and dancing."

The jubilation faded considerably when the *Kilauea* rescuers told the men of *Saginaw* about the ordeal and fate of those who had gone for help so many weeks before. Capt. Sicard and the rest of the crew vowed to never forget that sacrifice. When they returned to civilization, Sicard and the others paid for and designed a memorial tablet that still hangs on a wall in the chapel of the United States Naval Academy at Annapolis. The inscription on the tablet names the four dead men and briefly describes their deed. It ends with this simple line: "Greater love hath no man than this, that a man lay down his life for his friends."

## Splendid Isolation

Coast Guard Chief Warrant Officer Jim Aschenbrenner has served 10 months of his one-year Kure tour of duty. He's the station's executive officer, the second in command under Lt. j.g. Lurilla Lee. Isolated duty is not new to him; he has served two other "isolated tours," in Alaska at other Coast Guard outposts. He knows the special problems of such duty and he knows the specialized mission of a Coast Guard LORAN station. He's the ideal guide for our tour of the station facilities.

The Coast Guard contingent here numbers 23: two officers (Lee and Aschenbrenner) and 21 enlisted personnel (nine of whom are female).

## Life and Death at the End of the Chain

Eight of the 23 are electronics technicians responsible for the functioning and maintenance of the LORAN equipment, and the rest are support personnel (engineers, cooks, a corpsman, etc.).

LORAN is an acronym for "long range aids to navigation." The system sends out an electronic signal from atop a red and white, 625-foot antenna at the center of Kure's Green Island. The station here is one-third of a three-station network used by planes and ships in the central Pacific to fix their position. Kure's sister stations are at Johnston Island and Upolo Point on the Big Island. A craft traveling over or on the sea receives signals from all three stations and, using simple triangulation, can determine exactly where it is. "LORAN tells *them* where *they* are," stresses Aschenbrenner. LORAN stations cannot tell what craft are out there and where they are. It's not some kind of Star Wars radar. And since the signals are sent out 24 hours a day, indiscriminately in all directions, the system can be used by any Pacific traveler, no matter what nationality.

At least one of the eight electronics technicians is on duty with the LORAN equipment at all times. Normal work day for station personnel is "tropical hours"—6 a.m. until 1 p.m. The tour of duty is one year, with a midtour leave granted anytime after the first six months. The enlisted men and women earn "foreign duty pay," from an extra $8 a month for an E-2 to $22 for an E-7. "They bring at least two weeks' worth of clothes when they first come here," says Aschenbrenner, "because if the water supply happens to be low, they might need that much." There is no underground water table; rain water is gathered by means of a rooftop catchment system and stored in holding tanks.

We visitors to Kure are curious about the LORAN equipment and the water system, but our questions soon turn to the social interactions within an isolated group of young males and females. "It's amazing how well people do get along here," says Aschenbrenner. The station SOP is to simply "keep 'em busy" during off-duty hours. There are power boats and water skis, a 16-foot catamaran, two Sunfish sailboats, volleyball, tennis courts, piano, pool table, video games, computer, library, weight room, TV and movie room, dark room, and hot tub (out back). "We have dances and beach bonfires," says Aschenbrenner. "And we do have beer and ale, but no hard stuff—although I wouldn't be surprised if there were one or two bottles of that floating around." What isn't floating around is dope, at least as far as Aschenbrenner knows. "I think it's kind of passé these days," he says.

Aschenbrenner then tells about his recent search for volunteers to paint the station's beach shack. "I couldn't get anybody until I announced there'd be free beer. Then we got a crowd. That's the way you get things done. In fact, as long as the job gets done, we don't hassle the people much."

## Vanished

The Kure LORAN station was constructed in 1960 and commissioned in March 1961. It was not the island's first permanent structure, however. Seventy-five years earlier, King Kalakaua ordered a wooden house built on Kure and stocked with water, food, and other provisions that would assist any future castaways. The king, of course, had sent his steamer *Kilauea* to rescue the *Saginaw* crew in 1871, but now, in 1886, there had been another disaster.

The British ship *Dunnottar Castle* hit Kure's reef on July 15, 1886. The crew struggled to Green Island. Within a few days the men decided to take a page from *Saginaw*'s book and attempt to reach Kauai by gig rather than wait for rescue. Again, the landing at Kauai proved treacherous and several crewmen drowned.

After the disaster, in September 1886, Kalakaua sent his special commissioner, Colonel J. H. Boyd, to Kure to take possession of the island for the Hawaiian Kingdom. Kalakaua also ordered the rude house built and amply stocked. But within a year, all the provisions were stolen and the house had crumbled.

Kure was acquired by the United States on July 7, 1898, when Hawaii became a U.S. territory. In April 1909, President Theodore Roosevelt, alarmed at the bird depletion due to poaching on Kure and the other Northwestern Hawaiian Islands, issued Executive Order 1019 declaring Kure part of the Hawaiian Islands Reservation, "a preserve and breeding ground for native birds." In 1940 President Franklin Roosevelt proclaimed most of the Northwest chain the "Hawaiian Islands National Wildlife Refuge."

It continued to be a refuge for human life as well. On April 24, 1961, about a month after the Coast Guard station was commissioned, the 82-foot tug *Port of Bandon* ran aground on the southeast edge of the reef. Coast Guardsmen from the station rescued the five-man crew using motorboats. The remains of the tug's rusted hull are still on the

## Life and Death at the End of the Chain

reef, but its recovered nameplate hangs on a wall in the Coast Guard dining hall.

At times Kure's unexpected visitors have come from the air as well as from the sea. Twice during the 1960s passenger planes made emergency landings on Kure's coral airstrip. Both times, station personnel fed and berthed scores of bewildered travelers. In neither case were there any injuries and the planes continued their journeys the next day.

But not every Kure tale has an ending.

The last communication from the Japanese fishing vessel *Houei Maru No. 5* came on February 3, 1976. The captain reported he was leaving Midway waters for fishing grounds about 190 miles east northeast of Kure. *Houei Maru No. 5* had put in at the U.S. Naval Station at Midway to seek medical treatment for an injured crewman. But now it was back at work, chasing fish.

The next day, Wednesday, February 4, 1976, the worst storm of the season hit the area. Two days later a Navy C-117 on a routine logistics flight from Midway spotted *Houei Maru* hard aground on Kure's north reef. The 17-man crew had disappeared. No one had come ashore on Green Island; no bodies were floating in the lagoon or on the ocean side of the reef. There was no sign of life—or death.

The search began and the mystery deepened. Despite the continuing foul weather, a sailor was lowered from a helicopter onto the rocking deck of the stuck vessel. He searched the darkness below but found no one. A few days later, search parties approached by sea and boarded the wreck. Again, there was no sign of the crew. But the searchers did find three sextants, charts, and a logbook. The last log entry was dated January 17, two weeks earlier. Among the crew's abandoned personal belongings were bottles of wine, sake, and cognac and brand new underwear and shirts, still in cellophane bags, ready for use at the next port. The most significant find: a makeshift rope hanging over the bow, possibly the escape route of the terrified crew.

For six days Coast Guard and Navy search-and-rescue ships and planes crisscrossed the area around Kure. Meanwhile, *Houei Maru No. 5* was slowly breaking up on the reef. Finally, the search was abandoned. The only thing that had surfaced were theories:

- Perhaps the hapless crew was picked up by another craft in the fishing fleet or by some passing vessel. But a rescuer would have made a report. There was none.

- Perhaps *Houei Maru No. 5* was scuttled deliberately in an insurance scam. But to make a phony insurance claim, you don't have to lose a crew.
- Perhaps the 17 were still out there somewhere, men against the sea, drifting in a lifeboat. Maybe. The ship's life raft was also gone. But they surely would have been within the wide search area. Also, the prevailing current and weather patterns would have pushed a raft in a wide circle, back into the Kure region, not far into the vast Pacific.

The most likely scenario is probably the simplest. The violent storm pushed *Houei Maru* off course and onto the reef. The crew assumed the vessel would break up quickly. The men panicked. They scrambled down the rope into the pitching life raft or into the churning sea. In their haste, they left behind a sailor's most valuable tool on the open sea: a sextant. The crashing waves capsized the raft; the raging water pulled the 17 men under and out to sea.

And during those dark, awful moments the Coast Guard men and women at the LORAN station, unaware of the disaster across the lagoon, stayed inside, out of the weather, watching a movie, drinking beer, and writing letters home.

## Only the Strong

The flat, blue water of the lagoon is as clear as a country creek, as warm as a midnight bath. We spend the last hour of our half-day stay enjoying the beach just steps from the Coast Guard buildings. A few hundred yards up the shoreline is a newborn monk seal in a cage-like enclosure, protected from bull seals who often attack the young, mistaking them for breeding females. The cage also protects the seal pup from curious homo sapiens like us. We have been reminded to keep our distance—at least 100 feet.

Hawaiian monk seals have remained virtually unchanged for 15 million years and are sometimes called living fossils. But what is changing is their numbers. They are an endangered marine mammal, with only about 1,000 individual seals still in existence, primarily in the Northwestern Hawaiian Islands. Their troubles began in the nineteenth and early twentieth centuries when sealers, shipwrecked crews, feather

## Life and Death at the End of the Chain

hunters, and guano diggers killed many of them and disrupted their sensitive breeding cycles. More contact with humans in the 1950s and 1960s further depleted their ranks. Protection of the seals now falls under the jurisdiction of the U.S. National Marine Fisheries Service, as well as the state Department of Land and Natural Resources. In addition, under terms of its lease with the Hawaii state government, the Coast Guard is obligated to protect monk seals, all species of sea turtles, and all other animal, bird, and plant life on the island, except rodents. A seal pup out here has no shortage of guardians.

While the monk seals are rare, the gooney birds are everywhere. Many other birds—tropic birds, frigate birds, booby birds, sooty terns, petrels, and shearwaters—also inhabit the island, but gooneys seem always under foot and over head. These Blackfooted albatrosses and Laysan albatrosses are stately when airborne, their wingspans stretching six feet across. On land they are awkward, scruffy, and noisy, creatures only a mother could love. They return to Kure and other Northwestern Hawaiian Islands every November to begin their eight-month breeding cycle. Their courtship ritual is an amazing sequence of posturing maneuvers and dance steps. The eggs hatch after two months, and the young remain on the island another five months, fed periodically by their parents. Then in July and early August, as the days of summer are shrinking, the fittest of the young and the adults leave the island. They'll roam the ocean for an incredible six or seven years, drifting on the air and feeding off the sea. Then they'll return to the island where they were born, to begin the breeding cycle again.

But many of the young and a few of the old—those too feeble to struggle up into the air—will be left behind. They will gradually starve. A few will get airborne for a short distance but will then plop down weakly into the sea. The sharks will do the rest.

Our C-130 rumbles along the coral runway and lifts off gently. The garter does its magic; we do not hit a bird. We circle Kure several times for a last look, for a few final photos. We gaze down at the lonely buildings and the erector-set antenna. We marvel again at the crystalline lagoon, and we stare at the surrounding reef and the white water breaking across its coral heads. We look for pieces of hulls, broken masts, twisted metal—the traces of tragedy.

# The Hawaiian Education of Henry Adams

ALFRED L. CASTLE

*The eminent author and intellectual spent a month here in 1890. Although he left Hawai'i feeling more refreshed than he had in years, he was deeply disturbed by much of what he saw.*

*Interestingly, one of the greatest literary and intellectual figures to visit Hawaii is rarely mentioned in standard histories of the Islands. Indeed, only intimate biographies of the Boston Brahmin, Henry Adams, even acknowledge his brief stay here.*

*Henry Adams, a descendant of presidents John Adams and John Quincy Adams, was already a nationally known literary and political figure when, at age 52, he departed in August 1890 for a tour of Hawaii, Samoa, Tahiti, Fiji, Australia, Ceylon, and Europe. The author of numerous historical works and novels, Adams was one of the most important interpreters of the age in which he lived. His* Education of Henry Adams, *published in 1918, is today considered one of most vital statements about the period that exists.*

✦ In August of 1890, Henry Adams was ready to embark on a whimsical search for nirvana. He had talked of such a "search" for five years and now, after completing the last volumes of the *History of the United States During the Administrations of Jefferson and Madison*, he de-

---

First published November 1981.

sired a quick departure. The last five years had been hard ones for Adams. In 1885, his wife Maria had died by her own hand; the memories of her at his H Street mansion in Washington, D.C., had become insufferably oppressive. As his private world was impoverished by loss, his public world dissolved. His hopes for Washington's politics declined with the elections of mediocre presidents Garfield, Hayes, Arthur, Cleveland, and, most recently, Harrison. Hoping for a spiritual renewal, he and his companion, the noted painter John La Farge, departed on *Zealandia* on August 23, 1890.

After the week-long voyage, Adams first sighted the island of Molokai on August 30. His boredom on *Zealandia* had been relieved only by La Farge's instruction in water color painting. This instruction in colors, shapes, and hue prepared him for recording his impressions of the Islands in uncharacteristically daring and florid imagery. In a diary-letter to his close friend Elizabeth Cameron, he wrote:

"Molokai is in sight on our left, a dim bank of fog, and Oahu ahead, a higher range of hills behind which is our port, Honolulu. The air is still soft as the clouds, which are always a delicate violet that makes sunset and moonlight equally refined. At ten o'clock we shall arrive, and already the Sandwiches seem companions of one's youth."

Disembarking at Honolulu, Adams and La Farge were taken to Alfred Hartwell's large and gracious home in Manoa Valley. W. O. Smith, Hartwell's brother-in-law, served as their guide while on Oahu. Here Adams found:

> The sense of space, light, color . . . superb, and the greater from the contest behind, where the eye rests on a Scotch mountain valley, ending in clouds and mists, and green mountain-sides absolutely velvety with the liquid softness of its lights and shadows . . . As for the grounds, they were a mass of palms, ferns, roses, many-colored flowers, creepers interspersed with the yellow fruit of the limes, and unknown trees and shrubs of vaguely tropical suggestions, all a little neglected, and as though waiting for us.

After two days of staying close to home, Adams experienced his first mango and the attractive laziness of a "Kanaka paradise."

On September 3 and 4, Adams was invited to breakfast with Judge Dole and to dinner by Mr. Dillingham. He toured the new Bishop Museum and took in a view of the Pali, one of the finest he had ever seen. In

## The Hawaiian Education of Henry Adams

his diary-letter of September 5, he reflected on the difference between his anticipation of Hawaii and the reality he had found.

> I conceived it as a forest-clad cluster of volcanoes, with fringing beaches where natives were always swimming, and I imagined that when I should leave the beach I should be led by steep paths through dense forests to green glades where native girls said "Aloha" and threw garlands round your neck, and where you would find straw huts of unparalleled cleanliness always in terraces looking over a distant ocean a thousand feet below. The reality, though beautiful, is quite different.

The "reality" for Adams was that Oahu's mountains were as barren as the Scotch moors. Reality also included the existence of paved roads, modern horsecars, and railroads—plus centipedes and omnipresent cockroaches. Most strangely, for Adams, it included a much cooler climate than he had expected. He could even recommend that Washington residents suffering from July heat visit Hawaii to escape the tortures of summer.

On September 12, Adams journeyed to the Big Island. Ironically he noted to Elizabeth Cameron that the journey around the island's southeastern end was a laborious one.

"As I detest mountains, abominate volcanoes, and execrate the sea, the effort is a tremendous one; but I make it from a sense of duty to the savages who killed Captain Cook just about here a century ago. One good turn deserves another. Perhaps they will kill me. I never saw a place where killing was less like murder."

Feeling nauseated from the rough voyage on the steamer *W. G. Hall*, Adams was irritated to see white men at the spot where Capt. Cook had been killed. Also, he found the Hawaiians to be, on the whole, strangely melancholy in their appearance. He concluded that this was because of the cultural displacement they had suffered at the hands of New England missionaries years before. This conclusion was to reach fuller expression in his novel published three years later, *Tahiti*.

On September 15, Adams stayed at the Kilauea Volcano House. In his letter-diary of that day he described the ritual of placating Pele and noted wryly that the ritual could be performed only by the rich. Adams also noted with interest that Hawaiians with a Christian education were still able, or perhaps best able, to participate in the sacrifice. For the agnostic Adams, deities were really quite interchangeable.

In Hilo, on September 18, Adams and La Farge visited a waterfall. The waterfall was behind the Severance house where he was staying. In at least a semiserious lamentation about the commercialization of a pristine scene, he reported that:

> She [Mrs. Severance] said nothing about the girls, but she did say that the boys used habitually to go over the fall as their after school amusement; but of late they had given it up, and must be paid for doing it. The last man who jumped off the neighborhood high rack required fifteen dollars . . . A Bostonian named Brigham took a clever photograph of a boy, just half way down, the fall being perhaps twelve . . . feet. So passes the glory of Hawaii, and of the old-gold [native] girls—woe is me!

On several other occasions, Adams was to bemoan the growing lack of "naturalness" in the Islands.

On Friday, September 19, Adams and La Farge left Hilo to ride 80 miles on horseback to Kawaihae, where they would catch the steamer Kinau back to Honolulu. Adams recorded his delight in the beauty of the many ravines and canyons they traveled through on the four-day journey. Adams was, on the other hand, bored with the several plantations that provided them shelter for their overnight rests. At one of Claus Spreckels' plantations they were entertained by "saturnine Scotchmen and a gentle-spoken Gloucestershire housekeeper" until seven Saturday morning. The next day they visited the Laupahoehoe plantation run by a German-American family who pleased their company by playing them Weber's last waltz. Finally, they paid short visits to the Horner plantation and the Jarrett cattle ranch. They were treated well by all their hosts and were escorted the last several miles to Kawaihae by two native girls who were working at the Jarrett ranch. Met by Jarrett, they were then entertained in a native house in the village.

"The mistress of the house brought her guitar and sang Hawaiian songs. They were curiously plaintive, perhaps owing to the way of singing, but only one—Kamehameha's war dance—was really interesting and sounded as though it were real."

Adams found this touch of "half-native life" the redemption of an otherwise dull, hot stay in his least favorite Hawaiian town.

After returning to Honolulu, Adams and La Farge had an audience with King Kalakaua. In a very condescending passage written on Sep-

## The Hawaiian Education of Henry Adams

tember 27, Adams gave the following description of the Merry Monarch. Received by the king in his drawing room, he found the king to be:

> half Hawaiian, half Negro; talks quite admirable English in a charming voice; has admirable manners; and . . . seems to me a somewhat superior Chester A. Arthur; a type surprisingly common among the natives. To be sure His Majesty is not wise, and he has—or is said to have—vices, such as whiskey and others; but he is the only interesting figure in the government, and is really what the Japs call *omusurvi*—amusing. . . . I would not be thought to prefer Kalakaua to Benjamin Harrison, but I own to finding him a more amusing subject.

Finally, in his last "Hawaiian letter" to Elizabeth Cameron, he judged white Hawaiian society in a negative fashion. Coming from the highest social circles of Boston and Washington, D.C., Adams clearly had expected a warm and perhaps even deferential welcoming in Honolulu. He noted that no real invitations had been tendered and that he had not been put up at any of the city's social clubs.

> Almost no one has called on us. As for dinner or parties, we have as yet cost Honolulu not a bottle of wine. Apparently in order to see the interior of a white man's house here, one must invite oneself into it, as we did on our journey last week. I should suppose we had given offense, except that no one seems to do more than we do, or to have more social vogue.

It seems Honolulu society ignored this eminent writer, although the reasons for this are unclear. Perhaps it was because of the brevity of his stay and his own reluctance to impose his presence on strangers. As Adams concluded, "I cheerfully forgive society for ignoring us, for I have caught glimpses enough of it to imagine worse than Washington horrors." In any case, the peregrinations of La Farge and Adams continued as they departed on *Alameda* for Samoa, the next scheduled stop on their tour of Polynesia. Although not happy with the inroads civilization had made here, or the passing of a virile archaic culture, Adams felt his short time in Hawaii had refreshed his nerves and sharpened his perceptions. Hawaii had, despite its drawbacks, given him "a sense of living, more than I had done in five years." He was "glad to be dead to the old existence which was a torture, and to forget it in a change as complete as that of another planet."

The last major comment Adams made on Hawaii was in his book *Tahiti*, published first in 1893 and reissued and revised in 1901. This little-read book was a strange one to many who had read Adams' other works. In *Tahiti*, Adams pretended to be, and to some extent was, merely the editor of the memoirs of Taimai, the last pre-Westernized queen of the Teva clan of Tahiti. In the privately printed book, Taimai discusses the history and genealogy of her family, and the traditions of her clan prior to the alterations wrought by the Western world. But, as one critic noted, the book manifests Adams' own style and power of generalizations; the reader is never far from the intellectual presence and predilections of the author.

Henry Adams entered the 1890s with a feeling of revulsion for the Western world. Particularly offensive to him was the advance of materialistic values, the growth in huge armaments, the concentration of capital, and degradation of the arts. Additionally, he carried the covert burden of his wife's suicide. Thus, in the short work *Tahiti*, Adams vented his growing dislike for a world he felt had grown mad and corrupt.

Of specific interest in *Tahiti* are the insights which Adams gives his readers about the conditions he perceived in Hawaii. The book's essential message is simple enough. The Polynesian social world was, as Adams saw it, a healthy and stable culture prior to contact with the West in the eighteenth century. Shortly after initial contacts with the British and French, this ahistoric society suffered rapid political and social decline at the hands of whalers, merchants, and English missionaries. Perhaps, understandably, Adams viewed the Tahitians as victims of many of the same forces that had "defeated" him. The key point is that Adams had come, by 1893, to see Hawaii as a slightly later version of Tahiti. In the single most revealing statement by the Arii (chiefess) Taimai, we receive Adams' view of Hawaiian history:

> When England and France began to show us the advantages of their civilization, we were, as races then went, a great people. Hawaii, Tahiti, the Marquesas, Tonga, Samoa, and New Zealand ... contained a population of no small size, better fitted than any other possible community for the conditions in which they lived. Tahiti ... was first to suffer. The people who numbered, according to Cook, two hundred thousand in 1767, numbered less than twenty thousand in 1797, according to the missionaries. This frightful mortality has been

often doubted, because Europeans have naturally shrunk from admitting the horrors of their own work, but no one doubts it who belongs to the native race. Tahiti did not stand alone in misery. What happened there happened everywhere, not only in the great groups of high islands, like Hawaii, with three or four hundred thousand people, but in little coral atolls which could support only a few score.

Furthermore, the islanders led happy, if somewhat hedonistic, lives until the usurping Europeans arrived.

"The Europeans came, and not only upset all their moral ideas, but also their whole political system . . . and for the social and moral depreciation, they were the active cause."

After his Tahitian parable was completed, Adams chose not to comment further upon his 1890 voyage to the South Pacific. When, in 1893, Charles A. Dance of the *New York Sun* asked him to do several articles on the Hawaii question, he refused. Apparently he had concluded that a lengthy recounting of Hawaii's history would be too painful and politically controversial. For Adams, Hawaii was a later version of downtrodden Tahiti; any further colonial venture in the form of U.S. annexation would be noxious. In any case, having left us with a brief account of his feelings on Hawaii, Adams began the last and most vital stage of his own writing career. Only much later would Americans fully appreciate the dire descriptions he had made in the final rendering of his Hawaiian and Polynesian voyage.

# An Artist-Adventurer in Turn-of-the-Century Hawaii

## PAT PITZER

*Theodore Wores, a widely traveled and widely acclaimed painter, captured on canvas the beauty and charm of the Islands in the early 1900s.*

♦ An artist with the instincts of an explorer, Theodore Wores had a lifelong interest in recording in his paintings the people, customs, and scenes of other cultures. His artistic quest for colorful, exotic subjects led him to paint his native San Francisco's Chinatown, then Japan, Hawaii, Samoa, and Spain.

By the time he came to Hawaii in 1901, he was already famous, having earned international acclaim for his Japanese paintings.

The artist stopped briefly in Honolulu in 1892 on his way to Japan, his second trip to live and paint in that country. Hawaii captivated him at first sight, and he declared his intention to return.

In both Hawaii and Japan, Wores sensed that the colorful and distinctive older ways of the culture were rapidly changing, and only a few precious years remained to capture them. He expressed his desire to "immortalize the vanishing spirit of Old Hawaii."

The road that ultimately led him to Hawaii was paved with artistic adventures. Born in San Francisco in 1859, he was the son of German-Hungarian immigrants, who encouraged his artistic gifts. At the precocious age of 16, Wores set off to train as a painter at the prestigious

---

First published May 1987.

Royal Academy of Munich. In his fourth year there, he won the academy's highest prize.

He lived and painted in Europe from the age of 16 to 22, spending the latter couple of years with noted artist Frank Duveneck and a vanguard of young artists and intellectuals in Florence and Venice. Another famed American expatriate artist he met while painting in Venice was James McNeill Whistler. It was Whistler who fired the imagination of the young man with the idea of going to paint in Japan, which had only recently opened its doors to the outside world.

Wores nurtured the idea and meanwhile, in 1881, he returned to San Francisco. Pursuing his interest in colorful, picturesque subjects, he immersed himself in painting scenes of that city's Chinatown, which won him recognition. During this period the young artist was also commissioned to do a portrait of celebrated Irish poet and dramatist Oscar Wilde.

When Wores made his long-planned pioneering journey to Japan in 1885, he was one of the first foreign artists to record the then little-known culture of that country. It was a time when Japan was a remote and exotic place, just emerging from its long self-imposed isolation. For the next three years, and for two later years, from 1892 to 1894, he lived among the Japanese people, painting scenes of their daily life.

Wores' Japanese paintings, which offered many Americans and Europeans their first views of that country, won resounding praise at exhibitions throughout the United States and in London and Paris and brought Wores fame.

Before coming to Hawaii, he also became well known as a portrait painter, and his subjects included many of San Francisco's social luminaries.

Upon his arrival in Honolulu in 1901 to live and paint here for a year and a half, one of the Territorial newspapers observed:

> Theodore Wores, who took London by storm a few years ago with original paintings of Japanese life, and who has lately been doing portraits for the society buds of San Francisco, has come to Hawaii to find something new. Two days of observation have convinced him that he made no mistake in coming to Hawaii . . . He hopes to do work that will immortalize the fast vanishing spirit of old Hawaiian life.
>
> He was told that he came too late. He does not believe it.

## An Artist-Adventurer in Turn-of-the-Century Hawaii

Wores had his own positive views about the Hawaiian subject matter at hand, praising "these pretty native girls in Honolulu" and "these tropical gardens, gorgeous in color, rich in variety." He noted in particular, "The flower girls upon the street corners afford an abundance of material for paintings of originality with wealth of local color."

The latter comment proved to be a prelude to the creation of his most famous Hawaii work, the beautiful painting, "The Lei Maker."

Other initial impressions of the Islands voiced by the newly arrived artist were that nature had juggled with color in Hawaii as never before or elsewhere, and he hoped to paint some many-hued landscapes. He said, "This is an ideal land for the artist and the painting of it would be a labor of love."

One of the locales in Hawaii that particularly appealed to Wores as an artist was Ainahau, a lovely tropical garden-like estate in Waikiki. It was the home of Archibald Cleghorn, who landscaped and designed it, his wife, Princess Likelike (sister of King Kalakaua), and their daughter, Princess Kaiulani. Kaiulani, heir to the throne of Hawaii, died at the age of 23, two years before Wores came to the Islands.

One Honolulu reviewer wrote of Wores' work: "Studies of tropical gardens, painted in the open at Ainahau . . . and many glimpses of Hawaiian life and scenery, bear the true local coloring and quality, while showing the masterful technique first made widely known to the art world in Wores' pictures of Japan."

Another island landscape setting that attracted Wores was Waialua, where he sometimes spent a couple of weeks at a time, painting its coconut groves, taro patches, and cane fields, often with the purple and emerald mountains in the background.

During the time he lived and worked in Honolulu, his exhibitions here drew enthusiastic audiences and glowing reviews from critics in the press.

Interestingly, the two paintings that drew the widest admiration and the highest praise at the time they were first painted and exhibited are his most famous Hawaii paintings today: "The Lei Maker" and "Hawaiian Child and the Poi Bowl." Both capture the spirit of old Hawaii that Wores sought to immortalize.

Among the many raves accorded "The Lei Maker" when it made its debut on the exhibition circuit was a 1902 description of it as "a vivid study of a charming native type in lei stringing pose . . . vigorously painted, and full of rich color effects."

Ever looking for picturesque lands and people to record on canvas, during his 1901–2 period in Hawaii, he also made a trip to Samoa, where he eagerly painted the people and scenery. Compared to Hawaii, Wores found Samoa a much more unspoiled native culture, almost wholly unaffected by outside influences.

On his return to Hawaii, a major exhibition of his Samoan and Hawaiian paintings was held. One newspaper account said: "The present exhibition is a display of the work of the first really prominent visiting artist who has made a careful and continued study of Hawaiian and Samoan life and character with perhaps the exception of Tavernier, who, however, kept within narrower limits." Still, the highest accolade was reserved for "The Lei Maker," described as "the most striking canvas in the gallery."

In addition to his paintings of the native Hawaiian people and landscapes, during his 18-month initial stay in the Islands, and particularly on his return here to paint in 1910, Wores was commissioned to do numerous portraits. The list of his subjects reads like a "Who's Who" of Island society of the day, and includes Archibald Cleghorn. Another of his prominent portrait subjects was Sanford B. Dole, president of the Republic of Hawaii after the overthrow of the monarchy in 1893, and first governor of the Territory of Hawaii.

While Wores was an enthusiastic admirer of Hawaii, its beauty, and its people, he also voiced a cautionary criticism that strikes a contemporary-sounding note. He regretted, even then, the "modernization" of Honolulu. As he was preparing in September 1902 to dismantle his Beretania Street studio and go to the mainland, in an outspoken interview he took the local government to task for despoiling Honolulu's environment and charm.

"The curves of the road with the pencilled cocoanuts against the sky, and a glimpse of the surf between, are all gone, the lily pond gone," said Wores. "The old cathedral has been spoilt and the town given an appearance of a third-rate American city instead of preserving the quaint charm of a semi-tropical town. The road to the Pali and Nuuanu Avenue present the only drive that still retains individual and characteristic charm . . . The drives near the city here should be beautified, not laid out as if they were military highways."

After leaving Hawaii in 1902, he spent most of his time on the mainland, though with his customary thirst for new artistic adventures, he made a painting trip to Spain. During his eight-year absence from the Islands, his Hawaii paintings, exhibited at art centers throughout the country, won acclaim and also became, in effect, a promotion of Hawaii. In addition to being admired for their artistic merit, they helped spread Hawaii's fledgling fame.

When he returned to Hawaii in 1910, an extensive exhibition of his works was held at the Alexander Young Hotel, including many Hawaii scenes and portraits as well as scenes from his Japanese and Spanish travels. Even with that competition, the most admired painting was "The Lei Maker," which by now had been celebrated and complimented across the continent.

A writer hailed the artist's return:

> Theodore Wores, artist, teller of tales through the power and delicacy of his gifted brush, is back in Hawaii.
>
> Eight years ago Mr. Wores came to the Islands in his never-ending quest of the new, the picturesque, the striking in life and color and beauty. A Ulysses in the field of art, he has wandered over the world, seeing with the eyes of a painter subjects and objects that would escape anyone else. From the brown mat-makers of Samoa to the gatherers of the purple grape in Spain, he has taken types and transferred them to canvas with a sympathy and a technical perfection that has won him recognition all over the world.

When Wores returned to Hawaii in 1910, he brought with him his new 17-year-old bride, Carolyn Bauer Wores. During their Hawaii honeymoon of several months, the artist was commissioned to paint many portraits of Hawaii's leading figures, and prominent Island families hosted parties for the famed artist and his bride.

Theodore Wores died in 1939 after a long, remarkable, adventurous, and successful career.

In 1971, his widow made a sentimental journey to the Islands for the opening of the first Hawaii exhibit of her husband's work since he lived here. In an interview with the *Sunday Star-Bulletin & Advertiser*, she reminisced about their experiences here in 1910 when she was a young bride: "It was all so romantic. We lived in the Alexander Young Hotel. Every day, groups of Hawaiian men walked along the streets with their ukuleles and stopped under our windows to serenade us.

"Every night, in one of those lovely old Island homes, there was a beautiful party to which the men wore formal dinner suits and the women dressed in long gowns. Everyone wore flower leis, day and night."

She recalled riding horseback at Parker Ranch with the Sam Parkers, who hosted a luau in their honor, taking the Dillinghams' railroad out to Haleiwa for a weekend house party, and being entertained by the Damons at Moanalua after polo matches.

On the occasion of the 1971 Wores exhibition, the state senate passed a resolution honoring the artist "for his outstanding contribution to the perpetuation and preservation of Hawaii's culture . . . to the world of art and to Hawaiiana."

The 1971 exhibit, at the East-West Center, featured more than 60 of Wores' paintings from Japan, Samoa, San Francisco's Chinatown, and Hawaii. Most of them, including "The Lei Maker," were from the collection of Drs. Jess and Ben Shenson, who with their mother accompanied Carolyn Wores to Hawaii.

The Drs. Shenson, two brothers who are physicians in San Francisco, knew Theodore Wores in his later years, and the artist and his wife were close friends of their parents. The brothers recall, "Although Wores was in his 70s when we knew him, he continued to have the same zest for life that had taken him to many lands in his earlier years."

Drs. Jess and Ben Shenson have the most extensive collection of Wores' works in existence, and over the years they have provided opportunities for Hawaii residents to share them through exhibitions.

While Wores' paintings are in many permanent collections, including the Smithsonian Institution, the White House, and the Bishop Museum, the Honolulu Academy of Arts has the prized work, "The Lei Maker," a gift last year from the Shensons.

For many years the only thing known about the model for the painting was her name, Lizzie Victor, remembered by the artist's widow who died in 1976 at the age of 96.

Along with their numerous Wores paintings, the Shensons have in their collection a photo of Lizzie Victor, holding an 'ilima lei, which the artist shot in his studio at the time she was posing for the painting.

In December 1970, *Honolulu Magazine* ran "The Lei Maker" on its cover and, in the accompanying article on the artist, sought clues about the model. It identified her as Lizzie Victor and posed the question, "Who in Hawaii might know of the beautiful girl who graces our cover?"

Letters came in with various leads, including one from an 85-year-old woman who wrote:

I knew Lizzie Victor when she was only 20 and an operator for Hawaiian Telephone Company. She never married but adopted two girls and one boy who were part Hawaiian and part *haole*. She educated them in public schools and then moved to Hilo where she became a sampan bus driver.

She and her mother, Mrs. O. T. Shipman, lived together and Lizzie was a wonderful hostess. Her Hawaiian food was excellent and everyone enjoyed her parties. Her children now live on the Mainland. Lizzie was a very nice woman. She died in 1945.

Following these and other clues, the Shensons were able to trace some members of the Shipman/Victor families to invite them to the presentation of the painting to the Academy of Arts last October. One of Lizzie Victor's adopted daughters, who now lives in Missouri, and a step-nephew from California flew to Honolulu for the event.

While some of "The Lei Maker" model's background is now known, there is an aura of mystery still about her, including the unsubstantiated rumor, told to the Shensons by various people who knew Lizzie Victor and her family, that Lizzie herself was fathered by King Kalakaua.

"The Lei Maker," in a handsome koa and mango wood frame designed by the late renowned Hawaii artist Jean Charlot, is now in its permanent home in the academy's collection of Hawaiian art.

In making their gift of the painting, the Shensons said they felt it should remain in Hawaii, where it "truly belongs to the people."

# IV

◆

*Places, People, and Prejudice*

# The Path of Progress over the Pali

## RICK STEPIEN

*"Johnny Wilson's road" replaced the footpaths and the horsetrails; the "Puka in the Pali" replaced "Johnny Wilson's road."*

*Whether prompted by necessity or sheer adventurism, blazing new trails has always been a fascination for man, testing his courage, resolve, and intelligence. Land, sea, and now space barriers have fallen to his perseverance and ingenuity, even when the obstacles seemed insurmountable. Such was the case at the turn of the century in Hawaii when two young, relatively inexperienced engineering students assumed the formidable task of constructing a roadway over the rugged Koolau Mountains on the island of Oahu.*

✦ The Koolau Range divides Oahu in half. From the famed hanggliding cliffs of Makapuu in the southeast, the range reaches heights of over 3,000 feet and extends 40 miles to Kahuku in the northwest. Its gentle leeward slopes, fissured by deep valleys, trace the path of lava from the island's volcanic beginning and extend like fingers toward Waikiki, Honolulu, and Pearl Harbor. But the windward side of the range is a wall of volcanic rock—massive cliffs (pali) that plunge into the rural towns of Kahaluu, Kaneohe, Kailua, and Waimanalo.

Immediately above the city of Honolulu is Nuuanu Valley where ancient Hawaiians carved a maze of footpaths through the dense, trop-

---

First published November 1980.

ical vegetation. But these paths abruptly ended at the dizzying heights of the windward cliffs. The Nuuanu Pali virtually isolated the windward coast for centuries.

In 1795, King Kamehameha the Great landed his war canoes on Oahu during his island-unifying campaign. During the Battle of Nuuanu, his forces drove the Oahuans to the upper limits of Nuuanu Valley where many of the defenders leapt to their death from the 1,000-foot cliffs. The site today is one of Hawaii's most popular tourist attractions, the Pali Lookout. It offers a panoramic view of Oahu's windward coast, a sight which many consider one of the most spectacular in the world.

Eventually, a crude walkway was carved into the windward face of the Nuuanu Pali. The trail was only five feet wide and ropes were needed to scale the nearly 50 percent grade. Those accustomed to the trek made it with relative ease, but newcomers found it necessary to remove their footwear and cling to the rocks and ledges on the inside vertical wall to keep from slipping or being blown off the path by the gusty winds. In the 1830s, missionaries worked to improve the ease and safety of the path by constructing steps along the steeper portions. But the inherent dangers of the trail over the Pali discouraged cross-island trips. All but the most daring travelers took the long, circuitous route around the mountains.

Continuous but minor improvements were made to the trail during the 1830s and early 1840s. In 1845, changes financed by the government and by Honolulu businessmen hungry for windward trade made the route suitable for horseback riders. King Kamehameha III and two members of his royal court made the first horseback trip over the Pali and, in essence, opened the Pali for public travel.

Queen Liliuokalani, Hawaii's last monarch, is purported to have composed one of Hawaii's most famous songs, "Aloha Oe," while descending the Pali Road on horseback.

But the Pali Road still remained a treacherous journey and accidents were frequent. Horses often slipped and sometimes were so paralyzed by fear they refused to proceed. Travelers were constantly bombarded by falling rocks, and residents continually petitioned for improvements.

In 1857, the Legislature authorized $2,000 to improve the road so it could safely accommodate carriages. The first horse-drawn carriage ride over the Pali by the Rev. E. Corwin and Dr. G. P. Judd on September 12, 1861, added another page to the colorful history of this famous passage.

## The Path of Progress over the Pali

Windward farmers no longer had to rely on rickety, unsafe sailing vessels to transport their produce and livestock to the Honolulu business district.

Despite the improvements, many people still refused to risk life and property by traveling over the Pali. They kept the issue of a safer road alive in political and business circles. Government officials and planners searched for ways to construct a safe, easy-grade, smooth-surface road against a sheer cliff.

Although everyone favored a safe passage, and legislatures continually approved funds for different concepts, the project needed someone with the necessary courage and expertise, someone who could work within the budgetary limitations.

In 1896, the Legislature, at the prompting of Sanford B. Dole, president of the Republic, appropriated the largest sum ever for a new Pali Road: $40,000. Mr. W. W. Bruner, chief highway engineer for the Republic, staked out a route. Accompanying Bruner as he walked the terrain of the proposed route was a young Honolulu man who would leave his mark on the development of cross-island travel on Oahu. His name was John H. Wilson.

Wilson, one of Stanford University's first engineering students, spent his summers in Hawaii working for the Oahu Railway Company. Although he had barely completed his junior year of studies, Wilson was intrigued by the engineering challenge presented by the New Pali Road concept. He summoned his close friend and fellow student at Stanford, Louis M. Whitehouse. Wilson borrowed $200 for the required deposit and submitted a bid of $37,500. The only other bids were $81,000 and $67,500; Wilson and Whitehouse were awarded the contract on May 24, 1897.

John Wilson was well known and respected by his friends in Honolulu. He was the great-grandson of Capt. Blanchard, who commanded the ship that brought the first missionaries to Hawaii in 1820. While his friends recognized Wilson as a bright lad, they could not help but believe he had bitten off more than he could chew. Those who didn't know him personally scoffed at the idea of so young and inexperienced a man attempting to build the "road that couldn't be built."

But in eight months, Wilson and Whitehouse were to prove their skeptics wrong and gain the notoriety which many believed they were seeking when they submitted such a low initial bid.

On May 26, 1897, ground was broken. The New Pali Road, to be constructed about 20 feet above the old windward trail, would start 600 feet on the Honolulu side of the Pali Lookout and extend two miles down and alongside the vertical windward face of the mountain. It was to have an 8 percent grade and be about 20 feet wide, 16 of which would be trafficable. As Wilson and Whitehouse began their monumental task, the hearts of all islanders were with them, but logic said the project was impossible.

An initial work force of about 40 Hawaiian, Japanese, and Chinese laborers had been increased to 250 by September. The work was backbreaking and perilous. Black powder blasted out sections of the cliff, then the labor force, perched on precarious, narrow ledges, hand shoveled the loose dirt to build up the 20-foot "bench" on which the road would be built. One slip meant a 500-foot drop straight down.

Windward residents witnessed months of blasting operations which culminated on October 4, 1897, when nineteen 250-pound charges were detonated to dislodge a rock ledge over the proposed route. Hundreds of people, President Dole included, came to watch the well-publicized event. Brothers from St. Louis School even hiked from Honolulu with some of their students to view the spectacle.

Employees lit the fuses with cigars and dashed for cover. For the next 15 minutes, mighty but muffled roars shook the stately Pali and hurled over 8,000 tons of rock and lava down onto the old Pali trail.

Daniel Logan's description of the event in the *Hawaiian Annual—1898* paints the picture:

> The observer might easily have imagined himself transported back ages unknown for just a blink of Oahu's molten period . . . Daring hands light one fuse after the other and scamper for safety. . . . Breath is held for a few seconds. . . . Then the fated ledge belches out smoke and dust . . . Great windrows of forest trees inverted, mingled with boulders tons heavy, all involved in avalanches of red earth, rise and hurtle reluctantly a few yards high, then crash and roll down the abyss, the conglomeration piling itself an everlasting barricade across the ancient trail a thousand feet below.

Not only did the blast cover the old trail, it also buried forever the skeletal remains discovered by Wilson and Whitehouse of over 800 Oahuans who died at the Battle of Nuuanu.

The last and most difficult portion of the road construction was only a few hundred feet past the Pali Lookout, at the first turn on the

## The Path of Progress over the Pali

windward side. Here Wilson and Whitehouse faced a curving, vertical rock wall which many said couldn't be cut to form the final 35 feet of roadbed. Wilson and Whitehouse agreed so they decided to bridge the gap.

Thirty of the most powerful laborers were harnessed with slings. From a narrow ledge above the chasm the workers lifted three 40-foot iron beams and gently lowered them down, resting the ends on the completed portions of the road flanking the gap. When the cross pieces were in place and the concrete poured, Hawaii had its first reinforced concrete bridge. The gap was bridged and so too were windward and leeward Oahu.

The route from Honolulu to windward Oahu began on Nuuanu Avenue. Halfway up the valley, the road snaked its way through tropical shade trees entwined with philodendron and passed waterfalls, blossoming ginger, bamboo, and lush fern. Curves in the road were numerous. At a place called Morgan's Corner, the road made an especially sharp zigzag "S" turn.

Further on, loosely hanging vines cascaded down from the thick canopy of tree limbs and draped the road. Emerging from this natural tunnel near the Pali Lookout, the Nuuanu Pali Road connected with the New Pali Road of Wilson and Whitehouse. Few could pass the lookout without stopping to take in the breathtaking view.

Past the lookout, the marvel of Wilson and Whitehouse's achievement became readily apparent. When the Pali traveler peered over the wooden railing, he could not help but wonder what was holding the road against the wall. For almost half a mile the new road twisted and turned to the contours of the cliffside. Then it veered from the grasp of the Pali with a sharp 180 degree turn and began its main descent. This "hairpin" turn was harrowing for even experienced travelers. Newcomers prayed.

In the foothills of the windward cliffs the road forked. One artery led to Kaneohe; the other to Waimanalo.

The New Pali Road was officially opened on January 20, 1898. Despite its narrowness and nearly 120 curves, many of them blind, travelers heralded the new transisland route as the greatest engineering accomplishment in Hawaii's history. Wilson and Whitehouse were heroes.

The two young engineers, either individually or as partners, were responsible for many other distinguished construction projects in Hawaii including the Oahu Railway's roadbed around Kaena Point, the Laupahoehoe Pali Road on the Big Island, the first pali road on Maui, and the trail to Haleakala Crater. Lou Whitehouse became the city engineer for Honolulu in 1912 and the commissioner of public lands for the territory in 1936. John Wilson, a Honolulu favorite son, climbed the strata of city government and was deeply involved in Oahu's growth for the next half century.

Many people felt the New Pali Road was the end of an issue which had been extremely controversial for nearly a hundred years. But the real controversy had not yet begun.

The New Pali Road was completed when horses were carrying riders and pulling carriages. The road was most adequate for this type of travel and for the existing population of the island. But when mechanical horsepower burst onto the scene, the kettle began to boil again.

Automobiles changed lifestyles and created the need for drastic improvements in all roadways. And roads like the one over the Pali headed the list.

Piecemeal improvements were made to the New Pali Road during the first decade of the twentieth century, particularly when John Wilson was Oahu's road supervisor in 1909. But as Model Ts became as numerous as carriages, more changes were needed.

Wilson became mayor of Honolulu in 1920, a position he held for eight of the next 10 years. With his road becoming the target of criticism by concerned citizens, he helped initiate many improvements.

By 1931, 2,000 cars were using the Pali Road daily. Each year automobiles became larger, faster, and less maneuverable. Their limited turning radius forced them to slow almost to a stop at sharp turns.

Tens of thousands of dollars were spent widening narrow portions, straightening curves and installing concrete barriers at danger points. But the improvements still could not keep pace with the ever increasing vehicular use of the Pali Road. Windward Oahu residents were especially vociferous in their demands for improvements. Their livelihood and very lives depended on a safe, cross-island route.

In 1937 some headway was made, and Oahuans saw what they considered the first serious efforts by government officials to improve the Pali Road. Three plans were submitted: (1) construct an entirely new road; (2) build a tunnel through the Nuuanu gap with safe approaches from both Honolulu and Kailua; and (3) widen and straighten the existing roadway.

## The Path of Progress over the Pali

The tunnel project intrigued everyone and won the immediate support of windward residents. Various tunnel concepts were proposed, but all were deemed too expensive at the time by government officials, even though matching federal funds were available. The idea was shelved.

In 1946, John Wilson was drafted by the Honolulu Democratic Party to run again for mayor. He won and was back in the turmoil over the road he had built nearly half a century before. The tunnel concept, originally proposed in 1937 and approved by the Legislature in 1939, was finally gaining momentum as Wilson took the reins of the city. But a new wrinkle developed which would further delay its construction. The city, supported to the hilt by Mayor Wilson, pushed for a new tunnel site in Kalihi Valley, a few miles west of Nuuanu. The city recommended continued improvements to the Pali Road but no tunnel; the territorial government supported the Nuuanu tunnel. Lines were drawn and the bureaucratic battle was on. When the territory outlined plans for a $2 million highway and tunnel project through Nuuanu Valley, Mayor Wilson accused the governor of attempting to "sabotage" the Kalihi project. The residents of Oahu watched in dismay and dejection as their elected officials played politics.

Then in 1949 the Legislature gave the go-ahead for the Kalihi tunnel, but the governor promptly vetoed the measure and the stalemate continued. Residents begged for relief as the hazards and congestion on the Pali Road became intolerable. The Old Pali Road was said to have been able to accommodate 4,000 cars daily. By 1953, daily usage was 11,000. The territory had already begun massive improvements on approach roads, preparing for the Nuuanu tunnel. Mayor Wilson, now 82, continued to object, but to no avail. The Kalihi project was eventually started but bogged down as funds were depleted. Windward residents were fed up with Wilson and were instrumental in his defeat in the 1954 primary elections.

In 1953, Gov. Samuel W. King ordered a complete restudy of the conflicting programs. The study confirmed the recommendations of preceding administrations: both routes were desirable but "the Kalihi Valley route . . . should be an adjunct to, but not a substitute for the Nuuanu route."

John Wilson's struggle to have the Kalihi project be the thrust of Oahu's transisland highway development failed. The Kalihi tunnel and road were finally completed in 1961, and his widow, Jennie, was on hand for the ceremony. The city paid "Johnny Boy" a final tribute by officially dedicating the bore as the John H. Wilson Tunnel.

The 8.3-mile Nuuanu Pali Highway and Tunnel project, financed by a state gasoline tax and matching federal funds, actually began in 1952. Sections were completed as funds became available.

Commuters still traveled John Wilson's Pali Road and watched the progress of the new highway 50 feet below. But they also had to watch for avalanches and landslides caused by the new construction. Rocks loosened by tunnel blasting and excavation often cascaded down on unsuspecting drivers. But the problem was not new; citizens had complained of bombardment by boulders as far back as 1850. Now in the 1950s accounts of near misses on the Pali Road were common. On January 3, 1956, a 500-pound boulder crashed through the roof of a car and landed on the floor of the back seat behind the woman driver. The rock scraped the nose of her five-year-old son sleeping on the back seat.

With the assistance of a California tunnel specialist, Anatole Eriman, the first bore was completed in 1957—20 years after the tunnel concept was first proposed. The tunnel was one-way to Honolulu, and windward-bound commuters still used the Old Pali Road.

The Windward Oahu Community Association proudly sponsored the tunnel opening ceremonies. Attending were Gov. King, Mayor Blaisdell, and a cast of thousands who all, unfortunately, tried to drive through the new tunnel almost simultaneously and created the worst traffic jam in Hawaii's history. The parade through the tunnel included the Aloha Week King on horseback symbolizing the first ride over the Pali in 1845 by King Kamehameha III. The "Puka in the Pali" was finally a reality.

Windward land values skyrocketed and extensive building programs began. Businessmen seized the opportunity and filled newspapers with advertisements beckoning consumers to buy windward real estate "only minutes from Honolulu" and newer and better cars to "keep up" with the New Pali Highway. Every merchant had "Pali Tunnel Specials."

With the completion of the leeward approach lanes to the tunnel on October 14, 1958, another milestone was achieved as vehicles could now bypass the winding Nuuanu Pali Drive. The drive would always remain a tourist attraction but would never again be a main thoroughfare. The widow of Dr. Morgan, after whom the infamous Morgan's Corner was named, said it was so quiet on the day the new highway opened, she could almost hear Nuuanu Stream. The driving time between Honolulu and Kailua was cut in half.

## The Path of Progress over the Pali

Until the second tunnel was complete, traffic flow through the one bore was one-way and regulated by hours. Schedules often changed, and motorists seldom knew whether to use the tunnel or John Wilson's windward Pali Road.

To permit construction of the last segment of the approach road to the second tunnel, the old windward Pali Road had to be closed. Only a few days shy of its 63rd anniversary, the old road was officially retired January 3, 1961. John Wilson had passed away in 1956 while his "pride and joy" was still serving the public.

In an attempt to clarify the confusion of the new traffic flow, the state division of highways published schedules in newspapers. However, the "clip and save" notices seemed to muddle the issue even more. An excerpt from the January 3, 1961, edition of the *Honolulu Star-Bulletin* read:

> Weekdays and Saturdays (except holidays)—6:30 p.m. to 9 a.m., tunnels open for Honolulu-bound traffic only; 9 a.m. to 3:30 p.m., tunnels closed to all through traffic; 3:30 p.m. to 6 p.m., tunnels open to Kailua-bound traffic only. Sundays and holidays—Pali tunnels will open to Honolulu-bound traffic only from 6:30 p.m. Saturday (or the day before a holiday), all day Sunday (or holiday) and until 9 a.m. Monday (or day after a holiday).

Whether they didn't read newspapers, were more confused after they did, or just didn't give a hoot, frustrated motorists began ignoring the directions, flashing lights, and barricades. Police called it "Pali Roulette." Some commuters would ride to the tunnel, remove the barricade and try to "slip through" hoping not to encounter cars that had the right of way. Some very serious accidents resulted.

The complete Pali Highway and dual tunnel project were officially dedicated on December 21, 1962. The cost was $25 million and almost half a century of frustration for island residents.

The man who guided the 11-year project was John C. Myatt, state highway division chief engineer. As he was attempting a U-turn on the highway to return to Honolulu after the dedication ceremony, his car was unceremoniously bumped by another. Total damage: $1 and a very red face for the infant highway's first accident victim. Said Myatt: "We christened it the hard way. Instead of using a bottle of champagne we used my car door."

With the new, easy, and safe access across the Pali completed, tourists, as well as banana wagons, bead sellers, and peddlers, flocked to the Pali Lookout in record numbers. Grandiose suggestions by state politicians and the Chamber of Commerce to construct restaurants, museums, and even a tram system at the lookout met strong kamaaina resistance and were eventually rejected. So too was a 1964 recommendation to change the road's name to the "J.F.K. Memorial Highway."

The new highway brought progress and controversy, but it was a necessity and accepted as such. It sealed the fate of the Old Pali Road just as the Old Pali Road had sealed the fate of the treacherous windward trail of the early 1800s.

While the leeward portion of the old road is still used as a residential and tourist drive, the windward portion has been closed for almost 20 years. A half mile of it is still visible from the lookout. Unchecked vegetation and erosion have reduced sections to no more than a path for those interested in a nostalgic walk back into Hawaii's past. The old road was a victim of that which waits for no one—time. And only time will dictate the future of its replacement.

# The Notches of Nuuanu Pali

## GERARD AULAMA JERVIS

*They once played a key role in the conquest of Oahu. Today they are silent memorials to the Hawaiian warriors who fought and died on that windy ledge.*

✦ In the spring of 1795 the stakes were high. Kalanikupule, king of Oahu, Maui, Molokai, and Lanai, had recently defeated Kaeokulani at Aiea and secured his undisputed reign. That battle was won with the help of newly acquired Western guns and ammunition that Kalanikupule had acquired from *Jackall*, a trading vessel anchored in Honolulu Harbor. Placing his confidence in the new-found firepower, Kalanikupule then set out to defeat Kamehameha, ruler of the island of Hawaii. But his attempt to sail with his army to Hawaii had to be aborted and he returned to Oahu. Kamehameha then launched his own attack.

Swiftly transporting his army in a fleet of war canoes, Kamehameha took Maui and Molokai in rapid succession. He then turned toward Oahu, crossed the Molokai Channel, and landed at Waialae and Waikiki. Kaiana, a longtime ally of Kamehameha, had slipped away from the main fleet during the crossing and landed on Oahu's windward side. He and his men then marched up to the Pali and joined the army of Kalanikupule.

Knowing well the military prowess of Kamehameha, the defector Kaiana directed the cutting of two notches into the Pali ridge. Each notch was to be approximately 30 feet wide and 12 feet deep. The ridge itself, only a few feet across, provided a commanding view of the valley

First published November 1982.

and flatlands below. The notches would face Waikiki and Kamehameha's now advancing forces. When they were nearly completed, Kalanikupule sent runners to Honolulu Harbor to bring back two cannon. These artillery pieces were then positioned in each of the now ready emplacements. The stage was set. The defending Oahu forces, implanted at the head of Nuuanu Valley, awaited the advancing army of Kamehameha.

Below the two cannon of Kalanikupule, Kaiana's men, armed with shoulder guns, lined the slopes of the Pali. Kamehameha's forces methodically marched up the valley, but cannon and rifle fire bore heavily upon them. Several times Kamehameha was at the brink of defeat but held his position. He realized he must find a way to end the slaughter inflicted by the cannon.

Kamehameha sent a division of his fastest and strongest warriors to double back and climb the ridge above Pauoa Valley. Meanwhile he sent a runner to instruct the reserves waiting in Waikiki to climb Manoa Valley and follow the ridge-top trail to the Nuuanu Pali. The two forces would converge on the cannon and the notches.

The Oahu warriors frantically tried to defend their position, but they were stunned by Kamehameha's men. The cannon were quickly captured. Kamehameha then pressed forward in the valley below. Kalanikupule's army was forced to retreat from one position to the next and was finally routed. Some of his warriors escaped over the mountain; others fought bitterly to the end and were pushed over the Pali; while others fearing capture more than death, plunged into the abyss below. Kaiana was killed and Kalanikupule escaped up a mountainous path. After wandering several months in the mountains, Kalanikupule was captured and sacrificed to the war god Kukailimoku. With this brilliant victory Kamehameha controlled the major islands of Oahu, Maui, Molokai, Lanai, and Hawaii. Only Kauai remained independent.

For years the path crossing the Nuuanu Pali was no more than a horse trail twisting around the base of the notched ridge. Then in 1897 the engineering firm of Whitehouse and Wilson was awarded a government contract to build what has become known as the "Old Pali Road." The firm used 17,500 pounds of blasting powder and 10,000 pounds of dynamite to complete the job. During construction, workers found an estimated 800 skulls and other assorted human bones at the foot of the cliffs—the 100-year-old remains of Kalanikupule's defeated warriors. The blasting operations buried these warriors under hun-

## The Notches of Nuuanu Pali

dreds of tons of earth, finally uniting them with the land they died defending.

Today the Nuuanu Pali Lookout attracts scores of visitors every day. Sightseers scurry up to the lookout point and its panoramic view of windward Oahu. Strong gusts of wind carry the scent of guava and yellow ginger from the valley below. The sightseers stroll around the paved lookout site and glance at the two plaques that commemorate both Kamehameha's victory and the road builders' feat. Then they return to their cars and drive off down the Pali Highway. Hardly a head turns toward Kaiana's notches.

Even Island residents who daily cross the Pali are often unaware that the notches exist. The exposed surfaces are now filigreed by a century-and-a-half of high winds and driving rains; the once clean lines and right-angled perfection demanded by their military engineer have now given way to rounded edges and partial erosion. Yet far above the bustle of twentieth-century concerns, in clear view for all to see, are the time-worn emplacements of Kalanikupule's cannon—nonmonuments to the drama of human struggle, built by the actors themselves.

# Ainahau:
## A Paradise for a Princess

MARILYN STASSEN-MCLAUGHLIN

*In the middle of Waikiki, among the high-rises and condominiums and a few dilapidated cottages, is a spot that once was a Garden of Eden. A hundred years ago, Ainahau was the home of royalty.*

◆ A pretty girl in a skimpy pink bikini bends to wash her Datsun's whitewalls where once Princess Kaiulani, dressed in a long, black skirt, yellow blouse, and ilima lei, rode her horse Fairy. The princess and Fairy would canter down Waikiki Road and return later to her father's grass-covered court for a game of tennis.

A rusted soft-drink machine proclaiming "Here's the Real Thing" sits in a laundry in an apartment parking lot, near the spot where years ago Kaiulani poured tea for Robert Louis Stevenson under the shade of a giant banyan tree. Stevenson would tell happy stories of his homeland, Scotland, to reassure the princess about her approaching journey to England where she would be properly educated for her future role as queen of Hawaii.

Ten acres of Edenlike splendor flourished in Waikiki for a while during the nineteenth century. The Ainahau estate, the home of Princess Kaiulani, her mother, Princess Likelike, and her father, A. S. Cleghorn, was a lush tropical paradise fit for royalty. The refreshing breezes wafting down from the Manoa and Palolo valleys had moved Princess

---

First published November 1986.

Likelike to name her home "Au-aukai," which was later changed to "Ainahau," meaning "cool place."

## A Garden Paradise

Ainahau was designed and landscaped by A. S. Cleghorn. In 1872, two years after his marriage to the young Princess Likelike, sister of King Kalakaua, Cleghorn bought the land as a vacation spot, a respite from the activity at their house in town located on the present site of the Pacific Club. In 1875, Princess Ruth Keelikolani, half-sister to

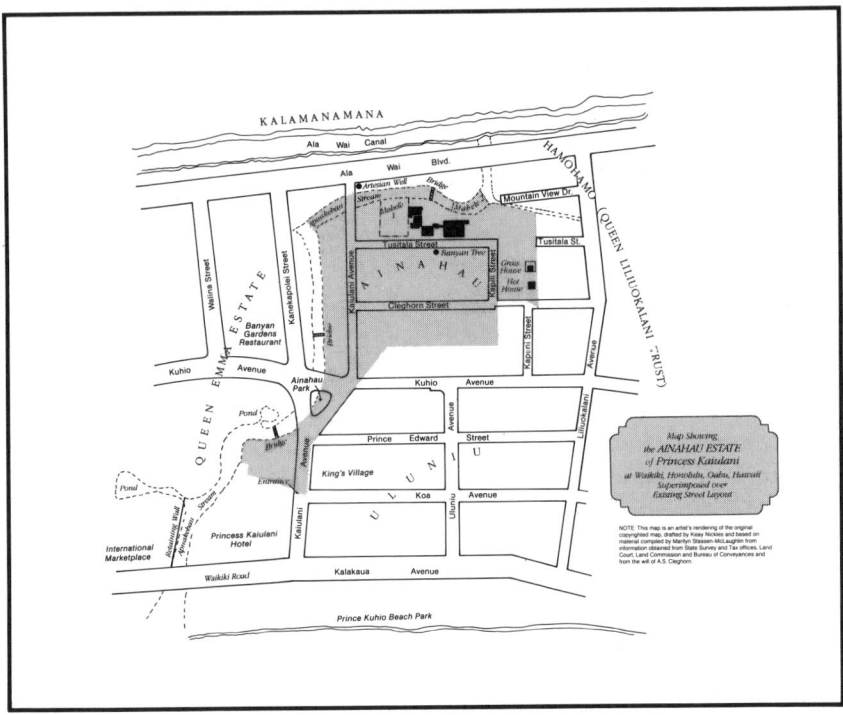

A map showing the Ainahau Estate of Princess Kaiulani at Waikiki, Honolulu, Oahu, Hawai'i, superimposed over the existing street layout. Note: This map is an artist's rendering of the original copyrighted map, drafted by Neay Nickles and based on material compiled by Marilyn Stassen-McLaughlin from information obtained from State Survey and Tax offices, Land Court, Land Commission and Bureau of Conveyances, and from the will of A. S. Cleghorn.

# Ainahau

Kamehamehas IV and V, added to the property by giving nearby acreage to little Victoria Kaiulani as her christening gift. Later, Princess Ruth presented an additional section of land to Princess Likelike. These properties constituted what was the Ainahau estate of Cleghorn's will.

Cleghorn intended the estate to be a botanical garden. (Landscaping and the study of plants were his avocation. He designed and supervised the landscaping of the Kawaiahao Church grounds, many palace and government properties, and other local sites that we still enjoy today.) It was Cleghorn's dream that after his death, Ainahau would be called Kaiulani Park and serve as a companion property to Kapiolani Park.

Through his work, Ainahau became a lush tropical garden. Stately peacocks strolled the beautiful setting. According to an 1891 issue of *Paradise of the Pacific* magazine, date palms bordered the long avenue from the gate to the residence, and a lake near the entrance was "thickly fringed with ornamental hedge, rose-colored blossoms of lotus." On the grounds grew eight different kinds of mango, soap trees, large evergreen camphor trees, Monterey cypress, 14 varieties of hibiscus, two varieties of kamani tree, Sago palms, and croton shrubs. Tall teak trees provided seeds which Cleghorn would give away to people wishing to grow their own. Cinnamon trees were scattered throughout the property, with not only the bark but the leaves tasting of cinnamon. Coconut palms were added when Princess Kaiulani was born. A banyan tree, planted in 1875 to celebrate her christening, flourished beautifully, boasting limbs the circumference of a man's body. Some believed the reason it grew so rapidly was that it had been planted on an ancient luau site, in soil enriched by years of soaking with the remains of fish, fowl, and pork.

Along the walkways, narrow Japanese bridges extended over lily ponds, one shamrock shaped and another containing gold fish. Cleghorn had dug an artesian well to feed these ponds. Stone lanterns marked the turn off the entrance road into the driveway. At the end of the driveway stood the bungalow and the giant banyan tree. On the right, beyond a grove of cocoa palms, was the grass tennis court, surrounded by date palms and hibiscus. Past the court was a magnificent, unobstructed view of Diamond Head.

Across the street was the bungalow where Kaiulani lived her childhood years. The house contained an immense drawing room which was used as a ballroom, and was the scene of many joyful birthday celebrations.

## The Story of Kaiulani's Banyan

A fascinating history lies behind the banyan tree that once graced Ainahau. It was planted by A. S. Cleghorn when Princess Kaiulani was a child, and it grew quickly into a huge, healthy tree. Located directly in front of the entrance to Kaiulani's home, it was frequently used as a background for family pictures.

This large tree, according to L. D. Fraser, former principal of Kaiulani School, was nourished by "refuse from early luaus." This enriched soil, no doubt accounted for the rapid growth of the giant tree.

Near the banyan, Robert Louis Stevenson, a friend of the Cleghorns', fearing the effects of the English climate on the young princess, who was soon to depart for England to be educated, wrote this poem in Kaiulani's red plush autograph album:

Forth from her land to mine she goes,
The island maid, the island rose,
Light of heart and bright of face
The daughter of a double race.

Her islands here in southern sun
Shall mourn their Kaiulani gone
And I, in her dear banyan's shade,
Look vainly for my little maid.

But our Scots islands far away
Shall glitter with unwonted day,
And cast for once their tempest by
To smile in Kaiulani's eye.

The banyan remained for many years after Cleghorn's death in 1910, offering shade when Kaiulani's new house became a hotel. Visitors often remarked about its impressive size and magnificent beauty.

When the Ainahau property was subdivided, William Chauncey Wilder and Percy M. Pond used the banyan as part of their advertising campaign. According to Pond, the men decided the banyan should be preserved. They divided the lot on which it stood (Lot No. 61) into three portions. The front part where the banyan reigned would be offered to the city and designated a park.

There were legal difficulties, however, one of which was the city's refusal of the offer because it already had enough parks to maintain. Finally, the deed was presented to the Daughters of Hawaii with the understanding that they would take care of the property and the banyan.

During the campaign to preserve the tree, a collection was taken at newspaper offices to provide a plaque for the banyan. When the

Daughters of Hawaii took on the responsibility for the tree, they enlisted the help of Earl Schenck. He suggested the marker be made of bronze, with "low relief of banyan foliage and roots to take away the cold aspect of a plain lettered emblem."

The October 17, 1930, *Pacific Commercial Advertiser* described the presentation of the bronze tablet that had occurred the day before, on Kaiulani's birthday. "Impressive Ceremonies Mark the Unveiling of the Banyan Tablet on Tusitala," the article read.

The tablet was inscribed:

This Tablet was Placed
in Memory of
Princess Kaiulani
1874–1899
The Daughter of a Double Race,
Her Islands Here, in Southern Sun,
Shall Mourn Their Kaiulani Gone,
And I, in Her Dear Banyan Shade,
Look Vainly for My Little Maid.
Written to Kaiulani By
Robert Louis Stevenson
Who often Sat Here with Her

Preparation for this impressive ceremony had been expensive. The previous June 17, 1930, Schenck had presented his plans and the price quote for the plaque, a bench, flagstones, and buffalo grass: $500. On August 25, the acting Territorial forester had declared that the property was in "very poor shape":

"It [the tree] has been burned and practically every limb of tree was at least half dead and the main trunk contains more dead than live wood. This dead wood distributed in such a manner that it would be impossible to remove it and retain the tree in its present form."

In 1947, the Daughters received letters from residents of the homes around the tree, offering to buy the little property. However, on the books, the land was considered "park."

On March 7, 1948, the residents signed a petition asking the Outdoor Circle, whom they commended for "saving the Keeaumoku Banyan," to please "abolish another—commonly known as the 'Robert Louis Stevenson orphan' . . . Rats, cats, red berries, leaves by the thousands, dead branches, and bird droppings have made this tree a first class nuisance over all."

Now the Outdoor Circle and the Daughters of Hawaii went to work. Finally, the park restrictions were lifted—the property could be sold. Then on February 7, 1949, the *Star-Bulletin* reported the destruction of the legendary banyan "which shaded a fern and flower filled retreat."

> But the story does not end there. On Arbor Day of the year that Princess Kaiulani died and the year that Kaiulani School was dedicated (1899), Principal L. D. Fraser had requested that a slip of the Ainahau banyan be planted on the school grounds. Cleghorn consented and gave Fraser a small cutting in a sake tub. (Today, the tree continues to flourish in the Waikiki-mauka corner of the school grounds on North King Street.) On May 1, 1954, Kaiulani School received the old bronze plaque from Donovan Flint, owner of the property. It now rests at the base of the Ainahau offspring.
>
> NOTE: The birth date on the plaque is incorrect. Placed now at the base of the sister banyan in the Waikiki-mauka corner of the Kaiulani school grounds, the date has been changed correctly to 1875.

Parties were frequent at Ainahau. Likelike had introduced croquet to the Islands, and it was welcomed enthusiastically. At some afternoon gatherings, guests grew so excited over the games that they would continue playing long after dark. Each player would make the rounds with a blazing torch in one hand and a mallet in the other. The ladies would be dressed in the latest fashion, in bustles, jewels, laces, and feathers, caressed by the Manoa breezes.

Kaiulani loved this home. According to Ruth Bancroft Powell in her unpublished story of Kaiulani, old Hawaiians on the beach would see the princess swimming out farther than "some of the best male swimmers dared to venture." A stream flowed through Ainahau and emptied into the sea a few hundred yards away (after passing through what is now the site of the Outrigger Hotel). Down this stream, known as the Apuakehau Stream, Kaiulani would paddle her canoe out to the surf, being an expert, according to *Mid Pacific Magazine,* both in the outrigger canoe and on the surfboard.

During her eight-year education sojourn in England, she sorely missed home. Soon after her return to Hawaii in 1897, she wrote to her aunt, Liliuokalani, who was traveling abroad: "About ten days ago Stella Lockett, Helen Parker, and I went over to your place and took a bath. The water was perfectly lovely. I have had only one dip in the sea so far. As my bathing suits have not arrived yet—we went in by moonlight in night gowns, when no one was around."

While she had been away from the Islands, her father, desiring a more elegant house for the future queen, had built a lovely Victorian-

Ainahau

style home. But Kaiulani was able to enjoy the house only a short time. She returned to Hawaii in November 1897. The following August, 1898, Hawaii was annexed as a Territory of the United States; Kaiulani would never be queen. A few months later, in March 1899, Princess Kaiulani died at the young age of 23.

## One Visitor's View

What would a guest of the Cleghorns see at Ainahau on a Sunday in 1893? Mary H. Krout, a Chicago journalist assigned to the Islands during the monarchy crises of 1893, visited Cleghorn in February, only one month after Queen Liliuokalani was deposed. Cleghorn had just completed the "proper" house for his daughter, Princess Kaiulani, who was being educated in England. (Although Kaiulani loved the bungalow, she was delighted that her father was building a new house. She wrote to her aunt, Queen Liliuokalani, in February of 1892: "I'm so glad to see that Father is putting up a proper house at Ainahau. It has always been my ambition to have a house at Waikiki worthy of the beautiful gardens.")

In *Hawaii and Revolution*, Mary Krout described her visit. She noted that she "drove up the winding carriage road to the house, halting under the shade of a giant banyan tree—one of the most magnificent of its kind—A carpenter's bench was strewn with chips and shavings and there was other evidence of incompleted work, which, however, was progressing rapidly towards completion."

The estate, she said, was "one of the most beautiful in the islands. The spacious grounds were ordinarily closed to visitors, with 'Kapu' (No Admittance) over the gate to the entrance. The new house was a white frame structure, of two stories, with wings at either end—the favourite form of Honolulu architecture—with a wide verandah extending across the front. The shrubbery had been cut away for several yards in every direction to allow the free circulation of the air, and just beyond the main entrance stood the one incomparable banyan tree, which the owner presently informed me was the handsomest thing he had."

A Chinese servant went to find Cleghorn and soon he arrived: "a tall, handsome man, erect as a field marshal, as dignified as a Spanish grandee, and altogether an impressive figure, with his keen black eyes, white beard and hair. He had been out amongst his flowers, he explained, and in proof of this he dropped a pair of pruning shears into the pocket of his loose alpaca coat. It was not every day that one met the parent of royalty so occupied. 'The house is nearly completed,' he said, looking up at the closed windows with a wistful expression. 'I built it for the princess, and expected to have it all in readiness, and now this overturn has come.'" Cleghorn gave her a tour of the house, including the drawing room, "40 feet in length and 30 feet in width, with many windows looking out upon the velvet lawn. The paneling was in beautiful woods highly polished, and the decorative tiles in the corridor had been brought from Chicago."

Cleghorn showed her another unique room "enclosed with Venetian blinds on two sides, the windows extending from floor to ceiling, and being provided with screens. This was the 'mosquito room,' in which the princess and the English companion whom she was to have brought back with her had expected to sit and sew, read, and talk. Much was made of the screens, so universal in the United States but which, strangely enough, were not in ordinary use in that mosquito ridden land."

At one point Cleghorn invited Krout to climb to an upper floor which was to be the princess's private suite. Krout noted: "The view certainly was most beautiful . . . Below us were acres of rice field, the most vivid and tender green; there were the solemn mountains, with great ragged masses of cloud floating down their summits and across the valleys; there was the sea blue as sapphire, with the white surf tossing along the curve of sunken reef; there was the harbour with its shipping; the shady streets, the blossoming hedges, and the gardens crowded with palms and algaroba and mango trees . . . The air was damp and soft and sweet, reminding me of an April day at home when the apple blossoms were in bloom, the gentle trade winds blowing across the Pacific and passing onwards to other islands whereof they knew."

Then Cleghorn showed Krout the bungalow: "a long, low building, the roofs sloping on the sides from an elevation in the centre. It was provided with a lanai. The floor of the main apartment was covered with matting, and it was very simply furnished, to secure coolness and space."

As she and Cleghorn walked the property, he commented: "When I bought this place a few years ago . . . there was nothing here. I have planted everything myself, and have seen it come to maturity." Wrote Krout: "It seemed incredible, for the trees that towered above us throwing their cool, dim shade down across the long avenue, might have been a century's growth. He stopped to show me some fine specimens of the croton. This curious plant is almost numberless in its varieties, both in the colour of its foliage and the shape of the leaf. It is yellow, green, dark maroon, crimson, and mottled yellow and green. The leaves on some are ovate, and others are perfect lanceolate. My host told me that frequently plants would send out a shoot differing in colour and form from the foliage of the shrub. This, broken off and planted, produced an entire shrub of its own kind. 'I am very much interested in their propagation,' he said, 'and I have already 40 varieties.'"

## A Gift Refused

In his will, A. S. Cleghorn offered the Territory the beautiful estate. He hoped it would be a quiet, garden retreat, a sister to Kapiolani Park. The offer was turned down. Two stipulations in the will discouraged the Territorial government from accepting Cleghorn's gift. First, Ainahau was to be maintained by the Territory; second, the park, to be known as Kaiulani Park, was to be closed from sunset to sunup.

At first, the announcement of the proposed park was greeted with much excitement. The *Hawaiian Gazette* reported in 1910 that Kalakaua's adjoining property, Uluniu, would be added to the Ainahau donation if the Legislature accepted the park plan. (These combined properties would have provided a perfect square of park area bordered by the present Liliuokalani Avenue, Ewa to Kaiulani, and from Kalakaua, mauka to the Ala Wai Canal.) A 1911 issue of *Mid Pacific Magazine* said that the Trail and Mountain Club wanted to use the grass hut as a rest house and would construct a trail through Ainahau, across the rice fields, and beyond the mountains into the Palolo and Manoa valleys.

But the two stipulations in the will worried legislators. They feared park upkeep would be costly, even if prisoners were used to maintain the grounds. A representative from the Fourth District voiced concern over the requirement that the park be closed from sunset to sunrise. The *Advertiser* quoted him as saying that after investing hundreds of dollars to maintain the property, "Someone may break that condition, then Cleghorn's nephew would step in and take it back."

Others opposing the gift claimed the park would not bring in revenue. (That objection raised cries of protest.) The chairman of the public lands commission wanted the land for an experimental agricultural station and a park for children. Cleghorn died in 1910; the legislators struggled with the question, finally refused the offer in 1911. The property was put up for sale. In 1917 James W. Pratt bought the estate, then sold most of it in 1919 to William Chauncey Wilder. Wilder, along with developer Percy M. Pond, had great plans. The property was offered to the public for subdivision.

The sellers had high hopes. Specifications for sale of the Ainahau property were stringent. "Care will be taken to preserve as many of the trees as possible in building streets into the famous grove," wrote the *Pacific Commercial Advertiser*; and "Houses [were] to be at least $2,000 and be twenty feet back from the roadway," said the *Hawaiian Gazette*.

The *Pacific Commercial Advertiser* ran a two-page ad with a map showing the division of the property. The ad offered a prize of $100 to the lady who sketched the best floor plan for her ideal two- or three-bedroom beach home, and promised that "No stores, shops or places of public amusement allowed at Ainahau . . . Houses not to cost less than $2,000 . . . Nothing but pretty homes at Ainahau."

Thus, amid much hoopla and grandiose plans, Ainahau became a subdivision.

As for the house that Cleghorn built—for the future queen who never became queen—it remained on the property for some years after his death in 1910. At one point it was used as a hotel, then rented out to various people. One August night in 1921, W. T. Aldrich, the "movie pictureman," was having dinner when his wife yelled "Fire!" He ran to the room where the gas heater stood and saw flames. Neighbors tried to help by beating them out with cloths. A fire truck was summoned from Kaimuki, but the pin holding together the steering gear fell out and the truck crashed into a fence. By the time help arrived, the building could not be saved. The Cleghorn house burned to the ground.

## Paradise Lost

Today, nestled among the assorted low- and high-rises that have sprouted since the 1930s, some of the subdivision bungalows and cottages still remain. Near the site that was once the entrance to a Garden of Eden sits the corner of Kalakaua and Kaiulani avenues; the entrance to the Ainahau estate began about where King's Village and the mauka annex of the Princess Kaiulani Hotel are now.

In place of matchless Washingtonia palms towering high over hundreds of coconut trees waving greetings to strollers, we are left with looming skyscraper condominiums glaring down on low-rise apartments and battered cottages.

And a decaying pink pottery flamingo ornament hanging on its spindly, rusted legs is the only reminder of the stately peacocks that once strolled an idyllic setting.

Gentle trades blowing in from Manoa and Palolo still cool the grounds that were once Ainahau. But long gone is the grandeur that Princess Likelike described in her song:

Sweet water, cool water of the rose
Drenching flower buds
Peacocks and birds with yellow feathers
Adorn my home.

Wind blowing gently from the sea
Brings the fragrance of lipoa seaweed
Love and delight and perfume from my home
My home, my home paradise.

So beautiful is my home
Aina-hau in a paradise
Swaying leaves of coconuts
Verdant beauty and fragrant flowers,
My home, my home paradise.

✦ ✦ ✦

### Princess of the Peacocks

During Ainahau's heyday, majestic peacocks strutted handsomely about the estate, enhancing the splendor of the setting. As many as 50 of the magnificent birds wandered on the property, especially near the house where they would pause to eat directly from the hand of the princess.

Peacocks became as much a part of the Kaiulani legend as did the banyan and her friendship with Robert Louis Stevenson. Hawaiians called Kaiulani the "Princess of the Peacocks," and since she loved the Chinese jasmine, they named that flower "pikake," their word for peacock.

In their book, *Kaiulani: Crown Princess of Hawaii*, Nancy and Jean Francis Webb describe this scene which took place on August 11, 1898, when Hawaii accepted annexation by the United States: "Ainahau seemed quite empty. Under her banyan, Kaiulani sat listening to the stillness. No single shout lifted, this morning, from the surf at Waikiki. The peacocks sulked and avoided the wet grass."

Another story says that when Kaiulani died, the peacocks screeched their mourning so intensely and so long that Cleghorn had to have some shot.

# The End of Hope

## BARBARA DEL PIANO

*The overthrow of her rule was not the end of the story for Lili'uokalani. There were more outrages to come— she was arrested, convicted of treason, and imprisoned.*

✦ Although it was midweek, the streets of downtown Honolulu were quiet. Most offices and stores were closed. At the harbor the usual sights and sounds of activity were missing. Patrols of soldiers were on nearly every street corner. The city was under martial law. In the Executive Building, formerly 'Iolani Palace, the cabinet members of the six-month-old Hawaiian Republic were meeting.

At 10 o'clock on this Wednesday morning, January 16, 1895, two carriages drew up in front of Washington Place, the residence of the former queen Lili'uokalani. Slowly, almost reluctantly it seemed, two men climbed out. Through the throng of silent Native Hawaiian guards clustered in small groups around the yard, they proceeded up the tree-lined walkway to the sprawling white mansion.

Deputy Marshal Arthur Brown and police captain Robert Waipa Parker, on orders from the government's adjutant general, had come to arrest Lili'uokalani. A short while later, dressed in somber black, the deposed queen emerged from the house and accompanied the officers to a waiting carriage. A single lady in waiting, Mrs. Charles Clarke, followed in the second carriage.

The queen's guards, whose leader, Sam Knowlein, was already under arrest, offered no resistance. Neither did the large crowd of curious onlookers that had suddenly appeared.

---

First published January 1995.

The carriages made their way slowly down Richards Street, then turned into the Kinaʻu gate which, during monarchy times, had been reserved for merchants and tradespeople. It proceeded to the mauka entrance of the palace. There, for the first time since her hasty departure two years earlier, Liliʻuokalani entered her former home.

The police officers delivered the former queen into the custody of Col. J. H. Fisher. Fisher courteously escorted her across the grand hall, up the koa stairs to the second floor, and into a sparsely furnished room on the makai—Diamond Head corner of the palace. There she would spend the next seven months and 21 days under house arrest.

The events leading up to the queen's imprisonment are often regarded as little more than a footnote to the overthrow of the monarchy that had taken place two years earlier, in January of 1893. But the counterrevolution, or War of 1895 as it is sometimes called, involved far more people, time, planning, preparation, and financial backing than the practically spur-of-the-moment coup that had deposed Liliʻuokalani. Unlike the bloodless revolution, this insurrection caused many injuries and some deaths. And, even more than the overthrow, it sounded the death knell of the Hawaiian kingdom.

When Liliʻuokalani relinquished her throne on January 17, 1893, the document drawn up by her attorney, Paul Neumann, and presented to Sanford B. Dole, the president of the Provisional Government, stated:

> That I yield to the superior force of the United States of America, whose Minister Plenipotentiary, His Excellency John L. Stevens, has caused United States troops to be landed at Honolulu, and declared that he would support the said Provisional Government. Now, to avoid any collision of armed forces, and perhaps the loss of life, I do, under protest and impelled by such forces, yield my authority until such time as the Government of the United States shall, upon the facts being presented to it, undo the action of its representative, and reinstate me in the authority which I claim as the constitutional sovereign of the Hawaiian Islands.

At that time, Liliʻuokalani was not abdicating. She and a large group of royalist supporters had not accepted the end of the monarchy as a *fait accompli*. Had not the British government, 50 years before, repudiated similar actions of Lord George Paulet, who had seized the Hawaiian government in the name of Great Britain? Had not Adm.

## The End of Hope

Richard Thomas, in a magnificent ceremony, ordered the British flag lowered and the Hawaiian flag raised as the sovereignty of the nation was restored?

On January 18, the day after the overthrow, a letter to U.S. President Benjamin Harrison was drafted and shortly thereafter dispatched to Washington with Paul Neumann. The letter, over the queen's signature, expressed "the certainty which I feel that you and your Government will right whatever wrongs may have been inflicted upon us." The matter was ultimately turned over to Harrison's successor, who would be taking office in March. Grover Cleveland was a personal friend of the queen, and she had every reason to expect a favorable disposition of her suit. Cleveland withdrew a U.S.-Hawai'i annexation treaty that had been submitted to the Senate and sent James H. Blount to Hawai'i to investigate the queen's claims.

Blount's first act, on April 1, 1893, was to order the lowering of the American flag and the reflying of the Hawaiian standard.

Blount's eventual report to the president, more than 2,000 pages long, was overwhelmingly in favor of the queen and stated Blount's belief that "without Stevens there could not have been a revolution." With Cleveland's declaration that "our interference in the Hawaiian Revolution in 1893 was disgraceful," Lili'uokalani and her supporters believed complete restitution would shortly be forthcoming. The new American minister, Albert S. Willis, who replaced Stevens and arrived in Honolulu in November of 1893, was charged with effecting the restoration of the monarchy and the rule of Queen Lili'uokalani.

For a while, negotiations with Willis foundered over the queen's unwillingness to agree to specific terms set forth by the American government regarding amnesty for the revolutionists. But realizing she was jeopardizing her cause, the queen reluctantly reversed her position and accepted the terms unequivocally. Willis, on orders from the president, then approached the leaders of the Provisional Government and asked if they would be willing to restore the queen to her throne. A few days later, Sanford B. Dole and his cabinet members responded: "The Provisional Government respectfully and unhesitatingly declines to entertain the proposition of the President of the United States that it should surrender its authority to the ex-Queen." In fact, the government accused the United States of meddling in its internal affairs.

Not willing to restore the queen by military force, Cleveland turned the matter over to Congress. Congress declined to annex the Hawaiian Islands, and the Provisional Government set about to turn itself into a republic.

Through it all, the hope of restoration continued to live on in the royalist camp, and Lili'uokalani continued to believe that the United States would ultimately set things right.

The Republic of Hawai'i was established on July 4, 1894, a year and a half after the monarchy was overthrown. Its founding planted the first seeds of doubt among the royalists, and they sent a delegation to Washington to nail down the American government's intentions toward the restoration of Lili'uokalani. President Cleveland's recognition of the *de facto* government of the new Republic of Hawai'i dashed whatever hopes they had. It was then that they began to entertain serious thoughts of armed rebellion.

Herman Widemann, a judge and former cabinet minister of the queen, convinced the royalists to delay their plans while he traveled to Europe to solicit help from England, France, and Germany. When he learned that these countries had also recognized the republic, Widemann returned home defeated. The royalists decided that a counterrevolution was the last remaining option if the queen were ever to reign again.

In the summer of 1894, the plotting began. The chief strategists were Samuel Nowlein, commander of the Queen's guards; Carl Widemann, the judge's son; Henry Bertelmann; and Charles T. Gulick. Robert Wilcox, a descendant of Maui royalty who had been sent to Italy by King Kalakaua to be educated, would play an important role.

The rebels purchased rifles and ammunition in San Francisco and loaded them on the schooner *Wahlberg*, which sailed for Honolulu in late November. Some of the rifles were unloaded at Rabbit Island and later secreted in various locations around Honolulu. The rest were transferred to the *Waimanalo*, then taken ashore at Diamond Head and buried in the sand near the home of Henry F. Bertlemann.

On Saturday, January 5, untrained recruits from all parts of the island converged quietly, in groups of two or three, in the Diamond Head area. They came by foot and by streetcar and included Hawaiians, part-Hawaiians, and haoles. They retrieved the buried guns and whiled away the time eating, drinking, or praying, waiting for their leaders to arrive and for the action to begin.

The police, whose spies had kept them informed of the imminent

## The End of Hope

uprising, soon had nearly 1,200 men on alert. On the evening of January 6, they confronted the rebels at Diamond Head. Both sides fired. When the smoke had cleared, there were wounded on both sides and one dead, Charles Carter, a loyal republican.

Stymied before their attack could get underway, the rebels fled in disarray up the slopes of Diamond Head with the police in hot pursuit. Several were caught that first night, but many of them escaped to the upper slopes of Manoa Valley and across the ridges into Pauoa and Palolo. With the rebels outnumbered by the government forces, and low on food and ammunition, the revolution had disintegrated within days to a game of hide-and-seek. The Hawaiians, being more familiar with heavily wooded mountainous areas, were able to hold out for several days longer, firing on the troops from behind stone walls, boulders, and clumps of trees.

On Wednesday, January 9, Wilcox and a few men faced a company of government sharpshooters deep in Manoa. Two Hawaiian men were killed and many were captured. Wilcox and several others managed to escape and continued over the mountain ridges to Nu'uanu.

On Thursday, January 10, although Wilcox was still free and Sam Knowlein's whereabouts unknown, the newspapers announced that "the back bone [of the insurrection] is broken." More than 30 high-ranking royalists had been arrested and jailed, along with the captured rebels.

Finally, on Monday, January 14, Wilcox, his bravado gone, surrendered. Sam Knowlein was found hiding out in the wilds of Wai'alae and arrested. The last holdout, Lot Lane, a powerfully built Hawaiian, finally came down from his mountain hideout on January 17.

Meanwhile, the prison was overflowing, not only with prisoners of war but political prisoners as well. The detainees included the editors of *Holomua*—the Hawaiian newspaper—and Queen Kapi'olani's nephew, Prince Kuhio.

Then on January 16, the unthinkable happened: The queen herself was arrested and charged with treason. (Later the charge would be changed to misprision of treason and Lili'uokalani would plead not guilty.) Her home was searched and all her personal papers, even her diary, were confiscated. The guns and ammunition that were found on the property were presented as evidence. She claimed they were part of a collection of antique firearms belonging to her late husband, John Owen Dominis.

On January 24, at the urging of her advisers, and believing that it would save the lives of her supporters, Lili'uokalani signed a formal abdication and pledged allegiance to the republic. With the signature she was ordered to use—"Lili'uokalani Dominis"—she relinquished for all time her claim and that of her heirs to the throne of the Hawaiian kingdom.

During her trial, which lasted three days, the former queen was treated as a common criminal. Many of her most trusted supporters testified against her in hope of lighter sentences for themselves. Lili'uokalani was convicted, sentenced to five years at hard labor and fined $5,000. Contrary to the rumors which spread through town, no one was sentenced to death and many of the insurrectionists were ultimately pardoned, as was the queen herself.

Lili'uokalani was released on parole on September 6. As her carriage returned her to Washington Place, many of her still loyal supporters gathered on the grounds to welcome her home. Although she would always be their queen, there was no longer any hope that she would return to her throne.

Most of those who had refused to sign the oath of allegiance to the new government relented and got on with their lives. Both Robert Wilcox and Prince Jonah Kuhio would represent the Territory of Hawaii as nonvoting delegates in the Congress of the United States.

# We Will Eat Stones

## MARTHA H. NOYES

*Written in protest against the overthrow of Queen Lili'uokalani, "Kaulana Na Pua" veiled its seditious message with its pretty melody and Hawaiian lyrics.*

◆ On January 17 the nation yielded. Queen Lili'uokalani, conceding to the superior armed force of the United States, retired to her home at Washington Place. There she would await response to her appeal to the American government to undo the wrong committed by its representatives and to restore the Hawaiian nation and return her to her throne.

There was lawlessness on the streets of the city. Hawaiians had been disarmed at once, but Americans fired their rifles in random bursts of celebration. Bullets ricocheted off rocks and tore into walls. The new Provisional Government of Sanford B. Dole, mindful that it represented but a minority of the populace, concerned itself more with courting America and warding off real and imagined counterrevolutionary conspiracies than with controlling any celebratory civil disorder.

Spies and intrigue abounded. The queen's own life was threatened. Newspapers were strictly controlled; in fact, were virtually censored. Attempting to bolster its support and isolate anyone loyal to the queen and the Hawaiian monarchy, the Provisional Government solicited oaths of loyalty from Hawaiians it felt might have influence or who were engaged in activities related to the new Hawaiian nation.

But most Hawaiians were not loyal to the new government. They were loyal to their homeland and to their alii and their queen. To some of these loyal Hawaiians, official or unofficial offers were made:

---

First published January 1993.

Sign the oath of loyalty to the new government and you will be paid money.

The Royal Hawaiian Band was thus approached. Band members were appalled at the offer. They were deeply angered. They would not sign, nor would they refuse in simple silence.

Ellen Keho'ohiwaokalani Prendergast was a close friend of the royal family, an intimate of the queen and loyal to the monarchy. She was also a composer of music. On an afternoon in late January 1893, every member save two of the Royal Hawaiian Band arrived at the Prendergast mansion in Kapalama. They told Mrs. Prendergast of the outrage. They told her they would not sign the haoles' paper. They told her they would be satisfied having nothing more than the stones—the pohaku—the mystic food of the land.

In response, Ellen Prendergast composed a song. Its original title was "He Lei No Ka Po'e Aloha 'Aina," but it soon became known as "Mele 'Ai Pohaku" or "The Stone-eating Song," and "Mele Aloha 'Aina" or "The Patriots' Song."

The words of the song are bitter.

*Kaulana na pua a'o Hawai'i / Kupa'a mahope o ka 'aina / Hiki mai ka 'elele o ka loko 'ino / Palapala 'anunu me ka pakaha*—"Famous are the children of Hawai'i / Ever loyal to the land / When the evil-hearted messenger comes / With his greedy document of extortion."

*Pane mai Hawai'i moku o Keawe. / Kokua na Hono a'o Pi'ilani. / Kako'o mai Kaua'i o Mano / Pa'apu me ke one Kakuhihewa*—"Hawai'i, land of Keawe, answers. / Pi'ilani's bays help. / Mano's Kaua'i lends support / And so do the sands of Kakuhihewa."

*'A'ole 'a'e kau i ka pulima / Maluna o ka pepa o ka 'enemi / Ho'ohui 'aina ku'ai hewa / I ka pono sivila a'o ke kanaka*—"No one will fix a signature / To the paper of the enemy / With its sin of annexation / And sale of native civil rights."

*'A'ole makou a'e minamina / I ka pu'ukala a ke aupuni, / Ua lawa makou i ka pohaku, / I ka'ai kamaha'o o ka'aina*—"We do not value / The Government's sums of money, / We are satisfied with the stones, / Astonishing food of the land."

*Mahope makou o Lili'u-lani / A loa'a 'e ka pono o ka 'aina. / (A kau hou 'ia e ke kalaunu.) / Ha'ina 'ia mai ana ka puana / Ka po'e i aloha i ka 'aina*—"We back Lili'u-lani / Who has won the rights of the land. / (She will be crowned again.) / Tell the story / Of the people who love their land."

Although the words are bitter, the melody is light, sometimes even lighthearted. The contrast was not without purpose.

Only a handful of the new rulers understood the Hawaiian language. The song could be sung in the faces of the oligarchy, and they would only hear a pleasant Hawaiian melody, ignorant that in fact the very singing of the song was spit cast in their eyes.

*Ua lawa makou i ka pohaku, I ka ʻai kamahaʻo o ka ʻaina*—"We are satisfied with the stones, the astonishing food of the land." The phrase is not mere lyric. Pohaku, stones, are possessed of spirit—mana, mystical and potent. One sense of the lyric, then, is that the mana of the pohaku is enough to sustain the life of those who refuse the offers of the new government.

In Hawaiian tradition, when Kamehameha I's people were on the windward side of Oʻahu, there was an occasion when food ran short. But no one had to go hungry. Instead, men were dispatched to Kawai Nui in Kailua to gather and bring back the *lepo ʻaeʻae*, the edible mud of Kawai Nui. Life was sustained from the dirt.

Pohaku are very much at the heart of Hawaiian life. House foundations, heiau, altars, the loʻi, all are formed of stone. In that sense, the song could be saying that it is enough that we have the pohaku, for the pohaku form the foundation of our life. In Hawaiian cosmology the goddess Papa represents Mother Earth, the earth as giver of life. Rock, as earth, in this way is Papa as life-giving rock.

Further, the word pohaku itself can be taken apart for meanings. *Po* means night and darkness and the realm of the gods. *Haku* means to put in order, and it also means master and overseer. *Haku* also means stone. *Ku* by itself means to stand, to anchor, and it means to transform and beginning and appearance. So the word pohaku could mean the anchor to the realm of the gods, or the transformation of the realm of the gods to physical form as stone, or it could mean that the stones stand as overseer of the realm. Or, it could mean all of these things.

The song quickly circulated among Hawaiians. Members of the Royal Hawaiian Band performed it until its meaning became more widely known. Then they were forced to stop. But others continued to sing it.

The new government changed the name of the Royal Hawaiian Band to the Hawaiian Band. Years later, when the band was again renamed the Royal Hawaiian Band, a principal attraction was the knowledge that Heleluhe, the singer, would be performing "Mele 'Ai Pohaku"—only now, it, too, had been renamed. It was called "Kaulana Na Pua"—"Famous Are the Flowers"—the name it is known by today.

In the 1960s, Eleanor Prendergast, the composer's daughter, wrote down the subtext of the song. Noelani Mahoe and the Leo Nahenahe Singers recorded both the song and the subtext on their album *Folksongs of Hawai'i*. The subtext says:

> This is a song of the Hawaiians' love for their land. The loyal subjects of the Hawaiian kingdom will long be remembered throughout the world for their firm and courageous defense of their beloved land. At the time of the overthrow of the Hawaiian kingdom, representatives of the new government attempted to bribe the Hawaiians to renounce their loyalty to Queen Lili'uokalani. Loyal Hawaiians from Hawaii, Maui and Kaua'i joined with their brothers and sisters on O'ahu in refusing to betray their homeland by selling their glorious heritage for a mess of pottage. All agreed their willingness to subsist by eating stones, the mystic food of the land. They supported the queen in her efforts to perpetuate the life of the land in righteousness. They sincerely prayed that the queen be restored to her rightful throne.

In 1964, not long after recording the song, Noelani Mahoe and Ka'upena Wong performed it at Orvis Auditorium at the University of Hawai'i. Folk singer Pete Seeger was in the audience. He was so struck with the song that he asked the performers to come to the annual folk music festival in Newport, Rhode Island.

Mahoe was hapai, but it was an honor she couldn't pass up. So in the summer of 1964 Noelani Mahoe and Ka'upena Wong joined renowned folk artists, including Theodore Bikel, Joan Baez, Jose Feliciano, and, of course, Pete Seeger, at the world's most famous folk music festival. There, in Newport, the rest of the world was introduced to "Kaulana Na Pua," both to its music and its meaning.

Others have recorded the song. Some, like Ike Lee, recorded the subtext along with the song. Some, like the Kahauanu Lake Trio, recorded the song as a lilting melody. Some, like the Hawaiian Nation, recorded it as a song of righteous protest. The Surfers recorded it. So did Vicki I'i, Jack DeMello, Webley Edwards, Marlene Sai, and the Mary Kaye Trio. Hui 'Ohana recorded it, and so did Peter Ahia, Leina'ala Haile, Myrtle K. Hilo, Nina Keali'iwahamana, Peter Moon,

Cyrus Green, Willie K., Ozzie Kotani, and Keola Beamer. Don Ho recorded it.

The song is widely performed. Palani Vaughan and the King's Own perform it. Moe Keale performs it. The Brothers Cazimero perform it, as do Keith and Carmen Haugen. Carmen dances it.

Some who know the song say it should not be danced to. The words of the song are like the words of a dirge, and a dirge is not to be danced to. Despite the contradicting melody, it is an *oli*, a chant that is not danced.

But it has been danced, and it is still danced. 'Iolani Luahine danced it in a black holoku. Lani Custino dances it, and so do Healani Youn, Palani Vaughan's Royal Court Dancers, and the Brothers Cazimero's Royal Dance Company.

Wherever it is performed today, whether sung or danced or both, its performance is greeted with recognition and with empathy. The sentiment the lyrics express are not buried, not veiled—not by the pleasant melody, not by the song's title, and not by contemporary circumstances.

Throughout history, a people dispossessed have always found a way in music and in dance to speak aloud their true feelings, while biding time for their dispossession to be remedied. "Kaulana Na Pua," written 100 years ago, remains to this day a melodic protest against Hawaiians' loss of self-determination, the loss of their sovereign nation.

# The Lynching of Katsu Goto

## GAYLORD C. KUBOTA

*The tragic fate of a successful "first ship" Japanese immigrant.*

*A Japanese storekeeper, K. Goto, was found dead this morning at 6 o'clock, hanging to a cross arm on a telephone pole about one hundred yards from the Honokaa jail. A two-inch rope, evidently purchased for the purpose, was used and from all appearances no bungling hands performed the work—the dead man's hands and legs were pinioned and a genuine hangman's knot under his left ear.*

Letter dated October 29, 1889, published in the
*Daily Pacific Commercial Advertiser.*

✦ This shocking incident has remained all but unknown in the annals of Hawaii's history. And, unfortunately, the few accounts of it that have passed down are based on an oversimplified, undocumented, and distorted interpretation of the incident. That interpretation holds that: (1) the Hawaiian authorities dragged their feet about investigating the incident because Japanese were not considered important, and that the investigative efforts of a Japanese, Eijiro Tatsumi, were really responsible for the arrest and successful prosecution of the culprits, and (2) that after being in jail for only a short while all of the men convicted of the crime escaped and left Hawaii, with the inference being that they somehow were allowed to escape.

The true story, however, is full of twists and turns and replete with

---

First published November 1985.

irony upon irony. Moreover, the names that emerge during the course of the story include prominent kamaaina families, missionary families such as Lyman, Hitchcock, Judd, and Dole.

A close look at the incident provides insights into the society and economic order of late-nineteenth-century Hawaii and, particularly, into the judicial system and justice of that day. The incident was also a potentially explosive diplomatic issue that could have had a serious impact upon Japanese immigration to Hawaii and, consequently, upon the history of these islands since that time.

## Goto, the "First Ship" Immigrant

Katsu, the oldest son of Izaemon Kobayakawa, was born in Kanagawa prefecture about 1862. The Kobayakawas had three other sons and two daughters. Even as an elementary school student Katsu had the reputation of being very smart, as did Sekijiro, the Kobayakawas' third son.

Prior to leaving Japan, Katsu was employed at the Oiso county office. It is believed that he learned English at the port of Yokohama.

According to Katsu's niece, Dr. Fumiko Kobayakawa Kaya, he changed his family registration to the Goto family because at that time eldest sons could not go abroad, since they traditionally succeeded to headship of the family.

Katsu Goto was among the 944 immigrants—676 men, 158 women, and 110 children—who came to Hawaii on the first of 26 shiploads of government contract Japanese immigrants between 1885 and 1894. Goto's ship, *City of Tokio*, arrived on February 8, 1885.

Goto was 23 years old when he came to Hawaii. His contract, like those of most of his male shipmates, was for a period of three years at $9 per month. A $6 monthly food allowance, free lodging, medical care, and cooking fuel were also provided. Goto's contract was reassigned by the Hawaiian Board of Immigration to Soper, Wright and Co. at Ookala on the Big Island. This sugar plantation had been organized and managed by John Harris Soper prior to his appointment as marshal of the Hawaiian Kingdom in 1884.

Goto's three years as a common laborer must have been long, difficult, and probably even humiliating in view of his background as a bureaucrat rather than as a farmer. However, his period of indentured service was not completely negative. He was able to send for his brother, Sekijiro, at the end of 1887 and to send him to high school in San

Francisco. Apparently, even at his low monthly wage Goto was able to save money. Goto, who would prove to be a good businessman, might also have found ways to make additional money on the side.

The hardships of a plantation laborer's life were probably made more bearable by his ambition and plans to open a store upon completion of his contract. Hawaiian Kingdom Interior Department records show that he obtained a retail license to operate a store in Honokaa in 1888. He was the first of the "first ship" immigrants to open a store after the expiration of their contracts.

Goto opened for business in a four-room house in which he also resided. The store was a few yards away from one operated by Joseph R. Mills. Goto's business was doing well by the end of the first year and he hired another Japanese as a clerk. Moreover, two months before his untimely death Goto opened a new store of "quite good dimensions" in a building right next to his former store.

Goto's general store carried a considerable stock of foodstuff, clothing, household goods, hardware, and so on, most of which were obtained from Honolulu. The heaviest merchandise was brought from Honokaa landing to his store for a fee by William Blabon on the Mills store wagon.

Goto's customers were mainly Japanese, though Hawaiians and Caucasians also bought from him. Goto was a very industrious businessman who actively went out to solicit orders.

When Goto was killed, his assets already exceeded debts incurred in starting the store, even after such a short time in business. The bright future that lay ahead was to be tragically denied him.

The lynching of any member of the Honokaa Japanese community would have been cause for dismay, anger, and fear. The fact that the victim was storekeeper Katsu Goto aroused the deepest emotions of his fellow countrymen. His store, the only one in the area owned and operated by one of their countrymen, naturally had become a community focal point and an informal gathering place. And, just as naturally, the man who had successfully established that store was looked up to by the others. The death of Goto meant the loss of the leader of their fledgling Japanese community.

## The Investigation

Hawaiian government law enforcement officials began a vigorous, careful, and extremely thorough investigation of Goto's death as soon as his body was found hanging from the telephone pole at six o'clock on the morning of October 29, 1889. Deputy Sheriff Rufus Lyman telephoned Sheriff of Hawaii Edward Hitchcock to inform him of the incident. Hitchcock ordered him to post a reward of $250, a sizable sum at that time, for information leading to the apprehension and conviction of the guilty party or parties.

Hitchcock also immediately asked the government physician in Hilo, Dr. R. B. Williams, to go to Honokaa to perform the autopsy. Dr. Sakichi Noda, one of the Japanese physicians brought over and employed by the Board of Immigration to attend to the medical needs of his countrymen, also participated in the postmortem.

Meanwhile, the body had been lowered by the coroner, Hamakua Police Court Judge Edwin Thomas, who had been summoned to the scene by planter Robert M. Overend. Helping the coroner lower the body was Thomas Steele, Overend's head overseer. A crowd of Japanese gathered and watched the scene.

A jury was called and the inquest was started before noon. Judge Thomas designated storekeeper Joseph R. Mills, who was also a special policeman, as the jury's secretary. The jury, which had to wait for completion of the autopsy, officially concluded the following day that Goto "was murdered by being hung by one or more unknown persons."

Edward Griffin Hitchcock, who as sheriff of Hawaii personally led the investigation of the Goto case, was the son of missionary parents and was married to the eldest daughter of missionary and Castle and Cooke cofounder Samuel N. Castle. Prior to his appointment as sheriff in 1888, Hitchcock, as manager of Hitchcock and Co.'s Sugar Plantation, had had personal experience in dealing with a multiethnic work force. He also had studied law and was later to become marshal of the Provisional Republic of Hawaii and a Circuit Court judge.

Two days after Goto's body was found, Sheriff Hitchcock wrote to Marshal of the Hawaiian Kingdom John Harris Soper that he was going to Honokaa immediately because, after talking to Deputy Sheriff Lyman, he was "of the opinion that the Hamakua murder was *not* committed by either Japanese or Chinese."

From the very outset, therefore, the law enforcement officers on the scene were well aware that white men had probably done the deed. The consequent social, economic, and diplomatic implications made the case much more important and urgent for them, while at the same time it made the investigation more complicated and delicate.

In Honokaa, the whites were concerned about possible retaliation by

## The Lynching of Katsu Goto

the Japanese. The following letter appeared in the *Daily Pacific Commercial Advertiser* on November 4, and in the weekly *Hawaiian Gazette* the next day:

### The Honokaa Hanging Tree

Mr. Editor: An inquest was held by coroner Thomas on the 29th and 30th, on the body of the deceased Japanese found hanging to the telephone pole at Honokaa jail. Some twenty witnesses were examined, but the jury did not succeed in eliciting any evidence of importance. All ended in about the same thing that the unfortunate man left his store about 8 o'clock p.m. and went to Mr. Overend's camp and stayed there until a little after 10 o'clock, when he started for home and on his way met with such a sad fate. There is a very strong feeling of regret among the foreigners here that such a cruel and barbarous transaction should have been perpetrated in this district, and apart from the guilt and shame of such a crime, it was decidedly bad policy, as retaliation may fall on some innocent parties. Should a suspicion of any party or parties arise in the minds of the Japanese, those parties are liable to suffer be they innocent or guilty, and we sincerely hope that the sheriff may succeed in fixing the crime where it belongs, and every law abiding citizen should help him, for a transaction of this kind reflects on the whole community.

Yours etc.,
J. R. M.

In Honolulu, high officials were concerned about the possible impact on Hawaiian-Japanese relations—particularly the immigration of Japanese laborers to Hawaii—as well as about possible further unrest in the Honokaa area. After years of fruitless entreaty the Hawaiian government finally persuaded the Japanese government to permit the steady emigration to Hawaii that had commenced in 1885. By the time of the Goto incident the Japanese were becoming the largest ethnic group in the plantation labor force, and this at a time when additional laborers were still badly needed by the plantations.

In view of the serious concern shown by some other officials, Attorney General Clarence Ashford's remarks to Sheriff Hitchcock in a letter right after the incident verge on being flippant:

In re Hamakua. I observe in the papers that the craze for Japanese decorative art has lately been carried to an extreme point in that District: this government can never admit the proposition that Japanese residents can be used to decorate telephone poles with impunity. I trust you may succeed in finding the "artist" responsible for that last extension of the craze, and duly impress him with the seriousness with such innovations.

Sheriff Hitchcock spent nearly a month in Honokaa and did not overlook any possible avenue of investigation. For example, he asked Marshal Soper to secure memoranda from Honolulu merchandising agents regarding any rope that they shipped to certain stores in Honokaa during the last few months prior to the lynching. Soper's reply included samples of rope shipped to the Mills store on October 1. Hitchcock questioned all possible suspects and witnesses.

The investigation proceeded more slowly than the sheriff would have liked because of the caution required by the delicate situation and the status of some of the suspects. In one letter to Marshal Soper he even expressed concern that his mail might be tampered with at the Honokaa Post Office; storekeeper Joseph R. Mills, who had become one of the leading suspects, was also postmaster at Honokaa. Hitchcock also was severely hampered by ill health.

Nevertheless, through perseverance and endurance, by the last week of November the sheriff had accumulated enough solid evidence to confidently swear out warrants for the arrest of a young Hawaiian known as Lala and three white men: John Richmond, stableman at Robert M. Overend's plantation; Thomas Steele, head overseer at the same plantation; and William Blabon, teamster for Joseph R. Mills.

By December 2 Hitchcock had obtained a detailed account of the lynching from Lala. In letters to both Soper and Deputy Attorney General Arthur Peterson that day Hitchcock also stated that he personally had no doubt about the complicity of Joseph R. Mills and plantation owner Robert M. Overend in the affair. However, since both of them were men of high standing in the community the sheriff felt that he must have stronger evidence before seeking warrants for their arrest.

To Soper he wrote: "I have no doubt, so far as common sense & reason go towards removing all doubt, that both R. M. O. & J. R. M. are as guilty as anyone else, but still the *evidence* is not, to my mind, sufficiently strong to enable me to take out arrests."

In his letter to Peterson the sheriff expressed confidence that Richmond was weakening and would soon tell all he knew about the inci-

## The Lynching of Katsu Goto

dent. Evidently the potential testimony of the Hawaiian Lala alone was not considered strong enough even though he had detailed Mills' direct participation in the incident. Therefore the sheriff was anxiously hoping to obtain corroborating information from Richmond, a white man.

On December 12 Sheriff Hitchcock finally had Joseph R. Mills—store owner, restaurant owner, Honokaa postmaster, Honokaa poundmaster, notary public, special policeman, and auctioneer—arrested. The same J. R. Mills also was undoubtedly the author of the letter from one "J. R. M." to the editors of the *Daily Pacific Commercial Advertiser* and the *Hawaiian Gazette*, which expressed regret over "such a cruel and barbarous transaction" and which concluded: "and we sincerely hope that the sheriff may succeed in fixing the crime where it belongs."

At the end of the month William Watson, head teamster for Overend and a former employee of Mills, was the last to be arrested. The sheriff apparently decided—no doubt regretfully—that, his personal feelings aside, he did not have sufficiently strong evidence against plantation owner Overend.

Meanwhile, on December 6 Viscount Chusuke Torii, vice consul of the Honolulu Japanese Consulate General and acting consul general of Japan, arrived in Hilo accompanied by G. O. Nakayama, the Board of Immigration's chief inspector of Japanese, and Keigoro Katsura, the first Japanese lawyer in Hawaii and inspector of Japanese for the island of Oahu. Their trip to Honokaa and their findings during more than three weeks on the Big Island were reported to the Japanese Foreign Ministry in dispatches marked *himitsu* (secret).

The dispatches indicated that, on the one hand, they were impressed by the great concern about the Goto incident shown by Hawaiian government officials, including the chief justice of the Supreme Court, and they fully appreciated Sheriff Hitchcock's exhaustive efforts to investigate the case. On the other hand, due to the difficult situation faced by foreign government officials trying to gather information from Japanese, they felt that by talking in person to their countrymen who had known Goto they could further the investigation. Furthermore, they believed the presence of the acting consul general would help to calm down the Japanese in Honokaa.

When they got to Hilo and met with Sheriff Hitchcock, he encouraged them to make direct contact with the Japanese witnesses. He also informed them that he was in the process of having J. R. Mills arrested and advised them to wait until that had been actually accomplished before going to Honokaa.

When the group arrived in Honokaa they assembled their countrymen. Acting Consul General Torii assured them that the Hawaiian government would do justice in its handling of the Goto case and asked them not to do anything rash on their own. He then urged them not to withhold anything if they had any information that could be used in the case.

Torii's party discovered that the Japanese in Honokaa had held back information because they were afraid of revenge. The arrest of Mills helped relieve some of that anxiety, as did the personal appearance and assurances of the head of their country's diplomatic mission in Hawaii. Their countrymen gave the following account of why they believed Goto was killed and who was most likely to have been behind his death.

There were about 70 Japanese working for Robert M. Overend at Overend's plantation. They would consult Goto when disputes arose between themselves and Overend and sometimes also asked Goto to interpret for their side. At times Goto had advised that they even go so far as to take a matter to court to be decided. Therefore Overend hated Goto. He had warned Goto not to go to the living quarters of his workers and that if Goto went there he would shoot him.

Another reason was that Goto's store was doing very well and his success was affecting the business of the white merchants. Among those affected was Joseph R. Mills, who everyone knew harbored strong feelings against Goto.

Overend's workers also related details of their meeting with Goto the night he was killed, and of certain comings and goings on the plantation before and after that meeting.

When Torii's party got back to Hilo and passed on its findings to Hitchcock, the sheriff was "thoroughly satisfied" because the information confirmed what he had found and provided more details.

The acting consul general also reported that evidence had been obtained to implicate Mills as one of the assailants. However, there was still no conclusive evidence against "Overend, who is widely thought to be the mastermind [*shubosha*]."

By January 2 of the following year a very confident Sheriff Hitchcock could write Deputy Attorney General Peterson: "Tuesday next, the 7th, is the day set for the examination before Judge Lyman for commitment of J. R. Mills, W. C. Blabon & W. D. Watson (the little red-headed luna of Overend's) and I do not have any doubts of securing commitments against each; nor do I think we shall fail of gaining conviction before Supreme Court at time of trial!" The main reason for his jubilant report was that: "Lala & John Richmond (Overend's stableman) have both turned state's evidence, and their story of the events that happened (both being present at the scene of the death of Goto) are very good & satisfactory." The sheriff also had the benefit of the information just obtained from Overend's Japanese workers by Viscount Torii's party.

January 2 was also the day that Acting Consul General Torii and Keigoro Katsura finally returned to Honolulu. Before leaving they informed the sheriff that they had hired his brother, David, the most prominent attorney in Hilo, to assist in the prosecution of the case.

The fact that the acting Japanese consul general was willing to leave Hilo at what normally would have been considered a critical point in the process of bringing the killers of a Japanese national to justice bespeaks his confidence in the manner in which the case was being handled by the Hawaiian government and, particularly, in the integrity, dedication, and ability of the man who had spearheaded the investigation, Sheriff of Hawaii Edward Hitchcock.

The examination for commitment went as well as the sheriff had expected it would. The Crown, represented by the brothers Hitchcock, had little difficulty in establishing a case against each of the three suspects in question. Judge Frederick Lyman concluded that "if the evidence produced is true, there is probable cause to believe that conviction would take place before a Jury of the Offense charged." The three defendants were committed for trial in May and sent to Oahu Prison for safekeeping; Steele, who had waived the examination proceedings, had been there since mid-December. Charges were dropped against Lala and Richmond in return for having turned state's evidence and they were bound over as witnesses on bonds of $3,000. Also bound as witnesses were three Japanese.

## The Trial

The long-awaited trial finally began in Hilo on May 6. Among those present to observe the proceedings were Acting Consul General Torii, Chief Inspector of Japanese G. O. Nacayama, and attorney Keigoro Katsura.

The Crown was represented by Deputy Attorney General Charles Creighton and former Deputy Attorney General Peterson, who had resumed private practice. The Japanese government had retained Hilo attorney David Hitchcock and Honolulu attorney Paul Neumann, giving the prosecution a battery of four extremely capable attorneys.

Peterson would become attorney general scarcely a month after the Goto trial ended. Paul Neumann was perhaps the best trial lawyer of his day in the Islands. A former attorney general of the kingdom, Neumann was well known to the Japanese government and also very familiar with the Japanese immigration situation because he had been the Hawaiian government's special commissioner for renegotiating the terms of the emigration agreement with Japan in 1887.

Two first-rate Honolulu attorneys represented the defendants. John M. Davidson appeared on behalf of Mills and his former employee, Blabon. Francis Hatch represented the two former Overend employees, Steele and Watson. Hatch would go on to become vice president of the provisional government, minister of foreign affairs of the subsequent Republic of Hawaii, and eventually retire as an associate justice of the Supreme Court of the Territory of Hawaii.

His appearance on behalf of Goto's alleged murderers was another one of the many ironies connected with the case. Attorney Hatch had represented Theo H. Davies and Co., one of Goto's principal creditor agents, in helping settle Goto's estate. For this service Hatch was later paid $25 from the estate of the man whose killers he had helped defend.

The case of *Rex v. Mills et al.* was widely perceived as one of the most important cases ever tried in the Islands. Supreme Court Chief Justice Albert Judd assigned himself to preside over it.

Defendant Mills—and his wife, Eugenia, who would offer controversial testimony during the trial—were no strangers to Judd. Nearly a decade earlier he had presided over a civil suit for damages brought against Mills by Robert Briggs because Mills "did carnally know Eugenia Briggs, the plaintiff's wife." That trial fully exposed the sordid character of the outwardly respectable-appearing Mills and was less than flattering to the character of Eugenia. The jury had taken only 17 minutes to find for the plaintiff and award him $2,000 damages.

Most of the opening day of the murder trial was spent arguing a change of venue motion submitted by the defense, a motion that the court denied.

## The Lynching of Katsu Goto

The second day was taken up entirely by the arduous task of trying to select a jury. Under Hawaiian laws of the day when "foreigners" (white men) were on trial the jury had to be drawn entirely from the same. The answers of the prospective jurors under questioning are of particular interest, since racial attitudes were exposed in the process. The prosecution lawyers' main concern was possible racial prejudice against Japanese, not so much because the victim was Japanese as because many of their secondary, corroborative witnesses were Japanese. The attorneys for the Crown were also careful to ask whether a prospective juror had any reservations about the death penalty. Their basic line of questioning was, in effect: Would you believe the testimony of a Japanese even if it were against that of a white man and even if a white man could be sentenced to death on the basis of it?

Most of the prospective jurors said they had no prejudice against either the Japanese or the death penalty. Two persons stated that they did have racial prejudice. One responded: "I have prejudice against the Asiatic race, enough to sway my judgment.... I would not take the testimony of a Japanese against that of a white man." At this point Chief Justice Judd expressed doubt as to whether the man should be disqualified. Neumann, however, pursued the questioning further, and Judd finally had to excuse the potential juror when he admitted that he was prejudiced against all Japanese because of trouble he had had with them. Another potential juror's reply to a similar question was: "If a case depended entirely on Japanese evidence, the fact would influence me; my reason is experience of Japanese on plantations." Neumann asked that the man be excused for cause. Judd, however, would not go that far, saying that "many fair-minded men would hesitate when life was at stake to act on exclusive Japanese or Chinese evidence." Although the chief justice's attitude seems startling today, it probably was an accurate reflection of racial attitude among "fair-minded" white men of that time. Needless to say, one of the Crown's peremptory challenges was subsequently used to excuse that person.

At the end of the day, both sides finally had arrived at a jury that they could agree on.

The following morning former Deputy Attorney General Peterson opened the case with a statement of what the Crown intended to prove. He told the jury that "a little over a week before the lynching, a fire occurred in the cane fields of Overend, and I hope to show you that it was set by the Japanese on the plantation." Returning to this point later he added: "We will show that the cause of the murder was the fire in the cane field. That the members of the plantation suspected Goto as the ring leader in the matter and that they were going to extract from him the facts and who set the fire."

This statement amounted to putting forth the theory that the suspects actually had not intended to kill Goto, but rather had only intended to extract information from him. In line with this theory, Peterson also stated: "We will not show that he was killed by the hanging, but by the pulling from the horse; that he was hung to the post as a mere matter of bravado." From the very outset, therefore, the Crown said, in effect, that it intended to prove manslaughter, not murder. Nevertheless, Peterson impressed upon the jurors that "this is the most serious case ever tried on these islands." He finished his opening address by squarely confronting the racial overtones of the case: "if the evidence is enough for conviction then never mind how much you may think of them as white men against Japs, it is your duty to bring in a verdict against them."

The Crown's case was presented according to a carefully thought-out plan. Testimony from several witnesses established the fact that Overend and Steele both believed that the fire had been set by some of the Japanese workers on the plantation, and that both harbored ill feeling toward Goto.

Planter Robert M. Overend, who the sheriff personally believed was connected with the incident resulting in Goto's death, ironically was a prosecution witness. Overend stated that every time he made any changes or new rules, his Japanese workers would say they were going to see Goto, that he was sick and tired of hearing that response, that he thought Goto was advising them, and that he had twice warned Goto not to come onto his plantation. Overend also said that he thought the fire was caused by his Japanese workers.

Deputy Sheriff Lyman testified that Steele had remarked that "Goto was at bottom of a great deal of trouble with Japanese" and that Steele believed the Japanese had set the fire.

The testimony that followed outlined the chronology of the fatal incident. Several Japanese workers employed on Overend's plantation testified that on the evening of the twenty-eighth they had left the plantation for Goto's store to consult him about $20 damages that Overend had demanded from each of them that afternoon for allegedly causing the fire. They happened to meet Goto while en route and he

## The Lynching of Katsu Goto

returned with them to their quarters on the plantation and spent more than an hour there. While on the way to the house with Goto they had met Steele, so Steele knew Goto was going with them. Goto left their house to return home sometime between 9:30 and 10 p.m. Other workers testified that Steele had left the plantation on horseback around 9:30 or 10 and that he and another man riding one of Overend's horses had returned around midnight. One worker also told the court that Goto said Overend had threatened to shoot him if he came to his plantation.

Knowing that his life could be in danger, and even knowing that Overend's head overseer had seen him, Goto had nevertheless continued on to the workers' quarters to hear about their latest trouble with Overend and give them advice; it was to be his last act of courage on behalf of his fellow immigrants.

Coroner Thomas then testified about the discovery and lowering of the body and the calling of a jury for the inquest. Dr. R. B. Williams followed Thomas to the stand. His opinion was that death was caused by suffocation, strangulation by hanging being one means. However, both he and the Japanese physician, Dr. Sakichi Noda, who examined the body with him, were also quite sure that the neck was broken. Dr. Williams emphasized, however, that this was not the cause of death. He explained that death would have come instantly had it been from this cause, and the various internal body signs of suffocation would not have been present in the corpse. This more or less left the conclusion, which was never explicitly stated by the doctor, that Goto had already died from some form of suffocation before suspension from the telephone pole presumably broke his neck.

The testimony of star witnesses Richmond and Lala, who had both taken part in the incident, yielded the following description of how Goto met his end.

The two of them were summoned separately on the night that Goto was killed. Richmond was summoned by Steele and sent to watch for a Jap who would be leaving the Jap living quarters on horseback and to report his departure to Steele. Lala was called out of his quarters by Blabon, who told him that Mills needed him. When they got to where Mills and the others were waiting, Mills told him to grab the bridle of the horse that a Jap would be riding toward them. After Richmond reported that the Jap was on his way they lay in ambush. Lala grabbed the bridle as he had been told to do while Steele and Blabon dragged the man off the horse. The surprised and frightened victim cried out, "Pau! Pau!"—his last words. Steele grabbed him by the mouth and the back of the head, while Blabon grabbed him around the body. Steele, Blabon, Mills, and Watson carried him to a location away from the road where he was placed face down and his hands and feet bound. Lala was sent to tie up Goto's horse and Steele's horse, after which he fled the scene. Mills sent Richmond to pick up a rope at the foot of the telephone pole, a rope that, he found, already had a hangman's knot at one end. When he returned with the rope someone in the group said, "My God! He is dead." Richmond then bent over and put his hand over the man's heart but could feel no heartbeat. Then Mills, who had earlier said something about asking Goto some questions, remarked, "Well, he won't sell any more goods." The body was then carried over to the telephone pole. Watson threw the rope over the crossbar, Mills put the noose around Goto's neck, and the body was hauled up and suspended.

Both Richmond and Lala claimed to have become involved unknowingly at the last moment, and both claimed they were never told what the others had really intended to do when they stopped Goto. Hence the difficult question of the defendants' intentions was left to the jury to decide without much clear evidence.

After the Crown rested its case, the defense made no opening statement but simply called a long string of witnesses who spent most of their time attacking the character and general credibility of Lala and Richmond, both of whom had very poor reputations for truthfulness. The lack of positive evidence to support the contention of the defendants that they were innocent was so obvious that even Chief Justice Judd, in his final instructions to the jury, remarked, "I would be glad to refer to the evidence for the defense, but it is almost all directed to discrediting testimony for the Crown." The notable exception to this was the testimony of Eugenia Mills, who attempted to establish alibis for her husband.

She gave an account of the activities at their home during the night Goto was killed, emphasizing that Mills was at home all night.

Subjected to intensive cross-examination, she denied having met with a kahuna named Poupou after the killing, denied having told Poupou that Mills was not with her between 10 p.m. and 3 a.m., and denied having asked Poupou to look into the matter as a kahuna to see who was implicated in the killing and particularly if Mills were involved. She also flatly denied having spoken to Poupou since coming to

Hilo, to try to get her to change her testimony regarding Mrs. Mills' saying that her husband was absent from their house the night Goto was killed.

The following day the Crown called Poupou as a witness. Poupou testified affirmatively about the conversations concerning Mr. Mills that Mrs. Mills had denied having with her, including the most recent conversation in Hilo when Mrs. Mills had tried to persuade her to change her testimony.

After Poupou had been cross-examined and the Crown had rested its case, a strange thing happened. Mrs. Mills suddenly and voluntarily admitted to the court that she had spoken to Poupou in Hilo, which she had flatly denied during her previous day's testimony. One observer reported that it "practically killed her whole evidence."

Defense attorneys Davidson and Hatch spent four hours presenting their closing arguments to the jury. Neumann, for the Crown, took just over an hour. His remarks included a statement to the effect that he could not believe that these men really intended to kill Goto and that he therefore could not sincerely ask for a verdict of murder.

Chief Justice Judd spent nearly an hour very carefully instructing the jury, prefacing his instructions by emphasizing the tremendous significance of the case: "I may say it is the most important case I have ever had to preside over since I have had the honor to occupy a position on the bench."

With obvious reference to the rather unusual way in which the prosecution had presented the Crown's case—from Peterson's opening address to Neumann's final arguments—Judd commented: "The theory suggested is possible: that it was not intended to kill Goto, that it was merely intended to pull him up and down to extort a confession. Malice aforethought need not have been formed for weeks or months beforehand. If without conspiracy defendants laid their hands violently on Goto and so used him that he died, it is murder. If you find the killing was not with malice you find in either of the three degrees of manslaughter."

Judd pointed out that the jury could acquit or bring in a conviction for either murder or one of three degrees of manslaughter for each of the defendants, and it was up to them to decide what, if anything, each defendant was guilty of.

After deliberating for more than six hours, the jury returned verdicts of manslaughter in the second degree for Steele and Mills, and manslaughter in the third degree for Blabon and Watson. Judd subsequently sentenced Mills and Steele to nine years imprisonment at hard labor, Blabon to five, and Watson to four.

A newspaper correspondent who had covered the trial reported, on the final day: "It is believed, as far as I can hear, that the prosecution was moderate in the presentation of the case, and that the verdict is a very lenient one."

Acting Consul General Torii, in his final report to the Japanese foreign minister, praised the fairness of Chief Justice Judd's handling of the trial and the sentences that he meted out. Not a word was said about the Crown's decision to prosecute for manslaughter rather than murder. The acting consul general indicated the difficult, if not delicate, situation to his government. On the one hand, if the outcome had been too severe, there would have repercussions in the white community. On the other hand, had the findings and punishments been too light, then there certainly would have been repercussions in the Japanese community. Thus, although his conclusion was that the Hawaiian government had done its best in this matter from start to finish, what Torii seemed to be saying was that the outcome was the best that could be expected under the difficult circumstances. The potentially explosive Goto case was handled diplomatically in this low-key manner with apparently no formal communications about the matter exchanged directly between the respective foreign ministers.

What the Japanese government and the Japanese community in Hawaii truly appreciated without reservation, regardless of the final outcome of the trial, was the tremendous effort Sheriff Hitchcock had made, even while in very poor health, to bring the men responsible to trial. This appreciation was expressed in a letter written by lawyer Keigoro Katsura, inspector of Japanese for Oahu, and signed also by the inspectors of Japanese for the island of Hawaii.

In it, they said: "The zeal, enthusiasm, and impartiality with which you have dealt with the case from beginning to end are most highly appreciated not only by Japanese Community in this Kingdom but also by our friends at home."

The letter is documented recognition of the sheriff's exhaustive efforts and dispels interpretations of the case that claim otherwise. Also, the total absence of the name of Eijiro Tatsumi, the man given credit by some historical accounts for solving the case, in any of the correspondence, court records, consular reports, or other official documents related to the incident also makes it clear that even if Tatsumi were somehow involved in the investigation, his role could not have been anything but very minor. An interview with Tatsumi's son, 90-year-old Seijiro Tatsumi, shed little light on the matter. He recalled that his father, who had personally known Goto, told him some 80 years ago that he was the one who found the body and was the one who figured out that the crime must have been committed by white men because Japanese did not know how to tie a hangman's knot. However, the latter was widely assumed from the outset and, as we have seen, the sheriff did not need anyone to point that out to him or to urge him to press the investigation.

If there is any question as to the diligence and thoroughness of the Hawaiian government in pursuing the Goto case it lies in the prosecution of the case rather than in its investigation. The prosecution clearly prejudged the case and pursued less than the maximum charge in presenting its case in court. This was not a tactical necessity in order to assure some sort of conviction. The laws of the time made it unnecessary to pursue a lesser charge as a tactic to avoid the risk of losing a case entirely. The jury could convict for either murder or manslaughter. Even the chief justice referred to the prosecution's line of argument as a "theory." What he left unsaid was how strange it was that such a theory was being put forth by the prosecution rather than by the defense.

It is not inconceivable that the Crown was forced into the awkward position of introducing and pursuing the accidental death theory because the Hawaiian government was unwilling to risk the possible repercussions of murder convictions any more than it would have been willing to risk possible repercussions of failure to secure sufficiently severe convictions short of murder.

And what of the other main tenet of the traditionally accepted account of the Goto case, that the four convicted men escaped, perhaps with aid, and left Hawaii?

All four were transferred under guard from Hilo jail to Oahu Prison immediately after the trial. In July 1892, attempts to secure pardons for Blabon, Watson, and Mills failed. Prison records show that on September 23 Steele escaped, and a newspaper report speculated that he stowed away on a ship bound for Australia. On December 15 Blabon also escaped; it was speculated in the press that he boarded a ship that left for San Francisco that very afternoon.

Mills initially had to endure a great deal more frustration. His unsuccessful escape attempt was followed by an unsuccessful suicide attempt. Then Eugenia filed suit for divorce before he had been in prison for even six months. In this light the abrupt undermining of her own testimony at his trial—which puzzled everyone—may well have been intentional.

In the end, however, it was Mills who had the last laugh. Over the objections of Attorney General William O. Smith and President Sanford B. Dole, Mills was granted a full pardon and restoration of his civil rights by a joint session of the Executive and Advisory Councils of the provisional government, effective on July 4, 1894, the occasion of the establishment of the Republic of Hawaii. The closing words of the pardon declared Mills "eligible to offices of trust, honor and profit." Those words must have made President Dole wince when he signed the pardon; attorney Dole had represented Robert Briggs in the successful suit for damages against Mills stemming from adultery with Eugenia Briggs. Another layer of irony was added when Foreign Minister Francis Hatch signed the document. Since Oahu Prison was the responsibility of the marshal of Hawaii, the bitterest irony of all occurred when execution of the pardon fell upon the occupant of that office, Edward Hitchcock.

Ever the shrewd businessman, Mills began a grocery store in Honolulu shortly thereafter and by the time he died in 1912 he was making his living as a notary public.

Watson was the only one to serve out his full sentence. After his release he gradually worked his way back to respectability, first in Honolulu, then in Hilo, the scene of the trial. When he died in 1924 the newspaper noted the passing of a kamaaina of 47 years residence in the Islands.

And when Robert M. Overend died in 1929, his passing received front page notice in *The Honolulu Advertiser* in an article headlined: "R. M. Overend Dies at Home in Kaimuki—Former Sugar Planter Succumbs after 10-Day Illness."

The Goto lynching incident had truly been forgotten.

# The Defiant Leper of Kalalau Valley

## WRAY JOSE

*When they came to take him away, he refused to go. Instead, he fled with his wife and child deep into the valley. His fight for freedom made him a legend.*

♦ One of the most haunting chapters in Hawaii's past is the legend of Kalua-i-koolau, known to history as Koolau the Leper, who in 1893—resisting separation from his family and resettlement at the government's leper colony on Molokai—battled the army of Hawaii from a tiny ledge on a cliff deep in the recesses of Kalalau Valley, along the Na Pali Coast of Kauai.

The story captured the imagination of novelist Jack London; he romanticized it in a book of tales about Hawaii, *House of Pride*. Indeed, this story has been told and retold so many times that it has become legend.

Although no two accounts of the affair are ever exactly the same, the basic elements of the story are well documented. Koolau had been a *paniolo*, a cowboy, in his early manhood. Born in Kekaha in 1862, he was schooled in Waimea and, at 17, began work on local ranches. In 1881 he married a beautiful island girl named Piilani. A son, Kaleimanu, was born to them two years later. For several years the young family lived happily in Waimea, on the west side of the island of Kauai. But in 1889 a strange rash began to develop—first on Koolau and then on little Kaleimanu. Three years later it was diagnosed as leprosy.

---

First published November 1982.

According to Aubrey Janion, who recounted the tale in a collection of true stories of Hawaii called the *Olowalu Massacre*, Koolau was at first willing to be relocated at the government's leper settlement at Kalawao, Molokai, where drugs and treatment would be provided. He insisted, however, that Piilani be allowed to relocate there as well. It was Koolau's intention that his family not be broken up, that he not be separated from his wife, and that Kaleimanu not be separated from his mother. When this was denied, Koolau vowed to resist.

They fled to Kalalau Valley by way of the Nualolo Path, a perilous journey through the mountains of Kokee. According to an article by D. Billam Walker published in 1934, this trail was named for its famous "Nualolo viaduct"—a narrow, 32-foot *alahee* log suspended across a deep precipice, a drop of hundreds of feet.

Once in Kalalau, the family joined a group of about two dozen other lepers who had already taken up residence in a ravine in the rear of the valley. Banding together under the leadership of Judge Kauai, an ex-magistrate of the land who had contracted the disease, the lepers were determined to resist any attempt to capture them. The ranks of the lepers grew as they were joined by others guided along the hazardous Nualolo Path by a leper named Kilohana, who sometimes carried the weak and faint of heart across the *alahee* log.

## The Mission of Sheriff Stolz

In May 1893, Kauai Deputy Sheriff Louis H. Stolz, an *ex officio* agent of the Board of Health, proposed rounding up the Kalalau lepers. He argued that the board should act immediately, before the Na Pali Coast's powerful autumn surf made landing on the coast impossible. Stolz reported that of the approximately 100 people in the valley, 28 were lepers. But the board was slow to act.

Stolz was concerned that the disease might spread if the Kalalau lepers were to remain free. Hoping to prod the authorities into action, he met with Edward G. Hitchcock, marshal of the Provisional Government of Hawaii. Hitchcock advised Stolz to wait until he could spare some of his foreign men. "You cannot rely on your Hawaiian officers as things are at present," he said. He was referring to the recent overthrow of the monarchy and felt the new government was not yet stable.

But Stolz was determined to act. On June 25, a Sunday, he entered

# The Defiant Leper of Kalalau Valley

Kalalau Valley alone. Deputizing several of the valley's residents, he announced the purpose of his visit and soon had a number of lepers in hand. Two days later, he neared the lepers' stronghold at the ravine and captured a man named Paoa. As Stolz led Paoa back to the beach settlement at about eight o'clock that night, he was confronted by Koolau, who stepped out from behind a rock.

Although various writers provide slightly differing versions of this encounter, a common thread runs through them all. Janion's account tells it this way:

"Stolz!" Koolau demanded. "You are carrying a gun. Are you after me?"

"Yes," replied the sheriff. "It is my duty to arrest you."

"One false move," Koolau warned, "and I'll kill you!" Stolz bolted in the darkness and Koolau fired. The bullet tore through the sheriff's stomach, and he fell to the ground.

"Is he dead?" shouted Koolau from behind a boulder.

"No!" cried Paoa in terror. Stolz struggled to a sitting position and desperately tried to aim his gun. But Koolau fired again, and Stolz toppled over with a bullet near his heart. According to Paoa, his last words were, "Give my love to my mother."

Taking Stolz's pistol, Koolau and Paoa proceeded to the beach settlement, where they told the resident kamaainas what had happened. They were satisfied with the story of Stolz's death, they said, and wanted no more trouble. But the residents were disturbed, and many spent the night huddled in caves.

Kaumeheiwa, the man whose house Stolz had used as a command post, had heard the shots and guessed what had happened. Fearing that the lepers might take vengeance on him for having cooperated with the sheriff, Kaumeheiwa jumped into a canoe and paddled out to sea. The canoe had a hole about 8 to 10 inches square, which was plugged with canvas and soap. With the craft sometimes half filled with water, Kaumeheiwa made his way to Mana, 15 miles away. Arriving at about midnight, he sped on horseback to a nearby mill and telephoned Kauai Sheriff G. N. Wilcox with the news.

## Shoot-Out in Kalalau Valley

On July 1, a hastily organized expeditionary force arrived at Kalalau. Landing at noon, they marched rapidly across the beach and assumed control of the base of the valley. They read a proclamation of martial law to the residents and declared a grace period of 48 hours during which all lepers could turn themselves in. After that, the troops would shoot to kill. They knew that the lepers were armed and, in view of Stolz's death, dangerous. They knew also that Koolau had threatened that, if cornered, he would kill his wife and child and then himself.

The next day the soldiers searched the houses across the stream and in the caves along the beach. They soon captured Judge Kauai, who was hiding under a bed. A doctor and an agent of the Board of Health examined the people in the lower part of the valley, while three messengers were sent inland to confer with the lepers. Some of them later turned themselves in, but five others, called the "Nihoa crowd," were reported to already have left the valley and were hiding out somewhere between Kalalau and Haena. Nihoa's brother was given a week to either bring them in or lose his property. By sundown the next day, the Nihoa party was in custody. Soon only Koolau, his wife, and son remained free.

The soldiers were from Company A, Auxiliary of the National Guard of Hawaii, then the army of the Hawaiian government. Led by Second Lt. George W. R. King, the army was serving as an escort to the civil police, whose captain, William Larsen, was the overall commander of the expedition.

At 9 a.m. on July 3, the 48-hour grace period was over. Now the troops would shoot to kill. "Our hunt has just begun," mused King, who provided his superiors in Honolulu with an almost daily account of the action. The troops fired three shells up the valley, one aimed at a pair of houses built closely together. King had heard that they belonged to Koolau but learned later that it wasn't true. He took four men and searched the valley above the houses, burning the structures as he went.

The next morning dawned sunny. It was the Fourth of July. Sgt. G. W. Pratt, a gunner in charge of a seven-centimeter howitzer led a squad of 12 men to search the valleys above the camp. At about one o'clock a note arrived from Pratt declaring that he was in pursuit of a party of lepers and that he needed more men. King went up immediately with every man in camp. Besides 10 special police officers, there were 24 enlisted men in the Guard force. Pratt had stumbled across an abandoned leper camp and upon crossing a stream found some taro and about a quart of spilled poi. With this as a guide, the men ventured up a nearby hill.

## The Defiant Leper of Kalalau Valley

"Here's the trail, boys!" cried Evanson. Instantly, three shots rang out from a rocky ledge 30 feet overhead. One man, named Anderson, tumbled over the side of the hill, shot through the chest. "Steady, boys!" shouted Pratt. Blum halted in his tracks, but others slid forward with their own momentum. Suddenly, Johnson stumbled over Evanson, and both hurtled 200 feet down the side of a cliff.

After sliding and falling in turn, the two men landed on the valley floor unhurt. Johnson had to be hospitalized with bruises. "How they ever escaped with their lives is a wonder to me yet," wrote King, "and always will be."

Anderson wasn't so lucky. Shot in the chest above the right nipple, he fell about 25 feet, then dragged himself farther down, to the bottom of the gulch. Stripping from the waist up, he gouged the bullet out with a pocketknife, then stuffed the wound with pieces of twisted ginger leaf to slow the bleeding. Fashioning a pillow from his cap, he lay on his back with his hands across his chest awaiting rescue. He was dead when they found him.

Pratt withdrew. Meeting King on the way down, Pratt said, "We have met the enemy, and have been cleaned out." By now they knew that it was Koolau, Piilani, and Kaleimanu who fired at the troops from the ledge—with the youngster wielding Stolz's .45 caliber revolver.

The ledge was a flat shelf about 20 feet long, and from one-and-a-half to five feet wide, broadening where Koolau had gouged out the loose rock. It was protected on the right by a tree reinforced on either side with stones and on the left by a steep stony bluff. Koolau lay flat on the ledge smoking cigarettes, resting the barrel of his gun in a cleft in rocks erected as a shield. The family had little to eat and no water. They got by on the dew of leaves. From the vicinity of this ledge, however, it was possible to reach the Nualolo Path and escape to Waimea.

The next day the soldiers again tried to assault the family's position. They advanced to within 30 feet of it, near the spot where Anderson had been hit. McCabe, a veteran of the American Civil War, scrambled behind a large tree, then peered up ahead. Two shots exploded from the ledge, hitting McCabe in the face and destroying the left side of his head. At the sound of the shots, Husberg swung his rifle around in his left hand, accidentally discharging it. The bullet tore upward through the left side of his throat and exited in front of his right ear. King ordered his men to advance no farther.

They shelled the ledge without effect, and King and Larsen fell to bickering. In a huff, Larsen journeyed to Kekaha and returned with Koolau's sister, Naholopaa, and her husband. Warned that they would pay for treachery with their lives, the couple cautiously approached the ledge.

They called out repeatedly to Koolau, reminding him of their kinship and exhorting him not to shoot. But when they finally reached the ledge, no one was there. Koolau and his family had escaped. Naholopaa returned with only a pair of blue overalls, a boy's pair of pants and white cotton shirt, and a piece of dried eel the size of a man's forearm.

## The Death of Koolau

The battle was over. The men of the expeditionary force cheerfully broke camp on July 12 and were back in Honolulu the next day. A price of $1,000 was placed on Koolau's head, but there were no takers. Koolau and his family lived the rest of their days hidden in Kalalau Valley.

It had been thought that Koolau had escaped to Waimea via the Nualolo Path. But in a book published in 1906 called *Kalua-i-koolau, the Hero of the Kalalau Cliffs*, Piilani, Koolau's wife, revealed the truth about the family's escape and their years of hiding. In an excerpt translated from Hawaiian by Frances Frazier, Piilani recalled the moment Koolau decided it was time to abandon the ledge. "My wife," he said, "I see that it is not good to remain here . . . The soldiers know we are here and are preparing our end. Therefore let us leave . . . the enemy will continue to think we are here and they will continue firing at this place."

With Koolau in the lead, they descended one by one in silence. Kaleimanu made no sound in spite of the sores on his hands and feet. They could hear the voices of soldiers as they crept breathlessly through the darkness. Crossing a stream, they settled down for the night in a depression called Koheo.

The next day they made for the houses of some friends but found the area crowded with government men laughing, smoking cigarettes, and playing cards. Finally, they reached a place called Limamuku, above the waterfall, where fresh water and ripening bananas could be found. Relaxing during the day, they could see the smoke and hear the fire of the howitzer aimed at the ledge where they had been. "We realized that

## The Defiant Leper of Kalalau Valley

God and Koolau's loving concern had saved us from the dark deeds of the enemy," wrote Piilani.

When the soldiers had left, the family moved to a place called Oheoheiki, near the banks of the stream. Here, taro and other food could be found in abundance. During this time they were seen only twice by friends. One of them offered Koolau a steer for food. Koolau thanked him but never availed himself of it. Another time, they were startled to see Kelau, a good friend, and his wife approaching with food and supplies. Overwhelmed, Kelau's wife and Piilani wailed together at their meeting.

It was the last time they would see another human being. For Piilani the loneliness was awesome. "We were living in the gloom of the mountain forest," she recalled, "enveloped and hidden away from the fringes of civilization . . . we were like wild things, looking and listening for signs of mankind."

In time, Kaleimanu began to weaken, as the leprosy overtook his tiny frame. He wept constantly with the pain in his stomach, and herbs administered by his parents brought only temporary relief. "We tried in every way to fend off the affliction of the child, but we knew that the end was near, with the noiseless hand that is finally the fate of all men in the world." Though weak in body, the child's mind continued to mature. "He talked with us lovingly," remembered Piilani, "in a way that my heart can never forget."

One day, Kaleimanu beckoned to his mother. He put his arms around her and rubbed his cheek against hers. He was crying. "Where is papa?" he asked. "I am going to sleep."

Piilani sobbed out loud, and Koolau came running. He embraced the child, calling to him, desperately trying to hold on to him. But Kaleimanu closed his eyes forever. "We, his parents, gave him into the hands of the One who made him."

Against a tall cliff, by a lehua tree wreathed with fern, they buried Kaleimanu. His grave was covered with the fragrant tips of young branches. "We gently placed his body there, praying and giving him to God, covering him over with leaves to garland him forever."

A year passed, and Koolau too began to suffer the dreadful stomach pain. For a while he seemed better, but then he began to weaken. "I had always thought," he told Piilani, "that you, of the two of us, would first depart from our life together. Now I see that I am the one that must leave you. What now?"

In the end, his mind began to wander, and he eventually slipped into a coma. "And in the middle of the night," Piilani remembered, "when the Milky Way turns, the light in the house that was Kalua-i-koolau was extinguished . . . When the sun rose and shone its rays over the beloved valley, I, his companion, laid him out with loving hands with a lei of lehua and fern on his breast, with his gun laid beside his right hand. I gazed on his features and remembered how he had been."

As Koolau had wished, Piilani left Kalalau and returned to her family in Kekaha, where she was born. "As I descended in the dimness I looked at the nooks and ridges where we had huddled together in the chill and a vision of their faces was before my eyes, and with my recollection, the tears fell." At Kekaha she went to the home of Kupui, Koolau's mother, and together the two women wailed for their lost loved ones.

In February 1897, Kauai Deputy Sheriff John Coney and a police officer, John I, dug into the earth at a spot deep inside Kalalau Valley. At about a foot-and-a-half down they stopped short. They had hit a few coarse boards. Removing them, they found a tin containing a hand satchel full of cartridges for a rifle and a pistol. A body lay beside it, wrapped in a gray blanket with an oilskin raincoat draped over its head. Its hands were crossed over a Mauser rifle. The police tore the covering from the body. They had found Koolau at last.

# Wedding of the Year: 1893

## BOB DYE

*He was a white naval officer. She, the Chinese-Hawaiian-Caucasian daughter of a prominent Island merchant. Their union was not condoned by all.*

✦ On December 5, 1893, in the midst of the political turbulence caused by the overthrow of the Hawaiian monarchy earlier that year, a storybook wedding took place at Central Union Church. The *Pacific Commercial Advertiser* described the nuptials as "the most notable wedding of the year."

For some of the guests in the church that evening, the bridal couple—Etta, "the belle of the islands," and William, a U.S. Naval officer and relative of George Washington—symbolized the hoped-for union between Hawai'i and the United States. But for others, the marriage of William Henry Whiting, 50, scion of a prominent white American family, and Henrietta Patrinella Kealaiki Afong, 22, the daughter of a Chinese father and hapa-haole mother, was troublesome.

In April, when the engagement had been announced, the *San Francisco Chronicle* had noted: "Naval officers at Washington profess to be skeptical about the report that Cmdr. Whiting is engaged to marry the daughter of a Chinese resident of Hawai'i." If the marriage indeed were to take place, it would be the first time that an elite member of the Navy's all-white officer corps would marry a woman whose blood was "tainted." The *Chronicle* predicted that the couple would be tabooed socially and Whiting forced to resign his commission.

According to the Hawai'i press, "The naval society at Honolulu has

First published November 1993.

not yet recovered fully from the shock occasioned by the announcement. Naval prejudices are intensely strong, and marriage into the [Afong] family does not meet with cordial approval."

Whiting, commended during the Civil War "for gallant conduct" in the burning of a Confederate blockade-runner, responded that his brother officers "should go slow," as he "might construe their skepticism into an impeachment of his choice." When he offered to meet Etta's detractors on the drill field with sabers, open criticism of his engagement stopped, and he was granted two months' leave for his wedding and honeymoon.

Etta's detractors were not persuaded of her good breeding—she was a descendant of Capt. George Beckley, one of Kamehameha the Great's haole advisers and the first commander of the Fort of Honolulu. According to family history, he had designed the Hawaiian flag. Etta's Chinese blood, though it flowed from mandarin scholars, and her Hawaiian blood, though it flowed from a king, damned her.

But they could not deny her beauty: "Of all the Afong daughters, it is fair to say that Miss Etta is the prettiest," wrote a military correspondent. "Petite in form, she has the lustrous black eye, raven hair, regular feature and dazzling complexion which is eminently characteristic of the Spanish races. In her manner and personal appearance, there is nothing to indicate the Oriental blood which courses through her vein. When her charms both of person and of mind are considered in the light of the dreamy alluring climactic conditions of the land of her birth, it is not strange that in the estimation of the male persuasion she is easily the belle of the Islands."

On that December evening in 1893, the auditorium of the new "bluestone" Central Union Church on the corner of Beretania and Richards streets (Central Union's original site) overflowed with the elite of Hawai'i society and officers from the warships in port. The polished yellow Ohio birchwood pews, which could hold 750 people comfortably, now, by squeezing, accommodated more than a thousand. Guests who arrived late stood against the walls. The school grounds across Beretania Street, where the horsedrawn carriages were parked, was chock-full.

A block away, sandbags fortified 'Iolani Palace, where the Provisional Government planned to make a stand against U.S. Marines sent to restore Lili'uokalani to the throne. The Provisional Government's Citizen Guard sharpshooters had made sniper nests on buildings along the line of march the Marines would follow to the palace (the same route the Citizen Guardsmen had taken 11 months before to topple Lili'uokalani's government).

If any of those who entered the church sought sanctuary from Hawai'i's political tension of those last months, they were to be disappointed. Rabid royalists and radical annexationists were seated side by side under the great chandelier that hung from the center of the octagonal dome above the auditorium. Many guests chose to stare at the geometrical figures in the stained glass windows rather than look at the enemy next to them.

Citizen Guardsmen, mostly Americans, and annexationists all, boasted that they would repel an invasion by "foreign troops." The Hawai'i attorney general affirmed to his friends that the executive council of the Provisional Government was "determined to resist any attacks upon the government from whatever source."

Some of the men in the church may have been armed: "Guns and pistols have been placed in the hands of all who are willing to take them," reported Albert S. Willis, the U.S. minister to Hawai'i. He had made provision for Queen Lili'uokalani's safekeeping aboard a U.S. warship if the mob violence he expected broke out.

For the Whiting wedding, the front of the church auditorium was profusely decorated with roses from the gardens of the Afong Nu'uanu mansion, as well as ferns and vines gathered from farther up the valley at La'imi, where the Afongs' stone "cottage" was nestled under the fanlike branches of great trees.

In the center front pews were seated three of the bride's married sisters and their pro-annexationist husbands: Emmeline and John Alfred Magoon (he was to be rewarded with a judgeship after annexation); Nancy Luhana and Francis Blakely McStocker (as deputy collector of customs he had secretly organized the 500-member Citizen Guard six months earlier); and Julia Kamakia and Arthur Johnstone (in six months he would become editor of the radical annexationist organ *Hawaiian Star*).

To their left was seated the U.S. minister to Hawai'i, Albert S. Willis, under instructions from President Grover Cleveland to restore Queen Lili'uokalani through diplomacy, if possible. Seated beside him was Rear Adm. John Irwin, who was under orders to support Willis with his gunboats, if needed. With them were the commanders of two of the American warships. The bigger guns of the *Philadelphia* were under the command of the best man. On the opposite side of the auditorium were seated "other notable guests," men with whom the Naval officers were prepared to cross swords.

Earlier in the day, Minister Willis had received from the royalists the procedures to be followed upon restoration of the monarchy. The U.S. Naval commander, backed by Marines, would advise the Provisional Government to turn over the archives and government buildings, a royal proclamation would be read and loyal citizens would register and surrender their arms. With the queen securely on her throne, proceedings would be instituted to try the revolutionists for treason. The queen's insistence on the matter of punishment for the revolutionists troubled Willis.

At precisely eight o'clock, all conversation stopped as Agnes Judd, wife of the chief justice of the Supreme Court of the Provisional Government, sounded the first note of "The Wedding March" from Wagner's *Lohengrin*. The Boston-made organ, whose pipes filled the front of the church, was flanked by American flags.

Julia Fayerweather Afong, mother of the bride, was escorted to her seat in the center pew. Though thickened by the births of her 16 children, she moved with the grace of all Hawaiian women. "Mahalo," she said in a soft and melodious voice to the two American naval officers who attended her.

The congregation then turned as one toward the back of the church to watch the entrance of four ushers in full dress uniforms, officers who had served under the groom aboard the USS *Alliance*. They were followed by four bridesmaids, younger sisters of the bride—Marie and Bessie in pale pink Bengalese silk dresses and Helen and Carrie in white silk crepe. They carried bouquets of chrysanthemums tied with satin ribbons.

William Whiting, the groom, entered by the right aisle. He was a favorite of Queen Lili'uokalani and in 1874 had accompanied her brother, King Kalakaua, aboard the USS *Benicia* to the United States. William was attended by his best man, Capt. Albert S. Barker. They were distinguished-looking officers, despite the unkind description of the groom in the *San Francisco Call*. The publication said William Whiting was a "gray-haired, pompous, worldly-wise gentleman of years and experience" about to pluck "a pink-cheeked, almond-eyed bud."

Then came the bride, "magnificently arrayed in a white satin gown trimmed in real lace and having a full court train," reported the local papers. "From headdress of orange blossoms with diamond ornaments fell the usual bridal veil of gossamery texture." Etta was on the arm of Chief Justice Judd, who was to give her away. Her father, the wealthy merchant Chun Afong, had returned to his native China three years before. For a time people expected that he would return to Hawai'i, but now they were convinced that he had decided to remain in China with his beautiful Chinese wife, Lee Hong, who had borne him three children. He had also fathered a child with a concubine.

The Rev. Dr. E. G. Beckwith stepped forward. His aquiline nose stood in sharp contrast to the curly white hair of his beard, which gave his face a crumpled look. On January 17, 1893, he had been a member of the committee that had notified Queen Lili'uokalani that she had been deposed, and not everyone who now listened to him begin the marriage ritual had forgiven him for that act.

Though Etta was a Congregationalist, the ceremony was Anglican, in deference to the groom, whose brother was the Episcopal bishop of Mississippi. Ironically, Bishop Whiting could not have performed his brother's wedding ceremony in Mississippi. There, the marriage of a white to a "Mongolian" was illegal.

The ceremony ended when Rev. Beckwith, a warm smile on his thin lips and a twinkle in his kindly eyes, instructed the groom to begin his married life "in the good old-fashioned way—by kissing the bride."

To Mendelssohn's "Wedding March," the newlyweds exited the church through the double koa doors, descended the 12 steps cut from Chinese granite, and crossed a carpet laid from the church steps to their elegant carriage.

The reception was held at the Afong Nu'uanu home, where a large canvas lanai, "gay with flags, flowers and vines," had been erected at the School Street side of the house to accommodate the wedding party. There, Sanford B. Dole, president of the Provisional Government, and his wife, along with Minister and Mrs. Willis, Adm. and Mrs. Irwin, plus members of the cabinet and the diplomatic and consular corps, were shown to "tête-à-tête tables." The U.S. consul general for Hawai'i, Ellis Mills, searched the gardens illuminated by the "fairylike light" of Japanese lanterns for the bride's sister, Marie Afong, with whom, it was whispered, he had developed "a romantic attachment."

"A number of naval officers lingered to bestow a volley of rice on the gallant commander and his bride as they took their departure for their temporary honeymoon quarters at Waikiki," reported the *Bulletin*.

The couple stayed at the Afong beach house, located in a lovely coconut grove, and in the morning looked out across the bright beach to a sparkling sea that rushed in to momentarily stain the white sand. William's colleagues at the Naval War College already had their eye on this land and the adjacent property and would later condemn the three-plus-acre site for coastal defense batteries. The Americans would name the place Fort DeRussy.

On Saturday, the newlyweds boarded the SS *Australia* for a honeymoon cruise to San Francisco. They found their cabin was "a bed of tropical flowers and evergreens." As the steamer moved out of the harbor, Etta and William threw kisses and flowers to their friends on shore.

Once in San Francisco, the couple kept to the privacy of their room at the Occidental Hotel until they boarded their train for New York City. There, the *Times* reporter complained, "The commander and his bride kept closely to their rooms all day. [They] received no callers." And with an almost audible sigh, he concluded his report, "She would command attention in a roomful of beauties."

When the honeymoon was over, the Whitings faced the reality of shore duty at Pensacola, Florida, where, it was reported, the "color line is strongly drawn and Mrs. Whiting's brunette charms of blended Hawaiian and Chinese tints were not admired."

After 2½ miserable years at Pensacola, brightened only by the birth of their only child, a daughter, Whiting was posted to Puget Sound, where there was less racial tension. After a year, he was promoted to commander and made captain of the *Monadnock*, a rebuilt Civil War monitor. In June 1898, amidst talk that Hawai'i would be annexed to the United States by presidential proclamation, a press dispatch from Washington stated that the *Monadnock* was ordered to steam to Hawai'i, where Capt. Whiting would haul down the Hawaiian flag (designed by his wife's great-grandfather) and raise Old Glory.

The newspaper report turned out to be nothing more than a trial balloon. A year earlier, Teddy Roosevelt, who was then secretary of the Navy, had told Adm. Mahan of the Naval War College that he would send a monitor to Hawai'i "and would hoist our flag over the island, leaving all details for after action."

Whiting instead was ordered to sail his monitor to Manila to join Adm. Dewey. On July 3, 1898, he put in at Honolulu to coal and repair the ship's machinery. Built in 1864, rebuilt in 1883, and finally commissioned in 1896, the *Monadnock* was not designed for long sea voyages. The *Hawaiian Star* reported: "On the trip down it was found that with everything closed above as was necessary at sea, the deck being so close to the water, the quarters where the engineers and firemen worked were so hot as greatly to exhaust the men." At his Honolulu stopover, Cmdr. Whiting immediately initiated work to better ventilate the engine and boiler rooms.

When U.S. Minister Sewall learned that Whiting would not immediately depart for Manila after refueling, Sewall sent a confidential dispatch to the secretary of state, with a copy to the Navy Department, that said, "It had been intimated to [Whiting] before leaving San Francisco that if he remained [in Hawai'i] long, it might not be necessary for him to proceed further."

Just before noon on July 13, 10 days after his arrival in Honolulu, Whiting pointed the bow of his monitor toward Manila. He was out of sight of land when Hawai'i learned that it had been annexed to the United States. U.S. Minister Sewall was applauded when he appeared on the streets of Honolulu that day, and was soon boosted as the choice of the local American Union Party for governor of the new American territory.

Though Cmdr. Whiting's brother-in-law, F. B. McStocker of the Citizen Guard, was a leader of the American Union Party, Sewall pressed his condemnation of Whiting. And despite the *Star* report that Whiting's men had worked "night and day" to make the needed changes to the ship "before it would be prudent to start on a long voyage to Manila," Sewall reported to his superiors: "I am confirmed in the opinion that his delay was unnecessary."

Whiting's enemies seized this opportunity to discredit the officer who had broken the all-white color code of the Navy. In October 1898, Whiting was hauled before a Naval court to answer charges of delaying at Honolulu to visit his Asiatic relatives. The court found no cause for action, and, in December, Whiting was given a letter of commendation for his good judgment and skillful seamanship in sailing a monitor across the Pacific Ocean.

Despite the prediction that he would be driven out of the Navy if he married a woman whose blood was "tainted with that of the Mongolian and kanaka," Whiting had a distinguished naval career as commander of the *Charleston*, *Boston*, and *Independence*. He also served as commandant of Pearl Harbor from 1902 to 1903, after which he was promoted to rear admiral and named commandant of the naval training station at Treasure Island in San Francisco Bay. He retired in 1905, and for the next 20 years he and Etta resided in Berkeley, California, where he died on July 26, 1925, at age 82.

Later, Etta married an old friend, Adm. Ammen Farenholt, a fleet surgeon and Naval historian. There was no adverse comment on their vows; William and Etta had forever destroyed the Naval taboo against mixed marriages. Etta, at 79, died on Feb. 11, 1950, in San Diego.

# V

♦

*Pearl Harbor and War in the Pacific*

# Death in the Depths:
## The F-4 Tragedy

### PETER F. STEVENS

*All eyes stared at the waters below, the waters of
Honolulu Harbor's fairway. Tensely, the men waited.
Suddenly, a twisted mass of metal broke the surface
and bobbed between huge pontoons that held the
wreckage from slipping back into the roiling depths.
In the debris—the crushed hull of what had once
been a submarine—21 men were entombed.
After five months on the bottom of the Pacific,
the crew of the F-4 was coming home.*

◆ On the morning of March 25, 1915, Honolulu's municipal piers rang with officers' shouts and the thumps of sailors' feet against metal hull plates. The four submarines of the First Submarine Division of the Pacific Fleet were about to put to sea, as they had three times a week since their arrival in Honolulu in August 1914.

As the 20 crewmen of the F-4 went about their tasks, the submarine's 27-year-old commander, Lt. j.g. Alfred L. Ede, probably had a lot on his mind. He had reason for concern: In early March an explosion, reportedly in the battery deck, had rocked the F-4, hurling men and debris throughout the 142-foot craft. Luckily, no one was seriously hurt. But the crew was uneasy, one sailor noting that since the sub's arrival in Hawai'i, one thing after another had gone wrong.

---

First published November 1990.

At 9 a.m., one by one the submarines slipped from their berths, eased between the ships clotting the fairway of Honolulu Harbor, and churned toward the open sea.

The F-4 cruised to a spot about a mile and a half south of the harbor. Crewmen securely closed the conning tower's double doors, and from the control room amidships, Ede gave the order to dive. The sub slipped beneath the beautiful blue-green waters. One hundred twenty battery cells, powered by two 310-horsepower engines and housed in the bottom of the hull, pushed the F-4 deeper. Bubbles frothing on the surface were the only visible evidence that moments before, a submarine had rested atop the waves.

By 10 a.m., the other three submarines bobbed alongside their berths at the municipal pier. The F-4's berth was empty, yet there was little concern, as Ede and his vessel were due in the fairway at any moment.

But as the hours passed and the F-4 was nowhere in sight, the first traces of anxiety gripped the men of the submarine flotilla. Around 3 p.m., Lt. Charles Smith, commander of the unit, hoping that the missing submarine had merely experienced a mechanical problem and was in need of a tow back to base, sent out a search party of motor launches. The launches spotted huge oil bubbles in the waters where the F-4 had slipped beneath the surface.

The oil was no cause for alarm, as Ede might have tried blowing oil from the tanks to lighten the submarine in an attempt to resurface. If that were the case, the vessel, whose underwater breathing apparatus could function for a week, could be raised by salvage ships.

Alerted to the crisis, Rear Adm. Charles B. Moore, commander of the Honolulu Naval Station, late in the afternoon ordered the submarine tender *Alert*, the Naval tug *Navajo*, and the F-4's sister subs to join the launches near the harbor entrance. The tug and the tender dragged cables through the deep waters, hoping to locate the F-4 in order to run the cables beneath the stricken submarine's hull in preparation for lifting her to the surface. (The *Alert* carried hoisting slips to attach to the heavy lifting shackles that were on the upper hull of all F-class submarines.) The submarine flotilla's crack deep-sea divers, G. B. Evans and Jack Agraz, slipped on their heavy helmets and descended to depths unprecedented in local annals; when Evans was hauled back from a depth of 185 feet and Agraz from 196, they were prostrate from the pressure their bodies had endured.

## Death in the Depths

The search grew more intense as darkness fell and underwater signals to the F-4 went unanswered. Rumors of disaster at the harbor's mouth spread from the piers into Honolulu, and hordes of citizens jammed the waterfront, staring solemnly at the distant lights of the search ships.

As dawn broke across the Islands on March 26, the bleary-eyed sailors of the search team continued to drag the waters outside the harbor. Hopes that the men of the F-4 were still alive ebbed with each passing hour; in diving tests, the hulls of F-class submarines had groaned and creaked from the pressure at 283 feet, and the waters where the F-4 had disappeared were more than 300 feet deep.

Meanwhile, the news of the drama unfolding in the waters off Honolulu had begun to spread across the Pacific. As newspaper readers from San Francisco to New York City pored over the first front-page accounts of the F-4's plight, fear for the trapped crewmen and sympathy for the men's families stirred the entire nation. President Woodrow Wilson expressed his concern and prayers for the men of the lost submarine.

While America awaited further news that day, rescue crews carried on their exhausting work. Morning gave way to midafternoon. Suddenly, one of the search cables pulled taut. It had snagged a bulky object in 305 feet of water.

The *Navajo* and a steamship lowered hooks to the object, caught it, lifted it slightly, and tried towing it slowly toward the harbor. Oil bubbles broke the surface again. The object was too heavy. Rescuers feared that if the find was the F-4, her metal hull may have sprung leaks from the pressure below and had flooded. They summoned a derrick and a crane from Pearl Harbor to help raise the object.

Although resuscitation equipment stood ready on the decks of the search ships, the crews sensed that Ede and his men would not need it. A Navy spokesman confirmed on the night of March 26 that any realistic hope of finding the F-4's crew alive was gone. Twenty-one men lay in a metal coffin on the bottom of the Pacific; and the Navy, already besieged by the public's outcry for answers, knew that the ill-fated submarine would have to be raised no matter how long the salvage operation took.

On March 27, the rescue ships tried time and again to raise the object—which had still not been confirmed as the F-4. To the frustration of the crews, chain loops repeatedly slipped off the object. Then the powerful dredger *California*, sent out from Pearl Harbor, succeeded in dragging a loop beneath the object; hopes rose as the chain gripped the mass beneath the waves. Slowly, a powerful winch began tugging at the object. The loop taut, the object stirred from the ocean bottom and rose 50 feet.

With sickening suddenness, the huge loop went slack. The object plunged back to the bottom. A rush of air bubbles broke the surface, indicating that the object was filling with water. Not only were the last fleeting hopes for the crew of the F-4 vanishing—if the object was indeed the submarine—but also any hopes for a quick salvage of the doomed vessel. Raising a water-logged craft from a depth of 305 feet would require a salvage operation unprecedented in maritime history.

Despite the endless setbacks of the rescue effort, the families of the F-4's crew clung to the hope that some of the men were alive. The relatives' anguish, detailed each day in America's newspapers, haunted readers' thoughts; but the people of Honolulu experienced a keener grief, sharing the sorrow of friends and neighbors reeling from "the agony the dark waters were concealing."

The search for the submarine continued. At one point, grappling hooks snared a heavy object, and the discovery was towed to shallower water. Agraz and Evans slithered down the cables, expecting to find the F-4 in the hooks' grasp. Evans found nothing at the end of one cable, and at a depth of 215 feet—a local diving record—Agraz met equal disappointment: The cable held a huge anchor.

Another object, resting about a mile and a half southwest of the lighthouse at Honolulu Harbor's entrance, was found on the evening of March 28. With the *California*'s chains clutching the object, several pieces of the F-4's superstructure were raised to the surface. On March 29, Moore confirmed: "We know the location of the F-4."

Knowing where the F-4 lay on the ocean floor and raising the ill-fated vessel were two entirely different matters. Day and night the salvage ships tried to move the water-logged submarine inshore, but the cables would invariably slip from the F-4's hull. Every time the submarine plunged back to the bottom, the chances increased that the F-4's hull would shatter piecemeal and prevent the salvage team from ever raising the vessel.

The salvage fleet received reinforcements on April 12, when the old armored cruiser *Maryland* docked at Honolulu. Aboard the cruiser was a crack team of deep-sea divers from the New York Navy Yard: Chief

## Death in the Depths

Gunner George D. Stillson, the unit's leader; Chief Gunner's Mates Frank Crilley, W. F. Loughman, and F. C. E. Neilson; and Chief Gunner's Mate S. J. Drellishak, who owned the world's diving record—274 feet.

Before Stillson and his men ventured into the waters imprisoning the F-4, they had to undergo dangerous tests designed to answer the question: Could a man descend 305 feet without succumbing to a diver's worst nightmare, the bends? In a huge steel tank placed on a dock, the divers subjected their bodies to the crushing water pressure at 305 feet. They emerged from the tank in good shape but were well aware that in the depths in which the F-4 lay, there awaited them any number of dangers that no tank could simulate.

Two days after the tests, Stillson's team, encased in cumbersome metal helmets and bulky diving suits, began diving into the waters imprisoning the submarine. They hoped to fasten lifting hooks to the F-4's hull. An Army dredger, two 600-ton mud scows, several barges, and other ships stood ready to begin salvage efforts if the divers reached the submarine. The divers relied upon the telephones in their helmets to maintain contact with the fleet, but if the men's air hoses failed, no telephone SOS would be able to save them from a violent, agonizing death.

The underwater team became the first humans to reach the submarine since her disappearance. During the third week of April, the divers attached the hooks to the F-4, and slowly the salvage fleet's "donkey" engines and powerful winches lifted the submarine high enough from the Pacific floor to nudge the vessel, still hidden far below the surface, shoreward. The ships and divers repeated the process each day until April 17, when the F-4 lay at a depth of 275 feet.

The operation began as usual that day. Loughman, having made a successful descent to the submarine, had started his ascent when, suddenly, his voice crackled into the telephone. His descending line had tangled tightly around a cable, trapping him 220 feet below the surface. How long a man could survive at such a depth was unknown.

George Crilley plunged to his fellow diver's side. Maintaining his composure in the desperate struggle, ignoring the peril to his own life, he grappled with the twisted lines. Minutes that seemed an eternity stretched into hours. Loughman slipped into unconsciousness as the line and cable squeezed his body in a viselike grip. For all Crilley knew, he was working on a dead man.

Four grueling hours later, Crilley finally freed his fellow diver. A doctor sprang into action as soon as Loughman's inert form was hauled to the surface. Crilley, exhausted by his torturous work, soon learned that his determination had paid off: Although Loughman had suffered severe head, shoulder, and chest injuries, he would survive. Crilley was later awarded a Medal of Honor for his heroic feat in the depths off Honolulu.

Although Loughman's ordeal underscored the dangers confronting the underwater operation, the divers and the crews of the salvage flotilla continued to perform their arduous tasks. As the months passed and the people of Honolulu went about their lives, the daily sight of the salvage ships working in the fairway continued to jar the city's—and the nation's—collective psyche.

The final phase of the salvage operation unfolded in late August 1915, when the F-4 sat in 60 feet of water. Fearing that further use of cables to lift the submarine, whose water-logged weight was about 250 tons, would split the battered hull into several pieces, the Navy decided to raise the F-4 with giant pontoons. The chances of success were anyone's guess, for in the history of underwater salvage, no one had ever used pontoons for such an imposing task.

Eight 60-ton-lift pontoons were built at the Mare Island Navy Yard and loaded aboard the *Maryland*. When the armored cruiser, its deck virtually hidden by the massive pontoons, reached the spot where the F-4 rested, tension and anticipation swept the men of the salvage flotilla. They sensed that the climax of the grueling five-month operation was at hand.

On the evening of August 29, a rumor that the F-4 had been raised spread from the Honolulu docks to the rest of the city. Rumor turned into fact as a twisted mass of metal held on the surface by the pontoons was towed to the Quarantine Station in Honolulu Harbor. The F-4 was coming home.

Faced with the American public's outcry for answers to the F-4 tragedy, the Navy lost little time in launching an investigation. As the search for clues in the silt-filled wreckage of the F-4 took place on the dry dock at Pearl Harbor, workers found the remains of six crewmen in the submarine's control room and 12 in the engine room. Fourteen of the bodies would be buried in Arlington National Cemetery.

The Navy Board of Investigation's efforts produced a 75,000-page report. Although the exact cause of the tragedy was not pinpointed, the examiners believed that the probable cause of the F-4's fate was a

## Death in the Depths

corroded steel plate, reportedly caused by sulfuric battery acid that had leaked through the protective lead coating of the forward battery tank of the F-4's hull; the acid-weakened rivets and steel of the plate, part of the top of the forward ballast tank, had likely allowed seawater to flood the submarine as pressure had increased during the F-4's fateful dive. One source suggested that once the water hit the battery compartment, deadly chlorine gas had probably formed and caused an explosion; a lighthouse keeper stationed near the entrance of Honolulu Harbor reported hearing an explosion moments after the F-4 had disappeared.

The F-4 investigation uncovered many alarming facts about America's submarines. All F-class submarines were found to have glaring defects: erratic performance by the engines; faulty battery linings allowing seawater to leak into the battery deck; the ever present threat of even small amounts of seawater producing fatal chlorine gas; and a litany of other potential problems. The investigators' preliminary report, sent to Secretary of the Navy Josephus Daniels within days of the raising of the F-4, also suggested that all F-class submarines were "in a dangerous condition for use on long dives."

Scarcely before the Navy's chilling assessment of the F-class submarines' flaws had made headlines throughout the nation, a steamer, the *Supply*, rammed the F-4's three sister ships. The submarines were heavily damaged and towed to dry dock. The ill-fated submarines were soon removed from active service, and the Navy, determined that brave seamen would never again slip beneath the waves in faulty submarines, quickly began seeking improvements in submarine construction and performance.

The F-4 tragedy soon became a historical footnote, eclipsed by the nation's entry into World War I. The wreckage of the F-4 was towed to a spot in Pearl Harbor, resunk, and forgotten.

Today, the twisted hull of the F-4 still rests on the harbor floor. Not far from the little submarine's grave, the USS *Arizona* Memorial honors the men killed aboard the battlewagon on December 7, 1941. But no memorial honors the victims of America's first submarine disaster, the sinking of the F-4.

# Pearl Harbor Reopened:
## The "Seaman Z" Story

### EDWARD OXFORD

*December 7, 1941. President Franklin D. Roosevelt was to call it, rightly, "a date which will live in infamy." And those who witnessed the havoc wrought at Pearl Harbor that Sunday morning would never forget it.*

The Japanese planes appeared without warning. At 7:53 a.m. the Japanese flight commander radioed "Tora! Tora! Tora!," the repeated code word for "tiger," indicating: "We have succeeded in surprise attack."

Two minutes later, the first wave—183 fighters, high-level bombers, dive bombers, and torpedo bombers, their rising sun emblems bright against the sky—roared in over the western half of Oahu. They hammered Battleship Row, Hickham Field, Wheeler Field.

It was a time of chaos, with no respite.

At 8:55 a.m. the second wave—171 fighters, high-level bombers, and dive bombers—swept in over Oahu's eastern reaches, smashing ships and harbor installations at will.

By midmorning, Pearl Harbor lay in smoke and ruins. The swarming planes disappeared, headed back to the carrier fleet that had borne them in secrecy across the Pacific. In a single stroke, Japan had devastated half of the U.S. Pacific fleet.

The roll call of ship losses bore grim testament to the fury of the

---

First published November 1984.

*attack. Eight battleships, three light cruisers, three destroyers, and four auxiliary craft had been sunk or damaged. One hundred and eighty-eight planes had been destroyed. And, most bitter of all, was the human cost—more than 2,400 sailors, Marines, soldiers, and civilians killed, and some 1,170 wounded.*

*Bewildered, enraged, resolute, the nation was galvanized by the smashing attack. Pearl Harbor became an instant call to colors.*

*America, its course clear, would take up arms against the Axis. Ironically, by unleashing the retaliatory might of America, the 110-minute attack had sealed the enemy's doom. With America in the war, the Allies would be certain of victory. Such was the scenario that became reality, over the four years of World War II that ensued.*

*But history has left some loose ends. Even after four decades, Pearl Harbor poses a tantalizing question. Did American leaders know beforehand of the impending Japanese attack?*

*The recollections of a former member of U.S. Naval Intelligence lend weight to the contention that indeed they did.*

✦ A reticent, even mysterious figure, this man was referred to simply as "Seaman Z" in John Toland's book about Pearl Harbor, *Infamy*, published two years ago [1982]. That brief mention induced the National Security Agency to reveal, last fall, that "Seaman Z" was, in fact, one Robert Danforth Ogg, a retired businessman living quietly in California.

Since World War II, Ogg had gone on to attain considerable success—as electronics expert, marine engineer, inventor, company chairman. But, through all the years, unspoken memories—particularly of the days just before the Pearl Harbor attack—troubled him. As time went by, he found himself in a dilemma. He knew "something" of which he did not wish to speak but of which history needed, sooner or later, to hear.

Probably better than most Americans, Robert Ogg realized that as historians tried to solve the Pearl Harbor "puzzle," they would be beset by conflicting testimony, elusive files, and time's passage.

Also, it became clear to him that he was one of the few surviving members of the U.S. Naval Intelligence community who had taken part in America's efforts to scan the Pacific in late November and early December 1941.

It was for these reasons that Ogg granted the author of this article

## Pearl Harbor Reopened

the opportunity to visit with him at his mountaintop home. There, amid the memorabilia—charts, photographs, diagrams—of a war long since over yet well remembered, a closely kept tale unfolded.

By late November 1941, the die had been cast. Japan's Kido Butai ("strike force") was gathered in an isolated bay in the Kurile Islands.

U.S. Naval intelligence reports revealed no sure sign of the main Japanese carrier force. The dangerous carriers were, for all practical purposes, "off the map."

To misdirect the "ears" of U.S. Navy radio listening outposts located in Alaska, Hawaii, and at points on the West Coast, the Japanese moved transmitters from ship to ship, switched radio operators around, changed radio frequencies, and repeated old messages. This enabled their task force to appear to be in the Inland Sea, but in fact to be on the high seas.

Undetected, on the cloudy morning of November 26, the 31-ship Japanese attack force sailed out into the North Pacific—bound for Hawaii. The six carriers sailed in two parallel columns, each column followed by four tankers. Two battleships and two heavy cruisers took guard positions, with the whole group encircled by a screen of nine destroyers and a light cruiser. Three submarines formed a lead-point 200 miles ahead of the strike force. Kido Butai moved eastward at 15 knots—aiming toward its first designated standby point, where the warships would refuel.

Meanwhile, at Twelfth Naval District Headquarters in San Francisco, Seaman First Class Robert Ogg, a lean, soft-spoken 23-year-old, continued to go about his rather unusual duties.

A brilliant student at the Berkeley campus of the University of California, Ogg had been recruited by the Navy to take on an assignment "of importance to the nation." His knowledge of electronics, radio, and navigation would serve him well in the James Bond–type work the Navy had in mind.

Along with a few select confederates, Ogg was assigned to the district's Naval Intelligence nerve center—several offices located behind double-locked doors on the seventh floor of 717 Market Street.

These Navy undercover experts wore civilian clothes rather than uniforms. They didn't turn out for daily muster. True to counterespionage tradition, they carried no identification cards. "If we were to be apprehended during a surreptitious job," Ogg explains, "we didn't know the Navy and the Navy didn't know us. It was that simple."

Seaman Ogg reported to Lt. Ellsworth Hosmer, a Navy veteran of

World War I who had been called back to service as America's relations with Germany and Japan became increasingly strained.

An intense intelligence officer, Hosmer put in long hours in the seventh floor inner sanctum—poring over bits and pieces of paper, searching through intercepts of Japanese messages for telltale signs that might presage war.

Hosmer kept Ogg busy. The "invisible" seaman—along with an assistant or two—was dispatched to tap the telephone lines of suspected Japanese espionage agents in various apartments and hotels throughout San Francisco. He also secreted microphones in the residences of Japanese agents. One delicate job involved bugging the Japanese Consulate itself.

Ogg also helped monitor incoming and outgoing trans-Pacific telephone calls. In round-the-clock shifts, Ogg and his cohorts recorded the conversations on large discs at the AT&T Long Lines overseas building near San Francisco's Chinatown.

Back at the Market Street intelligence center, U.S. Navy translators analyzed the taps and recordings.

Speculation was rife. How were the Japanese reacting to the oil embargo President Roosevelt had invoked against them? Could the ongoing Washington-Tokyo negotiations forestall a major conflict? If trouble were to come, where would it strike—the Philippines, the Dutch East Indies, Malaya, or someplace else? And, significantly, where were those missing Japanese aircraft carriers?

"At one point, about 2 in the morning, along with a couple of other intelligence people, Hosmer and I found ourselves in a warehouse on the San Francisco waterfront," Ogg relates. "Something like $25,000 in cash had been turned over to a radioman who served aboard a Japanese merchant ship. He had the Japanese Naval Reserve code book with him. We photographed it page by page, right there in the warehouse. Then one of our Intelligence people brought the film by plane to Washington."

Ogg remembers another intriguing incident: "Not long before the Pearl Harbor attack, we had word that a Japanese merchant vessel was to enter the Panama Canal loaded with explosives. Once in the canal, it was to be blown up by the Japanese, thus blocking the passageway. But the Navy stopped that ship and turned it around. So we knew the Japanese were on the prowl."

On Tuesday, December 2, Hosmer and Ogg took part in some very disturbing events. It began as most other days, with Ogg letting himself into intelligence headquarters through a back-alley entrance. But the day would change his life.

Ogg tries to reconstruct the scene: "That morning, Hosmer came out of his office. He was grim faced. He read some bearings to me from a scrap of paper and told me to mark them on the chart."

Ogg hunched over a big table, and worked out the longitude and latitude on a two-foot-by-four-foot great-circle chart of the Pacific. He roughed out the location—an area east of the international date line, thousands of miles from Japan.

"Hosmer was stunned," Ogg explains. "He had just gotten the bearings from one of the commercial radio services—Press Wireless, Globe Wireless, RCA, one of those. Their radio operators on the West Coast had picked up low-frequency signals coming from a place in the Pacific where no ships were known to be. They told us about it because the signals had to be coming from an area east of the international date line. Maybe—and here we kind of frowned—maybe they were signals between ships, out there in the middle of nowhere."

The operators gauged the signals as being at a "whispering" frequency. It was only because of "skip-distances"—the signals bouncing off atmospheric layers and spanning outward—that the operators could detect them in the first place. What had been picked up were not voices but radio signals in code. And, Hosmer was convinced, the code patterns were Japanese.

Hosmer sketched a version of the big chart on a small sheet of white paper, marked the signal area, and pinned the paper to a wall. He and Ogg pondered the dot. What did it mean? Ships? Whose? How many? What kind? And—where were they headed?

For Ogg, the mood of that day remains vivid: "We were worried. We really weren't sure what we had. As I was later to learn, Hosmer did the smartest thing he could do. He hurried to the office of Capt. Richard McCullough, down at the end of our floor. The captain was our intelligence chief. But he was something more than that."

McCullough, it turned out, was rather like The Washington Connection. A graduate of the U.S. Naval Academy, a decorated Navy veteran of World War I, he, too, had been called back from civilian life to serve his nation in newly troubled times. But something in his past made him special, even among the cloak-and-dagger types who made up the Market Street "irregulars." Years before, McCullough had come to the attention of Franklin D. Roosevelt when Roosevelt served as assistant secretary of the Navy. He had, indeed, become and remained something of a Roosevelt confidant. And he would go on to become a rear admiral.

"That was our tie to Washington," declares Ogg. "McCullough sensed the importance of the mysterious signals. And so, as he told me numerous times later, McCullough informed the White House as to what we had discovered. And by the White House he meant both Harry Hopkins, the president's personal adviser, and President Roosevelt himself. He did so by telephone using a special line. There's no doubt in my mind that he did just that. The White House knew what we knew."

But what did they know? At this time all they "had" was a pencil mark on a piece of paper.

The next day, December 3, it happened all over again. Hosmer once more came into the chart room. The commercial radio operators had heard new signals. Hosmer gave the bearings to Ogg, who meticulously plotted their position. He marked the new point. To their consternation, it fell considerably east of the previous day's position. Whatever the source of the signals, it was now northwest of Hawaii.

Alarmed, Hosmer again notified Capt. McCullough. And McCullough again informed the White House.

They now had two dots.

Remarkably enough, the Hosmer-Ogg-McCullough threesome was dealing with the signals on its own initiative, quite apart from the Navy's far-flung listening posts. To what extent the Navy's in-place "net" was picking up such signals—and what the outposts were doing about them—Ogg was never able to discover. The driven group at 717 Market Street simply pursued the signals as they would any intelligence—"for the sake of the nation." (During the war, Ogg was to come across a U.S. Navy officer who had been at a listening post in Alaska in the days before the Pearl Harbor attack. The officer told Ogg of his post's picking up similar signals.)

"Thinking back," Ogg now says, "the signals at first seemed impossible. An attack fleet would almost certainly keep strict radio silence. But the war was to see many impossibilities—cases where commanders said one thing and the people being commanded did another. There was also the matter of stormy seas—you'd almost have to use radio to communicate, ship to ship. And the Japanese fleet hit rough weather on its way to Hawaii."

## Pearl Harbor Reopened

Through the years, Ogg has come up with yet another explanation that seems to fit: "The Japanese oil tankers, the ones refueling the warships from time to time—they had merchant crews, not navy crews. The civilian sailors might well have been more lax than the Japanese navy men. That would account for the signals that were detected."

Ogg has no hour-by-hour memory of December 4 or 5. He kept no diaries. His intelligence unit committed little to paper. But he does feel that, at least once in that 48-hour period, signals had again been detected. Hosmer so informed McCullough, who in turn informed the White House.

What if it *were* an attack force? Would Washington take measures to warn the Hawaiian defenders?

"It was perplexing," Ogg says. "But the more Hosmer and I talked about it, the more we felt confident. Perhaps Washington would interdict the oncoming fleet, simply turn it away. Or, if an attack were to be launched against the Hawaiian Islands, we felt sure the Navy could handle the situation. At worst, it would be a glancing blow, and the Navy would inflict terrible retribution.

"That line, dot to dot, had a hypnotic effect on us. It's all we thought about. All we talked about."

It was like the moving finger, the writing on the wall, in the Old Testament. Each day, that line had traveled eastward. Whatever it was, it was heading right toward Hawaii.

Saturday, December 6. Something had to give. The mysterious signals were heard again. A careworn Hosmer brought them to Ogg.

The seaman, tired from long duty hours, plotted the latest advance of the line. The new dot indicated a position about 500 miles north of the Hawaiian Islands. Hosmer conferred with McCullough, who once more alerted Washington.

Ogg recalls: "It was on my mind more than ever. After duty, I went to Hosmer's home and we talked about the situation. In my mother's diary there's a one-line entry for December 6. It reads: 'Went with Bob. Something about radio.' Hosmer and I hoped that, somehow, Washington would make some countermove. We still felt that the situation—whatever the situation might be—was well in hand. But I spent a restless night."

Sunday, December 7. Seaman Ogg reported early and made his way to the barred room on the seventh floor of 717 Market Street. Midmorn-

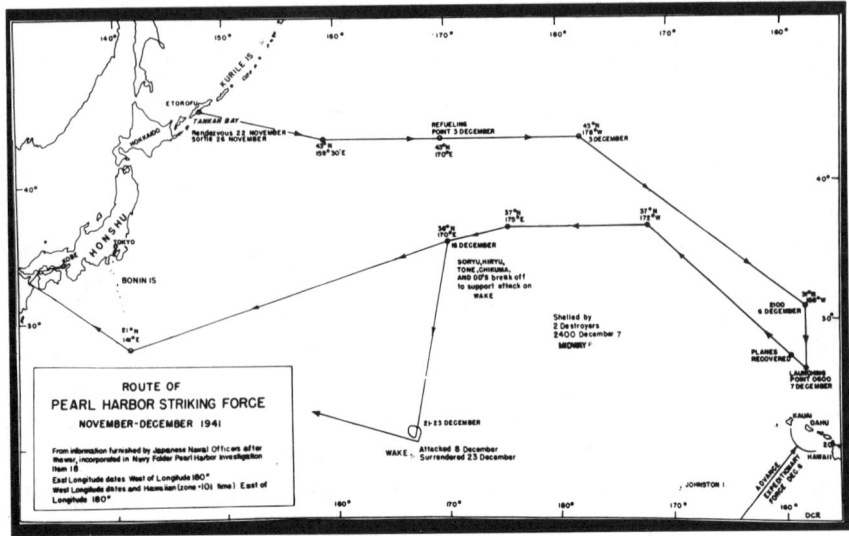

The route of the Pearl Harbor striking force, November–December 1941. From information furnished by Japanese naval officers after the war, incorporated in Navy Folder Pearl Harbor Investigation Item 18. East longitude dates west of longitude 180°. West longitude dates and Hawaiian (Zone +10½ time) east of longitude 180°. Drawing by David C. Redding for *The Rising Sun in the Pacific*, courtesy of the Naval Historical Center.

ing, word was received of the attack on Pearl Harbor. Ogg remembers calling Hosmer at home. "I just said to him, 'Al, it happened.'"

Robert Ogg, now in his mid-60s, still lean and limber, sits against a backdrop of shelves lined with books of science and of the sea. He looks out onto a lush valley. He thinks back upon Pearl Harbor with a sense of sadness.

Ogg recounts his Market Street experiences, not to diminish the reputation of President Roosevelt, "whom I consider a magnificent leader," but rather to "add my light" to the complex, controversial, and seemingly still-changing story of Pearl Harbor.

For Ogg, there is a touch of loneliness, thinking back upon these unforgettable days. "Whenever I pass the 717 Market Street building, I can remember the way it was," he says. "Of course, many of those I knew then are gone. Hosmer died about seven years ago and lies in a military cemetery in Tennessee. McCullough passed away in a naval hospital nearly 20 years ago. And President Roosevelt didn't even live to see the end of the war."

He explains what he thinks about the attack: "It's hard for me to believe that the White House—the president—didn't know about the forthcoming attack. There's evidence that warnings came from a number of sources. God knows, our intelligence unit at 12th Naval did our best with those signals."

He stares at a nearby globe, at the blue of the Pacific.

"To this day, there is no way for me to know how Washington took our warnings," he says. "All I can attest to is that we told them what we knew—day by day." There were other, earlier, indications of Japanese intentions. From the early 1930s, graduating classes at Japan's naval academy were asked on their final exam, "How would you carry out a surprise attack on Pearl Harbor?" In 1932, a U.S. carrier force on a fleet exercise showed how: Strike from north of Oahu at dawn.

Ogg, in company with a number of scholars and historians, feels that there was a Roosevelt strategy, and that it had a well-meant point: "From what I can see of the grand design, I think Roosevelt wanted an incident that would unify the nation. Maybe the way to get the people to unite—and save Europe—was to have a *Lusitania* incident, the kind of attack that brought America into World War I. He was sure our forces were well positioned to absorb and counter the blow."

But the blow struck by the Japanese was "a terrible one. Much more damaging than any of us, including the president himself, could have imagined it would be."

In his study, Ogg peers out the window. "It is easy to understand FDR's confidence. The Navy was his heart. And it was mine, too."

# The Battle of Niihau

BRIAN NICOL

◆ Two fighter planes circled low over the tiny Hawaiian island of Niihau. Black smoke streamed from one sputtering engine. The residents of Niihau, most of them on their way to church at Puuwai Village, watched the two planes buzz their small hamlet then head north out over the ocean. The villagers had noticed and recognized the rising sun insignia on the fighters' wings, but they had no knowledge of the events taking place in Honolulu on the island of Oahu, nearly 150 miles to the southeast. The people of this isolated isle continued their trek to church, curious about the two airplanes but never guessing that on this beautiful, quiet Sunday, December 7, 1941, the Battle of Niihau was about to begin.

The Eliza Sinclair family purchased these 73 square miles of kiawe bushes, grassland, and volcanic rock from King Kamehameha V in 1864. The Sinclairs, sheep ranchers from New Zealand, paid $10,000 for the entire island. Since that time the Robinson family, descendants of Sinclair, have kept the isle and its two or three hundred Hawaiian residents isolated from the complexities and disruptions of the modern world. Unauthorized visits to this "Forbidden Island" are strictly kapu. The Niihauans live a simple life of cattle and sheep ranching. They speak a relatively pure strain of Hawaiian that is closer in some respects to Tahitian—the origin of the Hawaiian tongue. They appreciate and treasure the privacy the Robinson family has afforded them. In the 1959 statehood plebiscite, Niihau was the only one of Hawaii's 240 districts to vote "no."

During the days of late 1941, the island didn't possess even a simple radio for contact with the outside world. Only Aylmer Robinson, arriving every Monday in his supply sampan from his Kauai estate, brought

---

First published November 1979.

any news. The United States Army had apprised the 180 Niihauans of the strained American-Japanese relations in the Pacific. As war clouds gathered, the Army asked ranchers to plow furrows across large island fields to prevent aircraft landings. It was into such a field that one of the Japanese planes crash-landed later in the afternoon of December 7. The two fighters had been unable to locate their carrier, and when the crippled craft finally plummeted into the sea off Kauai, his mate sought sanctuary on Niihau.

For about 15 minutes the plane buzzed the island, then bounced down into the plowed field, crashed over boulders, ripped through a wire fence, and stopped just short of the home of Hawila Kaleohano.

When the dust had settled, Hawila cautiously approached the cockpit. The dazed pilot attempted to draw a revolver from a holster, but Hawila quickly yanked him from his seat, breaking his harness. The pilot then began to fumble in his shirt for some papers. Again Hawila reacted quickly. He grabbed the packet of documents, which included a map of Oahu and Pearl Harbor, and held them and the revolver away from the agitated Japanese.

By now other villagers had converged on the two struggling men. Once the pilot was subdued, the Niihauans attempted to question him in English. When the aviator didn't respond, the villagers sent for Yoshio Harada, an American citizen of Japanese ancestry who had been working for a year as caretaker and beekeeper at the Robinson's Niihau house. The only other resident of Japanese descent was Ishimatsu Shintani, an alien who had married a Niihau girl and now lived with her on the island.

Through Harada, the captured pilot admitted he had just come from Oahu. The Niihauans decided to keep their prisoner under tight guard until Aylmer Robinson's regular Monday arrival in the supply sampan.

But Robinson didn't show Monday nor Tuesday nor Wednesday. The U.S. military had restricted any interisland travel in the wake of the Pearl Harbor raid and the subsequent fear of impending invasion. The people of Niihau were unaware of the tragedy so near their shores. Each day they marched their prisoner the 15 miles down from the village to the Kii boat landing. Mr. Robinson had always been punctual in the past.

During these first few anxious days the aviator finally admitted he had attacked Pearl Harbor, but he claimed he was the sole survivor of the Japanese force. He seemed penitent and humble, even suggesting that he settle on this splendid little isle once the war was over.

## The Battle of Niihau

By Thursday the villagers had decided (at Harada's suggestion) to leave the pilot at the Robinson house near the landing rather than trudge back and forth each day from the village.

When no sampan was sighted Friday morning, five villagers set a fire high on a mountain facing Kauai. This was the traditional trouble signal to the Robinson family's Kauai estate. But what the Niihauans considered a puzzling, burdensome situation was about to become a frightening, violent confrontation.

Late Friday afternoon the pilot indicated to his guard, a Hawaiian named Hanikiki, that he would like to see Harada, the Japanese caretaker, again. Hanikiki escorted the aviator to the honey house where Harada was working with the bees. There the pilot and Harada suddenly pulled guns on the startled Hawaiian. Harada had stolen a shotgun and a revolver from the Robinson house. He and his now comrade-in-arms locked Hanikiki in a shed and left to search for Hawila Kaleohano who had taken the pilot's papers and gun five days before. Within minutes, however, Hanikiki escaped from the shed and slipped away to warn the villagers.

On the road to Puuwai Village Harada and the pilot waved down a horse-drawn buggy carrying a Hawaiian woman and seven children. The two Japanese lined the woman and six of the children one behind the other in a single file. Harada translated the pilot's threat to kill them all with a single bullet if anyone moved or yelled. Then the two jumped into the buggy and ordered the remaining girl to drive them to the village.

On Thursday, the day before the escape, the pilot had tried to obtain his papers through intrigue. He ordered Shintani, the other Japanese resident of Niihau, to go to Hawila Kaleohano and offer the Hawaiian $200 worth of yen for the papers so they might be destroyed. If Shintani refused his secret emissary mission, the pilot would (somehow) kill him.

Hawila Kaleohano had rejected the bribe, and now when he saw Harada and the pilot armed and approaching in the buggy, he hid the papers and ran out the back door. The two Japanese then went to Shintani's house, but he had fled to the hills after his Thursday mission had failed.

The aviator and Harada went from home to home, threatening to shoot everyone if the papers weren't produced immediately. Most of the villagers ran into the nearby bush land and caves to hide. An old invalid woman, Mrs. Huluoulani, remained in her rocking chair reading the Bible. When the two threatened to shoot her, she merely said, "Only God has the power over life and death. Anyone else who interferes with that power will be punished." The puzzled pilot and the caretaker continued their search.

Meanwhile Hawila Kaleohano and five other men set out in a whaleboat to get help. They rowed for 16 hours, finally reaching Waimea, Kauai, at 3 p.m. Saturday. Before they could return with a detachment of soldiers and Mr. Robinson, events on Niihau came to a bloody conclusion.

Harada and the pilot stripped the wrecked plane of its two machine guns and then paraded through town with the cumbersome weapons, shouting they would shoot up everything and everyone if Kaleohano didn't come forth. They again ransacked the Hawaiian's home, this time finding the aviator's pistol and map of Oahu but none of the other papers. They searched other homes throughout the night Friday and finally set fire to Kaleohano's house and the Japanese plane.

The villagers, weaponless and frightened, were, none the less, planning to recapture their hamlet. Beni Kanahele and another Hawaiian named Kaahakila had slipped into town and stolen the machine gun ammunition while Harada and the pilot were busy ransacking houses.

Then at 7 a.m. Saturday, Beni and his wife tried to sneak into town to get food for the hiding villagers. They were both promptly captured by the two Japanese. Again there were the demands for the missing papers. But Beni Kanahele was tired of the whole mess. He told Harada, in Hawaiian, that the two of them, Beni and Harada, should jump the pilot and take his gun. Harada said he didn't dare because the pilot would kill him.

Then Beni grabbed the pilot's arm and tried to twist the gun free. Beni's wife jumped into the fray, but Harada pulled her away. As he struggled with the pilot, Beni yelled to Harada to leave his wife alone or he would come after him next.

But the pilot jerked his arm free and shot 51-year-old Beni Kanahele three times—one bullet in the stomach, one in the groin, and one in the thigh.

As Beni said later, "That's when I got mad." Despite his wounds, he lunged at the pilot and growled, "if I'm going to die, I'll kill you first so you can't kill anyone else." Beni picked the man up by his leg and his neck, the same way he had picked up hundreds of sheep on the ranch, and smashed out his brains against a stone wall. The pilot died instantly, his skull crushed.

## The Battle of Niihau

Harada, numbed only for an instant by the awful spectacle, quickly loaded his shotgun and turned it on his own stomach. Beni's wife tried to prevent the suicide, but Harada pulled the trigger and took both barrels. He died two hours later in the home of one of the villagers.

The military rescue party arrived from Kauai Sunday morning, one week after the two fighter planes had first circled the island and attracted the squinting gazes of the people of Niihau. But now the battle was over. The soldiers arrested Shintani and Mrs. Harada. She was released a short time later, but Shintani spent the war years in a mainland internment camp. Beni Kanahele was taken to the hospital on Kauai. He protested all the way.

Wartime security kept the details of the Battle of Niihau from the rest of the Islands for months. In June 1942, L. David Larsen, a Kauai sugar plantation manager, visited Niihau with Aylmer Robinson. Larsen interviewed witnesses and principals of the December violence and recorded the events in a letter to his wife. Local newspapers later published excerpts from the letter. In August 1942, two generals went to Niihau to present the American Legion Heroism Medal to Beni Kanahele and Hawila Kaleohano.

In those early war years some people saw the Niihau battle as evidence that the Japanese living in Hawaii couldn't be trusted. But the actions of Harada and Shintani stemmed more from fear of the pilot than from loyalty to the emperor. The lack of sabotage by Hawaii's Japanese citizens and the heroism displayed by the 442nd Battalion (made up primarily of AJAs from Hawaii) in the European theater finally dispelled any loyalty doubts.

In August 1945, on the day the war ended, the Army brought Beni Kanahele to Fort Shafter in Honolulu for presentation of the Purple Heart and the Medal of Merit. Special authorization from Washington was needed for a civilian to receive a Purple Heart. While Beni stood tall and straight, the Army band played "They Couldn't Take Niihau No-how."

*They Couldn't Take Niihau No-how*
*Words and Music by R. Alex Anderson*

On the tiny, isle of Niihau no one knew a war was on;
'Til a Japanese flier decided to retire and landed with a machine gun.

Then Big Ben Kanahele laid aside
    his ukulele,
He told the aviator he would throw him
    in the crater if he didn't get the heck
    right out.
But the Jap shot Ben in the shoulder, in
    the ribs and in the groin;
Kanahele took a swallow and tightened
    up his malo and then he girded up his other loin.
Then big Kanahele grabbed the Jap
    around the belly and threw him down against a stone wall.
And Mrs. Kanahele took a rock and
    made a jelly of his head 'til he was dead and that was all.

So THEY COULDN'T TAKE NIIHAU
    NO-HOW with the Ben Kanaheles around;
The Jap was a sap to think it a snap
    when he set his airplane down.
So THEY COULDN'T TAKE NIIHAU
    NO-HOW, when big Kanahele said "Pau!"
He made a grand slam for his Uncle Sam
    and THEY COULDN'T TAKE NIIHAU NO-HOW!

# The Forgotten Internees

## SUSAN MORRISON
## AND PETER KNEER

*During World War II, Japanese-Americans were
not the only victims of wartime hysteria.
Germans, Italians, and Austrians—resident aliens
and naturalized citizens—were also rounded up
and thrown into internment camps.*

✦ On Sunday morning, December 7, 1941, Alfred and Jana Preis were in their Waikiki apartment listening to a symphony on their phonograph. Over the music they heard distant explosions and thought that the military maneuvers seemed unusually realistic. Several miles away on Pacific Heights, Herb and Nikki Walther, wondering at the shooting practice so early on a Sunday morning, followed a fire engine up the hill to where a shell had exploded on the roof of their neighbor's house. Just below, on Kaloa Way, Joe Pacific and his wife and nine-year-old daughter also heard the commotion. In Kaimuki, Otto Orenstein and his father climbed on their garage roof and looked through field glasses toward Pearl Harbor, where they could see smoke rising. Across the Koʻolau Mountains in Kailua, Mario Valdastri was already working in his yard with his son and his Japanese gardeners. His wife ran outside from the kitchen where she had been listening to the radio. "Something is wrong. They're saying we're being attacked!" Curiosity turned to alarm and then to horror as the announcement came over the radio: "This is no maneuver; this is the real McCoy!"

First published November 1990.

By midday, Gov. Joseph B. Poindexter had placed the Territory of Hawaii under martial law and turned the government over to Maj. Gen. Walter C. Short, commanding general of the Hawaiian Department. The radio was silent except for occasional orders to stay off the roads, to black out all windows, and to heed the curfew set from 6 p.m. to 6 a.m. Rumors circulated of parachutists landing on the top of St. Louis Heights, and coded messages being transmitted by radios and blinking lights. The day passed in confusion, fear, and worry.

On Monday, Walther went to his office at Ready-Mix Concrete Co. where he was an accountant. Born in Germany and educated in England, he had come to Hawaii in 1932 and first worked as a maître d' at the Royal Hawaiian Hotel. Pacific, an Italian who had immigrated first to New York and then to Hawaii, stayed home from his shop, and he and his daughter put black paper on the windows. His German-born wife went shopping for food in hopes of stocking up against the inevitable shortages. Valdastri, also from Italy, remained at home with his family in Kailua. Preis, a young architect from Austria, spent the day with other architects helping Civil Defense prepare for the blackouts. Nineteen-year-old Orenstein, also from Austria, went to his job in the stockroom at Sears, Roebuck and Co.

During the day, Walther was interrupted at work by two men in suits and ties who asked him to come to the Immigration Station for questioning. "Wait until I call my wife and tell her where I am going," he answered. "No need to," one of the FBI agents said. "She is in the car." When he reached the car he saw his wife in the back seat, her hands black with paint from her attempts to black out the windows.

At the Valdastris', a car rolled up and stopped under the monkeypod tree. Two men asked Valdastri to come with them to the Immigration Station. He thought he was needed as an interpreter since he was multilingual. Dressed in sweatshirt and working pants, he asked if he could have a moment to change clothes. But the men said, "No, there is no time." He kissed his wife good-bye and said, "Mama, my country needs me."

When Orenstein came home that afternoon, two men were waiting to take him to the Immigration Station and told him his parents were already there.

At 7:30 that evening, after Preis had returned home, two men came to the house and asked him and his wife to accompany them. The men said they would bring them back soon.

## The Forgotten Internees

At the Immigration Station Preis was ordered by soldiers to empty his pockets. Then he and his wife were separated. He was pricked in the back with a bayonet and prodded up a steel stairway. The soldier yelled up the stairs, "Another prisoner coming up!"

Stunned and bewildered, Preis found his way into a room that was pitch-black except for the glow of cigarettes. Someone greeted him in the dark: "Ah, it's Preis." The voice belonged to Valdastri. Otto Orenstein, his father, and Joe Pacific were also there.

Pacific had been picked up that afternoon by men who asked him to come to the station to have his papers checked. They wouldn't let him bring his daughter and his wife wasn't home yet; but they assured him that he would be brought back immediately. When he arrived at the station a soldier took his name and emptied his pockets, then hollered up the stairs, "Another one." He learned later that his wife had also been picked up and that his daughter had been left alone at home.

Walther was also locked up in a dark room. It was filled with Japanese men who believed he had been put there to spy on them, since he was the only Caucasian among them. They kicked him and stepped on him where he lay on the floor trying to sleep. Later, when they realized he was also being held as an alien, they apologized.

Outside their door stood a guard with a bayonet. "Shut up, you spies," he yelled.

With the attack on Pearl Harbor, FBI and military intelligence units had immediately gone into action rounding up people in Hawaii who might be suspected of disloyalty to the United States. Because of the possibility of war, the agencies had been compiling notes and lists for several years. They had an "A" list of those considered "dangerous to the internal security of the U.S.," and a "B" list of those of "doubtful loyalty" to be kept under surveillance. By the end of the day on December 8, 482 people were in custody on Oʻahu: 370 of Japanese descent, 98 of German descent, and 14 of Italian descent.

What had young Otto Orenstein done that put him behind bars on December 8? Raised in Austria, he was imprisoned in 1938 by the Germans for being a Jew. He was released when they learned he was only 16 years old; however, his family thought it best he leave Austria. He began an odyssey that took him out of Austria through Germany and finally to Belgium. There he was arrested in 1939 as an enemy alien because of his German passport and spent six months in detention. His family finally obtained visas for the United States and he was released from the camp. The family was reunited in New York and came to Hawaii where they obtained resident status in 1940. Now, after fleeing Hitler and two incarcerations, he again found himself imprisoned, along with his parents.

Alfred and Jana Preis, also Austrian refugees, had fled Vienna when they realized that Hitler was taking over their country. They came by ship to New York and then to Honolulu where a job awaited Preis at the architectural firm of Dahl and Conrad. They had received their first U.S. citizenship papers in New York but by law had to wait five years before final papers could be signed.

Mario Valdastri immigrated to New York from Italy in 1909. He enlisted in the U.S. Army in World War I and fought in France. When he returned to the United States he became an American citizen. He came to Honolulu in 1926 and was put in charge of adding cast stone veneer to the Bank of Hawaii building. When he went to the owner of the construction company to be paid, the owner asked if his name was M. V. Morris. He said, "No, it's Mario Valdastri." The man replied, "Well, if you want to get paid, your name is M. V. Morris!" During internment a question he was repeatedly asked was, "Why did you come to Hawaii under a false name?"

Joe Pacific first went to New York from Rome in 1916. He married a woman from Germany in 1930 and they arrived in Hawaii in 1936. He operated a shoe and luggage repair shop and was expecting his final citizenship papers in February 1942. The FBI had tapped his phone, he said, and overheard his wife speaking in German, as well as her brother, the chef at the Royal Hawaiian Hotel. Pacific believed he was picked up because the FBI figured it was best to be on the safe side.

Herb Walther, who left Germany for New York in 1929 and then came to Hawaii, received his U.S. citizenship in 1934. In 1936, he took a short trip back to Germany. He returned via Chicago, where he met his soon-to-be wife, another German immigrant. They married within a few days and came to Hawaii. The FBI found their brief courtship suspicious and concluded it may have been part of a conspiracy. They also suggested that Walther, as maître d' at the Royal Hawaiian Hotel and very fluent in English, could have been planted there to spy on drunken American officers.

Such suspicion was common. War hysteria ran high. After the war, Gen. Delos C. Emmons, one of the military governors during the period of martial law, stated: "We leaned over backward in interning people in order to achieve as much security as we possibly could. Undoubtedly, mistakes were made."

On December 11, some of the internees were taken away from the Immigration Station. Christmas passed. More people disappeared. Finally on December 30, Walther, after a cursory hearing, was told to prepare to leave. Under heavy armed guard, he and other internees were bundled into trucks and taken to the harbor.

In boats guarded by armed soldiers they started off across the water. Soon they found themselves disembarking at Sand Island at the entrance to Honolulu Harbor. A quarantine depot had been established there in the late nineteenth century for ship passengers who were ill. It later became part of the Immigration Station. Now the Army had taken it over. Through a marshy land of coral tidal flats, mangrove, and kiawe, the internees were marched three abreast until they came to the entrance of the compound. There they found the internees who had disappeared earlier from the Immigration Station.

Tents stood in the enclosure surrounded by three rows of barbed-wire fences. They had only the wet earth for floors, and the cots, which had no mattresses, sank their legs into the ground. Each man was issued two blankets and a pillow. Cold, wet, and confused, and still not told why they were being held, the "A" list men, Japanese and European, American citizens and aliens, were now incarcerated within sight of Aloha Tower. Honolulu's own Ellis Island had become their prison.

The Europeans were in one cluster of tents, while the Japanese were in another. The European area was known as the "mixed camp" and included men from Germany, Italy, Finland, Norway, and Austria. Some were naturalized American citizens and others had been given status as resident aliens awaiting their final papers.

Life in the camp was fairly routine. The prisoners were given writing paper and pencil once a week, but in the early days they were allowed no magazines or newspapers. Most chose to work in order to pass the time. Several worked in the laundry; others in the kitchen. Some of Honolulu's best chefs were in the mixed camp, and the food was so good that the soldiers looked for opportunities to take their meals with the internees rather than in their own MP quarters. When the wooden building for the women was completed in February, the women interned at the Immigration Station were moved to Sand Island, and the men were allowed to join them for Sunday breakfast.

Without newspapers and books, the internees looked for ways to pass time and keep themselves mentally active. Thus began the "University of Sand Island." Orenstein's father was a talented pianist. He knew by heart nine of Anton Bruckner's symphonies. He could hum and analyze each one. A violinist from Germany and a composer from Norway also added their knowledge. Preis gave seminars on city planning and architecture. Others gave talks on human anatomy, history, religion, and astronomy. During the blackout at night, the group spent many evenings stargazing.

Treatment by the guards and officers varied. If a knife was missing from the mess hall, all internees were ordered to strip and be searched. On the other hand, overworked guards often asked to sleep in the internees' tents while on duty, trusting the internees to wake them if an officer approached.

The internees passed their days, trusting in the justice of the American system, believing they would be freed as soon as possible. But the waiting seemed interminable and was filled with anxiety.

Families of the internees suffered too. They often had no money for rent or food. Children took after-school jobs to help make ends meet, and in some cases families were forced to move out of their homes. Tragedy befell the Valdastris when their daughter fell from a balcony during the blackout and was killed. Valdastri, heavily guarded, was allowed out of the camp only for her funeral. In cases where mothers were also interned, some children were left alone at home. Pacific's nine-year-old daughter was alone for three days until his employer came to the house to find out why he wasn't at work.

When people suddenly left the camp, those remaining optimistically believed they had been set free. Sometimes this was the case, but not always. On February 17, 1942, 13 Americans of German and Italian descent, along with a large group of those of Japanese descent, were herded into the hold of an Army transport and kept below decks for a cramped and stifling voyage. When the ship reached California, the men were transferred onto trains. On one train, the internees noticed the landscape becoming bleaker and the weather colder. On March 9, they reached Camp McCoy, the Department of Justice Internment Center, at Sparta, Wisconsin. Valdastri and Walther, still in their tropical-weight clothing, stuffed newspapers into their clothes and shoes to shield themselves from the bitter Midwestern winter.

At Camp McCoy the German- and Italian-American citizens from

Hawaii sent a letter to the U.S. attorney general, Francis Biddle, asking his help in securing their release and pointing out the illegality of their imprisonment as American citizens being held without charges. Though habeas corpus had been revoked in the Territory of Hawaii under martial law, civil rights had not been revoked in the United States, and therefore, the internees wrote, they could not legally be held. In April, Secretary of War Henry L. Stimson wrote in his diary that American citizens from Hawaii were being sent "back to Hawaii which is under a state of martial law and where we can do what we please with them."

In the meantime, one by one, some of the Sand Island internees were released on parole. The Preises were paroled on March 28, 1942, to a man whose house had been designed by Preis, and who owned a quarry and concrete company in Halawa Valley. Preis worked for the company as an engineer and learned to drive a bulldozer.

Orenstein's father was paroled in February, and Orenstein and his mother were paroled in May. They attributed their release to efforts by the Hawaii delegate to Congress, Samuel Wilder King, and Mrs. Orenstein's brother in New York who had written to King on their behalf. They went to the Big Island, where Orenstein worked as a clerk in the company store of the Hamakua Sugar Co.

Pacific was released in April and reunited with his daughter. His wife, however, had been sent to a detention camp in Texas. Released in September 1943, she then moved to California. She never returned to Hawaii.

Walther and Valdastri were returned from McCoy on April 28, 1942, and were put back behind the barbed-wire fences at Sand Island, where they remained for almost another year.

The Sand Island Detention Center closed in March 1943 and became the Army Port and Service Command. Many internees were released at that time, including Valdastri, who was asked to do some consultant work for the Army Corps of Engineers, requiring his inspection of restricted areas including tunnels running from Red Hill to Pearl Harbor.

The Walthers were transferred in March 1943 to the Honouliuli Internment Camp near 'Ewa, having been informed in a letter from the Office of the Military Governor, "It appears necessary to continue you in internment for the duration of the war."

In Honouliuli Gulch, hot and mosquito-ridden, amidst red dirt and kiawe brambles, the camp now housed the Territory's remaining internees as well as prisoners of war.

Walther had written more than 50 letters to officials at various levels protesting internment, emphasizing his loyalty and patriotism, and expressing dismay over the humiliation and despair suffered by him and others. Often the letters were unanswered or referred to another office with the reply that the matter was not in the jurisdiction of that particular department. Even Hawaii's delegate to Congress, Samuel King, in his efforts to help the internees, had run into this impasse.

In August 1943, Walther made arrangements for an attorney to represent him in a suit against the government. The letter he wrote to the military to indicate his intentions was acknowledged and "forwarded to higher authority for whatever action they consider appropriate." On August 21, 1943, the Walthers were released on parole, after more than 22 months of internment. Because they had not been able to meet their payments, their house, their car, and their furniture were gone.

Martial law was rescinded in October 1944, and the writ of habeas corpus restored. The war ended the following year. Joe Pacific, who had lost his shoe and luggage shop during internment, built a new one at the corner of Union and Bishop streets, eventually acquiring four more. He received his final citizenship papers in 1946.

Herb Walther became the head accountant for Honolulu Roofing Co. and retired in 1984. An active member of the community, he belonged to the Elks Club, the Honolulu Symphony, and the Morning Music Club and was recognized for his volunteer work for Historic Hawaii, the Academy of Arts, and the Manoa Valley Theatre. He died in June of this year [1990].

Otto Orenstein, who became a U.S. citizen in 1946, spent 38 years with the Hawaiian Telephone Co. as a statistician and forecaster. Mario Valdastri continued his work in cast stone, contributing to buildings such as City Hall and the old Halekulani Hotel. The large eagle statue at the Hickam Air Force Base entrance was originally cast from an iron mold he made in 1932, and his last job was to restore the ornamental plaster at 'Iolani Palace in 1975. He died in 1978 at the age of 82, and his son now carries on the family business.

Alfred and Jana Preis received their final papers as American citizens in 1946 and built the house in Manoa where they still live. One of Preis's best known architectural designs is the USS Arizona Memorial.

## The Forgotten Internees

He was instrumental in the planning of the Honolulu civic center as Gov. John A. Burns's planning adviser, and he was the founding director of the State Foundation on Culture and the Arts. He has been designated a "Living Treasure" by the Honpa Hongwanji Honolulu Mission Temple.

What do the internment victims think about now, when they look back at those difficult days nearly 50 years ago? Says Orenstein, "I remember the place and I remember the people, but I don't think about it much." Walther, who had kept a thick scrapbook of his internment correspondence, said that after his release he had tried to forget the ordeal and to get on with his life. Pacific says, "To me it's gone and done with, but in a way, to recognize the Japanese and not the Germans and Italians is not fair. But then again who am I to say anything."

Do they feel bitterness? "No," says Mario Valdastri Jr., "my father never felt bitter. He was a patriot. After all, he had fought for the United States in World War I. He knew there was uncertainty and hysteria at the time and he had faith it would eventually be straightened out. He was sad. But not bitter. He said, 'I have served my country in both wars!'"

"Nobody was prepared for war," says Preis. "Everyone was nervous, anxious, edgy. The government did what it felt it had to do under the circumstances. Compared to what happened under the Nazis, Hawaii was still paradise."

But as Gen. Emmons said after the war, "Undoubtedly, mistakes were made."

# The Day After: December 8, 1941

## THELMA CHANG

*Our efforts to help as many people as possible with head injuries became a surgical marathon, no sleep. We worked around the clock, operating on one case after another. Head injuries—that's all I did. We took a short rest, put our heads down, while the room was being cleaned for the next patient. I only had two hands and we couldn't operate on everybody. So we had to pick and choose.*
—Dr. Ralph Bingham Cloward, Neurosurgeon

◆ Dawn's light on Monday, December 8, 1941, belied the darkness and tension felt by a stunned people. Remnants of black smoke rose from the vicinity of Pearl Harbor while Oʻahu was reeling from the devastation of the day before. Martial law—government under military rule—was one day old and firmly established over the U.S. Territory of Hawaii. The changes were profound. On this day, for instance, all territorial courts were closed. The writ of habeas corpus, an individual's right to be officially charged with a crime before being detained indefinitely, was suspended, and civilians were now tried for minor offenses in provost courts presided over by the U.S. Army.

"Army officers report 'all quiet' on Oʻahu on war's second day," announced a local newspaper. But all was *not* quiet on war's second day.

---

First published December 1991.

As the morning sun shone upon a hill behind the Kamehameha Schools, a group of tired and anxious students wondered, "What is going to happen to us?" The youths, part of the school's ROTC unit, had had little or no sleep since the day before when they were issued rifles and given the mission of patrolling Kapalama Heights. "We received information that there might be Japanese paratroopers landing in the hills," recalls U.S. Sen. Daniel K. Akaka, who was 17 at the time. "We were still so young and it was a really scary feeling being out there all alone in the hills."

Below, the city of Honolulu struggled with its own fears and priorities. Gravediggers were served their first meal since the bombing. They had been up all night at Nuʻuanu Cemetery burying the dead. In Waikiki, barbed wire stretched along the beaches. Freshly dug trenches could be seen along Ala Moana—from Kewalo Basin to the Ala Wai. And in what was to be an ominous symbol of things to come for Hawaiʻi's people of Japanese ancestry, large quantities of dynamite were unloaded at Kewalo Basin "in case it became necessary to destroy moored sampans in the vicinity," reported a local newspaper. (The fishing sampans were owned mainly by Island Japanese.)

The Neighbor Islands were also on alert. Ben Tamashiro, part of the Hawaii National Guard's 299th Infantry Regiment, was on Kauaʻi guarding a small airfield called Burns Field. "We blocked the field with oil drums so planes couldn't land, even our own," he recalls.

Throughout Oʻahu, military and civilian casualties from the bombings, wayward antiaircraft shells, accidental shootings, and other causes spurred a continuous flow of blood donors, medical supplies, doctors, nurses, volunteers, and other help. Hospitals were filling up with the dead and injured. Doctors doing major surgery the day before had quickly run out of scissors, surgical gloves, and other supplies. "They ran out of operating gowns and worked in pajamas and underwear," notes Gwenfread Allen in her book *Hawaiʻi War Years*. "Some doctors were extremely critical of the Army's lack of preparation."

At Pearl Harbor, many critically burned men in severe pain needed personal care. Honolulu nurses quickly donated their services.

Countless others, including Japanese-Americans, responded to the community crisis. Red Cross volunteers worked nonstop in the basement of ʻIolani Palace handling hundreds of people who answered the call for blood. The basement was crowded with other defense workers, including truck drivers and sentries who stopped by for hot chocolate or coffee. They were too exhausted to eat solid food. Crowds also packed

## The Day After

Queen's Hospital (now Queen's Medical Center), standing for hours in crammed hallways and elevators to donate their blood.

At the Honolulu morgue, people walked in and out trying to find or identify missing friends and relatives. "Dead, Portuguese girl, unidentified, age 10, address unknown, puncture wound, left temple," reported the *Honolulu Advertiser* on December 8. "Japanese girl, age 9, unknown, DOA at morgue."

Others surveyed the damage to their homes and cars from bombs and antiaircraft shells. "I remember a big hole on Lewers Street in Waikiki, and it wasn't learned until much later that much of the destruction had come from our own antiaircraft shells," says Nadine Kahanamoku, then the recent bride of Olympic swimming champion and Honolulu sheriff Duke Kahanamoku. "On Monday, we were absolutely in a daze. Duke was hard at work at City Hall."

Dr. Ralph Cloward and his surgical nurse, Edith Yoshioka, were also hard at work. Cloward was operating virtually nonstop ("I didn't get up on Monday morning because I never went to bed"), saving the lives of soldiers whose heads were injured mainly by shrapnel. The surgeries became a four-day marathon. "They only had 250 beds and about 1,500 casualties delivered to that one hospital," recalls Cloward, who, at 33, was the only neurosurgeon in the Pacific at the time. "The injured were on stretchers outside on the grass—no place else to put them. I would take a few minutes off, go out, and choose the cases that I could help. If a man had half his head blown off and there wasn't any chance we could save him, we had to choose the ones who would survive the operation."

Cloward did the best he could with equipment considered "primitive." (This was before the invention of gelfoam or thrombin—substances used to coagulate blood.) "We used large wads of cotton soaked in hydrogen peroxide, which coagulates blood. My suction apparatus was a portable machine run by a small motor used to aspirate the trachea of newborn babies. So we could suck out the damaged brain without damaging the uninjured part."

The day before, December 7, Cloward had been mowing the lawn of his Manoa home when he heard the call on the radio for doctors to report to Tripler Hospital right away. Cloward rushed over, got out of his car and nearly stepped into a pool of blood. "I called Edith right away and said, 'Go get my instruments from Queen's—we've got a lot of work to do.'"

Cloward's wife, meanwhile, was alone with two babies at their Manoa home. He could not let her know what was happening. "The first 24 hours after the bombing, telephones were out of order," says Cloward. "There were rumors that Japanese paratroopers were landing in Manoa Valley."

Cloward did not get home until December 10. He worked steadily at the hospital, performing 42 operations in 3½ days. "I was entirely oblivious of time and what was going on."

War or not, life went on. A newspaper "help wanted" ad sought a "barmaid" at a downtown inn. Businesses offered carpenters $1.20 an hour and car mechanics $7 a day, tidy sums for the time. Homes were for sale. "Diamond Head house for $12,500," said one ad. "Manoa house, fully furnished, $6,350," said another.

Seven babies were born between 6 p.m. December 7 and 6 a.m. December 8 at Queen's Hospital. Meanwhile, seriously injured civilians were being admitted and treated in its emergency room. Frightened patients and families inundated social service workers there with requests: "See if my house is still standing." "Feed my dog." "Contact my employer." "Feed the chickens."

"Our department became the hospital's clearing center for cables to anxious relatives and friends," said a 1941 Social Service Department report. "At noon on Dec. 8, we sent a volunteer to the cable office with about 60 messages. After waiting in line for an hour, he returned saying that, according to military instructions, our messages were wrongly prepared and had to be written all over again."

Life had taken on a now-or-never urgency. People made maximum use of Monday's daylight, since strict military curfews and blackouts were in force. "Everyone had something to do—they had to get it done that day, whether it was cleaning out the closet or whatever," remembers Mary Richards, the daughter of prominent businessman A. D. Castro.

Many went shopping. Fort Street stores were doing a "lively Christmas business," declared one news report. "Everybody was rushing around on Monday to buy food, rice, and emergency supplies," says Genoa Keawe, renowned Hawaiian entertainer and the mother of five children in 1941. "We headed to Kress Store, crowded with people, to buy candles for some light at night. We had to cook early in the day before the blackout. It was an eerie feeling. We kept the kids from going to school because we didn't know what was going to happen. We were told not to drink the water. We still drank the water. I didn't think it was contaminated."

Keawe was a singer with George Hookano's 14-piece dance band

## The Day After

before the war, performing such romantic tunes as "Embraceable You" and "As Time Goes By." The shows were canceled after December 7. From December 8, Keawe's evenings were filled with other activities. "We and our neighbors would go outside in the dark and talk story—everybody was friendly in those days—sharing our feelings."

Like Keawe, Mary Richards found herself rushing around in downtown Honolulu, but her Monday was complicated by the fact that her December 12 wedding was in jeopardy. Her fiancé, Ed Fitzsimmons, was a defense worker. "Invitations had gone out, the bridesmaids, the gown, the whole ball of wax," recalls Richards, whose family home was one of many used to shelter uprooted families from the destroyed area at Hickam and Pearl Harbor. "All I could think of that day was to find a priest, get married, skip everything else. But we couldn't find a priest. They were needed at Pearl Harbor."

Richards remembers the nervousness of the day, as she headed for Liberty House. "They were shooting at anything that even stirred—I felt sorry for cats and dogs." Upon her arrival, she noted the teary eyes of the saleswomen. "Everybody was undone, so undone. They asked, 'What are you going to do about your wedding?' People made a lot of fuss over weddings in those days. I said, 'I want to take the gown home.'"

With her gown carefully wrapped in a box, Richards headed for the Metropolitan Meat Market around the corner to check on her food order. A large "closed" sign was posted outside the market that had been a landmark for many food shoppers. "The reception was unimportant as far as I was concerned," says Richards. "We had enough stuff and wouldn't starve. I [later] got a call from the newspaper and that's how I learned about cameras and film being frozen. It was easier for the military government to just—whoosh—blanket everything, cut it straight across the board."

Richards stopped at Benson-Smith ("everybody's corner drugstore"), then headed for the bank. It was guarded by military police. "I was only 20, but the MPs looked like they were still in grade school, and they were scared to death. They were examining everything. This soldier asked, 'What's in there?'

'I'm getting married, this is my wedding dress, don't you dare touch it.'
'You'll have to open it.'
'Well, I'll open it, but I'm not going to haul it out.'
'Open it up.'"

As the soldier pushed at the box with the point of his gun, the crowd standing around Richards was getting angry. "He was obnoxious, arrogant as heck. I had to put the box on the ground. He looked and said, 'Well all right. What's in the other bag?' It contained personal items. He said, 'Open it up.' I was dying inside. I almost blanked out. Everybody's nerves were on edge. Finally it was over with. Nobody said a word. They felt for me. But this insensitive little guy was only doing his job."

Richards got married, not on December 8, but on December 12 as planned. "The priest had been out at Pearl Harbor since Dec. 7 and it wasn't until around Wednesday [December 10] that we made contact. He sounded as weary as any soul could possibly be. His heart was broken. He was sad, so sad. My father was sad too. He had been through World War I and now to have this happen."

While Richards, her family, and others struggled to make sense of the day, the skies and oceans off Hawai'i were busy with activity. American planes went on scouting missions, looking for aircraft carriers.

As fighter planes flew overhead that day, the Pacific Ocean below hid its fresh tragedies. For instance, the *Cynthia Olson,* an American freighter, had been hit on December 7 by a torpedo from a Japanese submarine about 1,000 miles northeast of O'ahu. The SS *Lurline,* a Matson luxury liner sailing between California and Hawai'i, picked up the *Olson*'s distress calls. The freighter and its crew, however, disappeared without a trace. (Matson's four luxury liners and 38 of its freighters would serve during the war.)

Nearer Honolulu, two sampans floated aimlessly on the ocean before they were towed into Kewalo Basin. Inside the sampans lay eight fishermen of Japanese ancestry—six dead, two wounded. They had left O'ahu days before to catch fish for the upcoming holidays. Newspapers on December 8 warned that all unidentified boats approaching O'ahu would be fired upon, but the fishermen were isolated from outside contact and had no way of knowing danger would come from the skies. Kaichi Okada and his three helpers were in one of the boats. Okada was the uncle of Harold Yokoyama.

"An American airplane shot dead the six men in the fishing boats," says Yokoyama, whose family's livelihood depended on fishing. "They were shot by .50-caliber bullets from the airplane. The other boat belonged to the Kida family. The Coast Guard towed the boats to Kewalo Basin in the early evening, and we saw the bodies. The boat had so much damage, it sank one week later. I went to my uncle's funeral. He was a single man, an American citizen."

## The Day After

While all civilians were subjected to restrictions under military rule, Hawai'i's Japanese were especially targeted. Their fishing fleets were ordered impounded at Kewalo Basin on December 8 and lost forever. The general public was asked to report any meetings of Japanese, especially Buddhist gatherings. Japanese could not enter certain security areas. The restriction included Japanese-Americans rendering valuable service for the U.S. Army's Military Intelligence Service (MIS). Community leaders were rounded up.

Joe Shimamura, today a decorated World War II veteran of the famed 442nd Regimental Combat Team, remembers the moment the FBI came to take his father away. "They turned the house upside-down and my five brothers and I were watching, angry," he recalls. "My dad had been a treasurer of a Buddhist church."

Pain and hope commingled in the hearts of many Islanders as the setting sun cast its last glow over Hawaii on the war's second day. On Maui, 13-year-old Patsy Takemoto surveyed a vegetable garden in her family's back yard. "There was no school on Monday, so we planted cabbage, eggplant, string beans and sweet potatoes in what later became known as a 'Victory Garden,'" says the gardener, who grew up to become U.S. Rep. Patsy T. Mink. "Victory, however, was the last thing on our minds that day as we went about our work."

Seedlings also graced the grounds at Queen's Hospital, where the kitchen staff had planted a "war garden" on December 8. Staff members replaced the area's beautiful dahlias with lettuce, eggplant, beets, carrots, sweet potatoes, parsley, Swiss chard, and green onions.

A crop of lettuce blossomed in 44 days.

Joe Shimamura, Harold Yokoyama, and Ben Tamashiro served in the U.S. Army. Shimamura was one of many Japanese-Americans involved in the epic rescue of the Texas "Lost Battalion" in France.

Eleven Matson freighters and four Matson-operated Liberty ships were sunk during the war.

Daniel Akaka, stationed on Saipan with the Army Corps of Engineers, watched the *Enola Gay* take off as it flew toward Hiroshima in August 1945.

Nadine and Duke Kahanamoku served Hawaii with warmth as goodwill ambassadors.

The wartime marriage of Mary Richards and Ed Fitzsimmons produced two children.

Dr. Ralph Cloward emerged from the war as one of Hawai'i's most noted neurosurgeons. Edith Yoshioka served faithfully as his surgical nurse, secretary, travel agent, bookkeeper, and confidante for more than 50 years.

Genoa Keawe blossomed as a versatile musician-singer and became a living legend in Hawaiian entertainment. In October 1991, Keawe left on a trip for Japan to share her love for Hawaiian music.

# The Night They Bombed Tantalus

JOHN J. STEPHAN

*It was one of the more bizarre episodes of World War II, but it held more significance than either side realized.*

✦ At 2:12 a.m. on Wednesday, March 4, 1942, moments after an air raid siren had cut through the rustle of a tropical shower, four heavy explosions rocked Honolulu. The blasts rattled windows downtown and shook houses in Makiki. At the home of Lt. Harrison R. Cooke (USN) on lower Tantalus Drive, shock waves smashed the glass panes of three sliding doors and ripped the frames off their tracks. Two miles mauka on upper Round Top Drive, Margaret Young was nearly thrown out of bed by jolts that she thought could only be a strong earthquake.

Thousands of startled citizens, already awakened by the siren, deluged police switchboards with phone calls. Others scurried in their pajamas and nightgowns through the rain to garden bomb shelters. Searchlights probed the low-hanging clouds over Waikiki and Kakaako. Anxiously cocked ears picked up what seemed to be the drone of planes overhead. Japanese bombers! Was this the beginning of what so many had been anticipating: an invasion of Hawaii?

Invasion was very much on the minds of Honoluluans on that morning of March 4. This was the first time that bombs had fallen on Oahu since December 7, 1941, when planes with rising sun emblems had rained destruction on Pearl Harbor in a surprise attack which crippled

---

First published November 1980.

the Pacific Fleet. In the intervening three months, Japanese forces had sliced through Southeast Asia and had leapt across the Western Pacific with breathless speed, eliminating all but isolated pockets of resistance. Guam, Hong Kong, Wake, Malaya, Borneo, and the "impregnable" bastion of Singapore had all fallen. Java was half occupied. The British were evacuating Burma. An undefeated Imperial Japanese Combined Fleet, commanded by the bold, resourceful, and unpredictable Admiral Yamamoto Isoroku, had scattered or demolished British, Dutch, and American squadrons in the South China and Java seas. As the Allies sought a haven in Australia, Japan controlled the waters and skies between the Indian Ocean and Wake. As Japanese momentum showed little sign of abating, many in Hawaii were asking themselves: "Is our turn next?"

With sunrise, Honoluluans could breathe a sigh of relief. Oahu and the Neighbor Islands were still in American hands. But the previous night's explosions remained a mystery. The *Honolulu Advertiser* quoted an Army spokesman as asserting that the siren had been "inadvertent" and that the cause of the detonations was being "investigated." This cryptic announcement only fueled speculation: Japanese warships had shelled Oahu. Japanese carriers were offshore. A disoriented American pilot had dumped bombs on the hills behind the city. The Army had staged the explosions to ascertain whether the local Japanese would, in the words of one housewife, "be loyal or ready to spring to arms for their native land."

All of these rumors turned out to be off the mark. Honolulu had in fact been baptized by what was then the longest bombing raid in the history of aviation, an extraordinary 4,000-mile odyssey that started and ended in the Marshall Islands. The raiders aimed for Pearl Harbor, but their bombs fell on the lower slopes of Mount Tantalus, a thousand yards from Roosevelt High School and seven miles from the intended target.

How the Japanese managed to cover such remarkable distances, to elude American fighters, and to penetrate the skies over Oahu, only to leave four 25-foot craters and some splintered algaroba trees, is one of the more bizarre episodes of the Second World War. It was an episode, however, that held more significance for Japan and the United States than either side realized.

Amid the euphoria sweeping Japan following the spectacular successes of the Imperial Navy, ranking officers of the Combined Fleet

## The Night They Bombed Tantalus

knew that they still had unfinished business in Hawaii. Carriers of the U.S. Pacific fleet had been at sea on December 7, escaping the fate of those doomed battleships anchored by Ford Island. Admiral Yamamoto and his staff were convinced that as long as the American carriers remained at large and used Pearl Harbor as a base, they posed a serious threat to Japan.

Intelligence from Hawaii was not encouraging. Submarines patrolling around Oahu noted heavy maritime traffic. A reconnaissance plane launched from a submarine off Kauai made a daring midnight swoop over Pearl Harbor on January 4–5, 1942, and reported "animated" reconstruction activity proceeding without even a blackout.

Yamamoto knew what this portended. It was only a matter of time before the United States, mobilizing its immense industrial superiority, would counterattack from Hawaii and put Japan's defenses to a severe test. Heavily engaged in the Southwest Pacific and contemplating a thrust against British forces in the Indian Ocean, the Combined Fleet was stretched too thin for an immediate general assault on the Hawaiian Islands. Besides, the army opposed an invasion. Yet something had to be done, quickly, to delay Pearl Harbor's recovery.

The answer came in the form of a second Pearl Harbor attack. Only this time, instead of being launched from carriers, the planes would have to fly across 2,000 miles from the Japanese-occupied Marshall Islands. Their task would be formidable, not only because of the distance but because the Americans were now reinforced, ready and waiting.

Well before the war, Japanese naval strategists had hoped to develop a long-range bomber that could reach Hawaii from the Marshall Islands (then under a Japanese mandate). Several models of four-engine flying-boats (*hikotei*) were in existence at the war's outbreak, but none could make the 4,000-mile round trip without refueling. Moreover, the most advanced models were only at an experimental stage and available only in limited numbers. These obstacles did not deter the Combined Fleet's chief of staff Admiral Ugaki Matome, who on January 17, 1942, issued orders to the Fourth and Sixth fleets and to the Twenty-fourth Air Group to prepare for night air attacks on Oahu with the object of disrupting repair work at Pearl Harbor and striking a blow at American morale.

During the five weeks between January 17 and late February, officers of the Twenty-fourth Air Group on Kwajalein worked out a plan of operations in consultation with representatives of the Fourth and

Sixth fleets. It was decided to use Type-2 flying-boats manufactured by the Kawanishi Aircraft Company in Yokosuka. These slow (cruising speed: 160 knots) planes had just under a 3,000-mile range with a two-ton bomb load, but they were all that was available. After several options were considered, the following plan of attack was adopted. The planes would take off from Wotje (in the Marshall Islands) and fly 1,605 miles to French Frigate Shoals (in the Hawaiian chain) where they would rendezvous with and be refueled by two specially outfitted submarines. Four more submarines would be stationed along the flight path to provide navigational assistance by radio signals: one between Wotje and French Frigate Shoals, one 10 miles south of Pearl Harbor, and two between Hawaii and Wotje. The sub off Pearl Harbor was also to report weather conditions over Oahu and—if necessary—to pick up survivors after the attack. The flying-boats were to cover the 482 miles from French Frigate Shoals to Pearl Harbor, drop 500-pound bombs on arsenals, dry docks, and warships, and return directly to Wotje without refueling. Full moon conditions were required in order to minimize hazards of debris and choppy waves during the nocturnal take-off run at French Frigate Shoals, so attacks were scheduled for March 2 (P-Day) and March 7 (Q-Day). Both missions were dubbed "Operation K" *(K sakusen)*, the "K" standing for *kyoryoku* ("cooperation") between bases, aircraft, and submarines.

Operation K ran into difficulties before it even got under way. The Kawanishi Company could only have two flying-boats ready for delivery from Yokosuka to the Marshalls by mid-February, although the original plans called for six. One of the two planes was damaged during a take-off from Saipan en route south and required time-consuming repairs. Second, the sudden appearance of an American task force east of Rabaul on February 20 forced a two-day delay of P-Day as all available Japanese naval units scoured the seas in a fruitless search for the elusive intruders. Third, although Japanese cryptographers had broken U.S. Naval weather codes and were monitoring radio reports from Hawaii during February, on March 1 the Americans changed their weather codes. Fourth, the submarine sent to wait outside of Pearl Harbor vanished on the way to Hawaii and was never heard from again. These setbacks not only deprived the attackers of precious time in which to train but insured that they would be flying blind into the target area.

Operation K was going to be even more hazardous than its planners

## The Night They Bombed Tantalus

realized. American naval intelligence had broken key Japanese naval codes and was able to warn the Pacific Fleet commander-in-chief on March 3 about enemy submarine activity around French Frigate Shoals. Furthermore, the Americans, unbeknownst to the Japanese, possessed radar whose electronic eyes could track any aircraft approaching the Hawaiian Islands. Under these conditions, Operation K promised to become an American turkey shoot.

Operation K was launched at 5:25 a.m. on March 3 (Honolulu time) when two flying-boats lifted off a moonlit lagoon at Wotje and headed northeast toward French Frigate Shoals. Each plane carried a crew of eight. Mission commander Lieutenant Hashizume piloted plane number one. Plane number two was under the controls of Ensign Tomano.

After a flight of about 13 hours, Hashizume and Tomano put their planes down in the relatively sheltered waters of French Frigate Shoals at 6:50 p.m., March 3. Two submarines awaited their arrival. No American patrols showed up to interrupt the delicate job of pumping 3,000 gallons of gasoline through buoyed hoses from subs to aircraft while both bobbed and rolled. Refueled in two hours, the planes lumbered into the air. It was just after 9:00 p.m.

By 11:30 p.m., Hashizume and Tomano were passing over the twin peaks of Nihoa Island. Calculating to avoid lookouts, they steered a course between Kauai and Niihau at 30 minutes past midnight on March 4 and then turned toward Oahu. Hashizume's plan was to sight Kaena Point on Oahu's western tip, continue east until directly north of Pearl Harbor, then turn south for the bombing run. This angle of approach was to enhance the element of surprise and to facilitate rapid escape.

Oahu's defenders were already alerted before Hashizume and Tomano had even started these maneuvers. At 12:14 a.m., the Army Radar Station on Kauai picked up a blip north of Niihau and immediately sent the first of a stream of reports to the Air Raid Defense Center in Honolulu where WARDS (Women Air Raid Defense Service) plotted its progress with markers on a board. Air Corps and Navy Air liaison officers at the Defense Center were unable to identify the blip as friend or foe, but at 12:43, as the blip crept by Kauai, the Air Defense Commander mobilized the Initial Air Striking Group. Thirty minutes later, five Navy PBYs armed with torpedoes started taking off with orders to search for and attack the carrier from which the intruders were thought to have come. At 1:36, four Army P-40s scrambled to intercept the enemy. Meanwhile, the naval base commander at Pearl Harbor ordered general quarters for all units. At 1:59, as the blip (now clearly showing two planes) approached Kaena Point, the Air Defense Commander ordered a full air raid alert. Minutes later, sirens shattered the sleep of thousands in and around Honolulu.

At this juncture, the weather intervened to disorient attackers and defenders alike. Giant cumulus clouds hovering over the Koolau Range suddenly rolled across the Schofield Saddle. Flying at 15,000 feet, Hashizume decided to change the attack plan and round the northern tip of Oahu to find a clearer avenue of approach. He radioed Tomano to follow him and veered northward. Hashizume detoured around Kahuku Point, flew along the windward coast to Kaneohe, and turned sharply south toward what he thought was the target area. At 2:10 a.m., catching sight through a break in the clouds of what looked like Hickam Field and Ford Island, Hashizume radioed Tomano to commence bombing and unleashed his own lethal cargo. Circling once to observe the fall of the bombs, Hashizume then headed south out to sea and made for the Marshall Islands. Hashizume's bombs fell on the lower slopes of Mount Tantalus.

Meanwhile, Ensign Tomano had received neither of Hashizume's radioed orders. Finding himself alone in the clouds off Kaena Point, he flew "by dead reckoning" toward Pearl Harbor and dropped his bombs. They landed harmlessly in the sea off the Waianae coast.

The clouds which frustrated the Japanese also saved their lives. None of the P-40s caught sight of the flying-boats, which would have been sitting ducks for the American fighters. Needless to say, the PBYs found no carriers.

While Army and Navy flyers accused each other of jettisoning bombs over Tantalus (no one believed that the Japanese could have sent planes to Hawaii without using carriers), Hashizume and Tomano returned safely to Jaluit and Wotje respectively. They reported that clouds had obscured the results of their mission. The Twenty-fourth Air Group command was disappointed and canceled the Q-Day attack on Pearl Harbor that was to have taken place on March 7.

Propagandists, however, filled in where the pilots were unable to observe. On March 9, the Navy Ministry announced that night bombers had raided Pearl Harbor with "pinpoint accuracy," destroying a marine barracks and exploding a gasoline storage tank. The same day, Radio Tokyo jubilated: "On March 4, a Japanese naval air squadron made a surprise attack at midnight on Pearl Harbor in Hawaii and rained tons of bombs, damaging important buildings of the navy arsenal and demolishing reconstruction work in progress."

The evening edition of the March 10 Tokyo *Asahi* newspaper editorialized that the raid would have serious domestic repercussions for President Roosevelt.

Indeed, the raid did have serious repercussions. After deducing how Operation K was executed, the U.S. Navy started to patrol the French Frigate Shoals. Consequently, the Japanese were obliged to cancel a reconnaissance mission over Pearl Harbor scheduled for May 30, 1942, in preparation for the Midway operation. Had French Frigate Shoals been available to his forces on May 30, Admiral Yamamoto might have learned about the American carriers that took him by surprise at Midway several days later. That piece of intelligence alone could have made the Battle of Midway a prelude to a Hawaii invasion rather than the turning point of the Pacific War.

Finally, Honoluluans can be thankful for Lieutenant Hashizume's timing. Released a few seconds later, his bombs would have fallen in residential Makiki.

# Contributors

**Alfred L. Castle** is a historian of U.S. diplomatic and intellectual history. He has published widely in various history, literature, and philosophy journals. Mr. Castle is president of the Samuel N. and Mary Castle Foundation.

**Thelma Chang** was the first recipient of the Carol Burnett Award for Responsible Journalism. She is the author of numerous travel, science, and human interest stories. Her 1992 book, *I Can Never Forget: Men of the 100th and 442nd*, received a best nonfiction award from the Hawaii Book Publishers Association.

**Gavan Daws** is the author of the classic works *Shoal of Time* and *Holy Man: Father Damien of Molokai*, along with other works about Hawai'i. He lives in Honolulu.

**A. Grove Day** was a leading authority on the literature of the Pacific. He wrote and edited over fifty books and was known for his anthologies of Mark Twain, Jack London, Louis Becke, and Herman Melville. He died in 1994.

**Barbara Del Piano** is a freelance writer. Born in Honolulu, she attended Michigan State University, Mills College, and graduated from the University of Hawai'i. She is the coauthor of *Ei Nei, Do You Remembah?"*

**Bob Dye** is a historian and frequent contributor to *Honolulu* magazine.

**Tom Horton** is the author of three Doubleday/Dolphin guides, including the *Dolphin Guide to Hawai'i* and *Super Span*, a history of the building of the Golden Gate Bridge. A former resident of Honolulu, he now resides in San Francisco.

**Gerard Aulama Jervis** was raised in the rough and tumble realm of Halawa Public Housing. An attorney, Mr. Jervis nurtures an avid in-

## Contributors

terest in Hawaiian history, a subject about which he has written many articles. He is a trustee of Kamehameha Schools Bishop Estate.

**Wray Jose** is a freelance writer.

**Herb Kawainui Kane** is an artist/historian and author with special interest in Hawai'i and the South Pacific. His books in print are *Pele, Goddess of Hawaii's Volcanoes* and *Voyagers*. In 1984 he was elected a Living Treasure of Hawaii.

**Mirka Knaster** is a freelance writer.

**Peter Kneer** is a freelance writer. He lives in Lanikai on O'ahu's Windward side.

**Gaylord C. Kubota** started, and continues to direct, the award-winning Alexander and Baldwin Sugar Museum in Puunene, Maui. He has published more than two dozen articles on ethnic history and heritage, sugar plantation history, and museum concerns.

**Victor Lipman** is a former senior editor of *Honolulu* magazine.

**Susan Morrison** is a freelance writer. Her work has appeared in *Honolulu*, *Historic Hawaii*, *Family Military Lifestyle*, the *Windward Sun Press*, and *Notable Women of Hawaii*.

**Brian Nicol**, a former editor of *Honolulu* magazine, is currently the editor and copublisher of *At Home & Away*, an AAA-owned travel publication.

**Martha H. Noyes** is a freelance writer.

**Edward Oxford** is a freelance writer.

**Pat Pitzer** is editor of *Spirit of Aloha* Magazine and an associate editor of *Honolulu*.

**Marilyn Stassen-McLaughlin**, a former English teacher at Punahou School, is a freelance writer. She has published extensively in professional journals and, most recently, contributed a chapter to the popular book *The View from Diamond Head*.

**John J. Stephan** teaches Japanese history at the University of Hawai'i at Manoa. He is the author of several books, including *Hawaii Under the Rising Sun: Japan's Plans for Conquest After Pearl Harbor*.

**Rick Stepien** is an administrator at Hawai'i Pacific University. He

## Contributors

holds a master's degree in Pacific Islands Studies and is the author of a monograph on the island of Niʻihau.

**Peter F. Stevens** is a full-time freelance writer. He is the author of *The Mayflower Murderer and Other Forgotten Firsts in American History* (1993) and regularly contributes to a wide range of publications including: *American Heritage, American History, Honolulu,* and *Grit*.

**Joseph Theroux** has lived in the Pacific since 1975. He has published a novel, *Black Coconuts, Brown Magic,* and many articles and short stories dealing with Hawaiʻi and the South Pacific. He is a school administrator in Hilo, Hawaiʻi.

**John P. Wagner** is a freelance writer.

# About the Editor

Bob Dye is a Kailua-based freelance writer. He taught in the honors program at the University of Hawai'i at Manoa and in the honors college at Western Michigan University. In the 1970s Dye served under Honolulu mayor Frank Fasi as his executive assistant. He has contributed articles, opinion pieces, and book reviews to scholarly journals, local and mainland newspapers, and popular magazines. Dye is the author of a forthcoming history of the Chinese in Hawai'i.